MAIN DEPARTMENT
MIDDLETOWN PUBLIC LIBRARY

Ohio Room

Middletown Public Library
Middletown, Ohio

D1127983

SOLDIERS' MONUMENT, NEW CALIFORNIA, OHIO.
The Monument stands on the northwest corner of the Square, facing
South. The building in the rear and to the right is the old Seceder
Church, now used as a Town Hall.

HISTORY

—OF—

JEROME TOWNSHIP

UNION COUNTY, OHIO

"Memory, a source of pleasure and instruction, is the only paradise out of which we cannot be driven away." – *Rogers.*

By

W. L. CURRY

COLUMBUS, - OHIO

1913

The Re-printing of this book was made possible by the encouragement of
the Jerome Township Board of Trustees:

Douglas A. Weakley
Eric R. Priday
Edgar Kauffman
John R. Woerner, Clerk

and

The Union County chapter of the Ohio Genealogical Society

Elaine Chapman, President
Ila LaRue, Editor (Index)
Margaret Markley, Librarian

Copyrighted, 1913
By W.L. CURRY
Published in October, 1913

A Facsimile Reprint
Published 1999 by

HERITAGE BOOKS, INC.
1540E Pointer Ridge Place
Bowie, Maryland 20716
1-800-398-7709
www.heritagebooks.com

ISBN 0-7884-1279-5

A Complete Catalog Listing Hundreds of Titles
On History, Genealogy, and Americana
Available Free Upon Request

CONTENTS

PREFACE.

In distinction from romance, history is defined as "A true story or record of important events," and the writing and publication of this little volume was undertaken with the desire that there may be a continuity of some of the facts already published in a county history some twenty years ago, as it was my fortune to furnish the greater part of the Jerome Township history for that publication.

By reason of the limited space in this volume, many interesting historical incidents must be omitted, yet we of the third generation from the pioneers who first settled in Jerome Township, have heard from the lips of our fathers and mothers many thrilling stories of Indian warfare, hunting, and other interesting incidents of pioneer life, which should be handed down to our descendants.

It has therefore been a pleasant duty to record for the future historian some of the facts that have not been heretofore published, to be utilized fifty years hence when he writes of the present progressive fourth generation. The story of the manner of living in the log cabins, the trials and hardships of the early settlers, will always be of intense interest to the young. The first generation has all passed to the other shore, and I hope they abide in a land where the birds sing as sweetly, the streams flow as gently as they did along the banks of Darby Creek and Sugar Run a century ago.

Perhaps the boys and girls of fifty years ago, whose hair is now sprinkled with the frosts of three score and ten winters, when they glance at these pages, may go back in memory as I have done, gaze into the wood fire at the old homestead, and live over again the days of childhood and youth.

Walking down the other side of the hill facing the sunset of life you can see in that flickering blaze the corner in the old fireplace where you conned over your lessons in the long winter evenings, read the weekly newspaper, cracked hickory nuts gathered from the old shellbark tree down in the meadow, ate Bellflower apples and drank cider.

As you muse, hear again the sweet strains of the old songs,
"Where are the friends that to me were so dear,
Long, long ago, long, long ago";
"Home, Sweet Home," listen to the thrilling stories of adventure, broken now and then by the bark of the faithful dog on the doorstep.

In the war history, writing in undue eulogy of any organization or arm of the service has been studiously avoided. It is not intended to extol the service of any soldier or officer, but to give credit where credit is due to any organization, and to give the service of each regiment as shown by official records.

Believing all soldiers, in whatever organization they may have served, to be equally patriotic, brave and faithful, wherever the fortunes of war cast them — whether heroes of the Revolution, Soldiers of the War of 1812, Mexican War, Civil War, or Spanish-American War.

W. L. CURRY
1913

JEROME TOWNSHIP, UNION COUNTY, OHIO.

The township was organized March 12, 1821, and the first election was held May 10, 1821, for the selection of Justice of the Peace. Clark Provin received the entire fifteen votes cast. James Ewing, Frederick Sager and Simeon Hager were the judges of the election. John Taylor and John McCune were the clerks.

When the first settlers came into the territory in Jerome Township along Darby Creek, it was the favorite "hunting grounds" of the Indians. In many places the traces of their wigwams still remained and the country was full of all kinds of game, including bears, deer, wolves, panthers, and small game.

Just north of Plain City, the Indians had a town where they lived in large numbers in wigwams covered with bark, until about the year 1800.

On the old Kent farm on Sugar Run was a sugar camp where the Indians manufactured maple syrup. Parties from Chillicothe often came here to trade for large quantities of raccoon skins and other furs. At this time the Indians were generally friendly.

The first sheep were brought to the township by James Ewing and he had to keep them confined in a high pen built of logs to keep the wolves from attacking them. One day, a number of Indians called at his cabin and one of the dogs belonging to the Indians jumped into the pen and attacked the sheep, whereupon Mr. Ewing took his rifle and killed the dog. This made the Indians very angry, and they had some trouble. As it happened, Jonathan Alder, who had been among the Indians for many years and understood their ways, interposed and peace was established between the Indians and the white men.

Wolves were very plentiful, but soon after the settlement was established, a bounty of $4.00 a scalp was paid by the county, which resulted in killing off the larger number of wolves.

Jonathan Alder lived in Jerome Township on the west side of Darby, just north of Plain City. He was taken prisoner by the Indians in Virginia when he was a small boy and lived with them until he grew to manhood. When he lived in Jerome Township he had a squaw wife. At this time he talked the Indian language entirely, but soon re-learned the English language. He finally parted from his squaw wife and she went northward with her people. He then married a white girl, but always seemed to be very much afraid of his squaw wife. The squaw wife did visit Mr. Alder's house during his absence and destroyed much of his white wife's wardrobe. She then left the neighborhood and that seems to have been the last he heard of her. The following is the inscription on his tombstone:

> " Jonathan Alder, born September 17, 1773.
> Taken prisoner by the Indians in 1781.
> Died January 30, 1849."

When the War of 1812 opened, apprehensions of trouble with these Indians were entertained, but they remained friendly and no hostilities or difficulties arose to mar their peaceful relations. Some of the rougher class of settlers were on intimate terms with the Indians and would go to their camps and join in the convivial feasts that were held there. The children of the earliest pioneers were for a time in mortal dread of them and it required a long time before they could be accustomed to their presence.

James Robinson had one of the earliest orchards in the vicinity, and after the trees approached the age of bearing he was greatly annoyed by the birds that had a strong liking for his choice fruit, and manifested the design of indulging their appetites before it was ripe enough to pluck. Some Indian lads, belonging to several families near by, were very expert in shooting birds with their small bows and arrows, and Mr. Robinson agreed with them, by means of signs, that for each bird they killed in the orchard he would give an apple. It

LOG CABIN HOMESTEAD OF STEPHENSON CURRY.
(Erected 1829.)

OLD SCHOOLHOUSE, NEW CALIFORNIA.
(Erected 1852.)

OLD SECEDER CHURCH, NEW CALIFORNIA.
(Erected 1852.)

CAVALRY WATERING, CHATTANOOGA VALLEY, TENNESSEE.

happened that the following day was Sunday, and as Mr. Robinson, who was a God-fearing Presbyterian, was engaged in the usual morning prayers, the Indian lads rushed in with a bird they had killed. The conscientious pioneer could not tolerate the idea of profaning the Sabbath by this unhallowed sport, and by shaking his head and gesticulting, intimated to them that they must not engage in it that day. They departed highly incensed, thinking he had withdrawn from his agreement, and after the old folks had gone to church that day, the Indian youths amused themselves by pointing their weapons at the children left at home, who fled to the house for protection and remained within with bolted doors till their parents returned.

When the troubles of 1812 had commenced, it was several times rumored that the Indians had taken up arms and were preparing to make a raid upon the settlement. Many families, panic-stricken, deserted their homes and fled farther south. At one time, a party of settlers, including Moses Mitchell, then a lad of sixteen years, fearlessly marched to the Indian villages far to the north to ascertain if they had concluded to put on the war paint and make the rumored attack. They found the Indians sitting in council, but with no hostile intent. The band of whites remained with them all night, then returned to their friends and quieted their fears.

FIRST SETTLEMENT.

The first settlers in the territory of Jerome Township were Joshua and James Ewing, two brothers. They settled in this territory in 1798 and erected the first cabin on the west bank of Darby Creek about one mile north of Plain City. This was the first cabin erected in the territory of Union County. Lucas Sullivant had laid out a town near this spot and called it North Liberty, about a year before the Ewings emigrated from Lexington County, Ky., but no house had been erected. At that time the Indians were very plentiful along Darby and seemed loath to leave their favorite "hunting grounds."

James Ewing established the first store in Union County,

2

at his farm in Jerome Township, and was appointed the first Postmaster.

Soon after the Ewings arrived in Union County, other settlers followed, prominent among whom were the Taylors, Robinsons, Mitchells, Kents, Currys, Cones, McCulloughs, Bucks, Provins, Notemans, McCunes, Sagers, Shovers, McClungs and Conners. Afterwards the Wises, McCampbells, Liggetts, Robinsons, Beards, Woodburns, Hawns, McCrorys, Flecks, Ketches, Dodges, Gills, Gowans, McDowells' Foxes, Converses, Kahlers, Ruehlens, Dorts, Crottingers, Nonnemakers, Beaches, Colliers, Bishops, Hudsons, Kiles, Stones, Donaldsons, Pattersons, McKittricks, Frys, Norris, Jackson, Laugheads, Evans, Stewart, Magill, Biggers, Moss, Rickards, Roneys, Adams, Herriotts, Hensels, Chapmans, Kilburys, Brinkerhoffs, Hagers, Morrisons, Wells, Dunboraws, Cooks, Arnolds, Channels, Warners, Bethards, Cramers, Hills, Hoberts, Greens, McCunes, Bowersmiths, Cases, Harringtons and Wagners, all of whom are among the older settlers of half a century ago. The majority of the early settlers came from the colonies of Virginia, Pennsylvania, and New Jersey, and a few of them from the New England States.

The large majority of these people were staunch Presbyterians and Seceders, the church now known as the United Presbyterian Church. In fact, the settlers along Darby and Sugar Run were always known as strongly Presbyterian people, and at the present time the U. P. Society is still retained at New California.

Many of the first settlers came from Revolutionary ancestors, and a number of Revolutionary soldiers settled in Union County. Among others was Colonel James Curry, who received 1,000 acres of land in part pay for his services as a Revolutionary soldier, which was for seven years as an officer of the Virginia Continental Line. Henry Shover, who settled in the township early in 1800, was also a soldier of the Revolution. Some of the land is still in the name of the Curry family.

Jessie Mitchell, born November 4th, 1799, was the first white child born in Union County, and removed from Darby

Township in 1823. He resided on the old Mitchell farm until he died, May 13th, 1881. He was a very highly esteemed and influential citizen, raised a large family, all of whom are deceased. A number of his descendants still reside in the township, and some of the land is still in the Mitchell name.

The citizens were strongly temperate, and it is a remarkable fact that there has never been a saloon within the territory of Jerome Township, although it has been settled for more than one hundred years. Another remarkable fact is that so far as is known, no one of the old settlers or their descendants has ever been convicted of a felony. Many of the old settlers were well educated and took an active part in establishing the common school system in the county.

THE LOG CABIN AND THE OLD FIREPLACE.

This chapter is particularly for the boys and girls of today to give them a glimpse of the manner of living, and hardships which their grandfathers and grandmothers endured in the early days and well remembered by the older residents who survive. Sixty years ago, as some of the now oldest generation of the township can remember, there were but few houses either of brick or frame in this section of the country. In fact many of the dwelling houses were erected of round logs not even hewn, but in time the better class of dwellings were made of hewed logs nicely matched and the openings between the logs "daubed" with mud mixed with lime, whitewashed, and presented a very neat appearance. When a citizen had his logs cut, hewed, and hauled to the location of erection the neighbors were invited to the "raising" and they came with axes and all necessary tools on the day set. There was great strife among the ax-men to see who could "take up a corner" the neatest and most rapid and it was very dangerous work for an inexperienced boy, but they were all anxious to try their hands, usually under the eyes of their fathers. There was also great rivalry in running the logs up to the workmen on skids by using long forked poles, and frequently one end of the log would be rushed so fast that the other end would fall and the workmen were sometimes injured by the falling timber. The house or stable, whichever it might be, was usually raised in one day and the ridgepole put on ready for the roof. The roof of clapboards, split usually from oak timber, was kept in place by long weight-poles instead of by nails.

It is well known to the older citizens, but may not be to many of the younger generation, the only way of heating the cabins or of cooking was by the old fireplace, about six feet wide, and many of the chimneys were made of sticks plastered with clay mortar on the inside. Cooking outfits were not very elaborate and usually consisted of an oven or two for baking corn pone, a skillet, an iron tea kettle, coffee pot and one or two small iron kettles and same number of large iron kettles for boiling hominy, making soap, and for washing clothes. The dishes were of the old blue pattern decorated with birds, animals and flowers, which are now considered the proper style and are quite rare. Before these old fireplaces and on the iron cranes that swung the kettles the good old mothers of the pioneer days would prepare chicken and squirrel potpies with accompanying side dishes fit for a king. How many men who live in luxury today long for the corn pone, the pies and "pound cakes" that mother made. The first improvement in cooking before the day of stoves, was the tin reflector. It was about two and a half feet wide with open front and one foot deep with a shed-like top running out toward the fire at an angle of 45 degrees, which reflected the heat from the fireplace to bread or cakes arranged on a tin or sheet-iron shelf raised six inches from the hearth on small iron legs, so that coals were placed under to heat below while the reflector heated above. The advent of the reflector was considered a great advance in the convnience of cooking and baking and was used in the majority of families until cook stoves were introduced in the vicinity about sixty years ago.

Nearly every cabin had a loom with spinning wheels for both wool and flax, and the linsey, Jeans and linen cloth was woven by the women in each household, cut out and made into garments for both men, women, boys and girls by the good mother and daughters. The loose wamus for men and boys was usually worn, and flannel dresses dyed by the same mother, using oak and walnut bark, and in these homespun dresses the girls were content, happy and pretty.

The furniture was both scanty and plain. Solid wood chairs or benches with a split-bottom rocker for mother, a plain table used for all purposes, and a "dough chest" for meal, flour and cooking utensils. Then beds with thick and wide feather ticks of sufficient height to require a step ladder, with a "trundle bed" under for the children, a bookcase, clock with wooden wheels, was about the usual outfit of the average family. No, do not forget the trusty rifle, bullet pouch and powder horn which always hung over the door.

HUNTING AND TRAPPING.

All kinds of small game was plentiful in this vicinity until the breaking out of the Civil War. It was common amusement to go out in the nearby woods on almost any farm and kill a "mess" of squirrels before breakfast or after supper in the summer season. When corn was planted the squirrels and chipmunks would commence digging it up near the side of the fields next to the woods and it was then the duty of the boys to "go the rounds" of the fields two or three times a day hammering on the fences with clubs and shouting to scare the game away, and some of the older men of today have devoted many an hour to this duty, skipping over the clods in bare feet and stubbing toes on stones or stumps. When roasting ears were in season the raccoons were very destructive and when the corn ripened wild turkeys visited the fields in great droves to get their share of the farmers' corn before it was husked. Every farmer had at least one deer or squirrel rifle, and hunting was not only great sport but was profitable as well. At least two hunting dogs were kept by each family and usually one was a "coon dog" or hound, and they were always anxious for the chase. In the late autumn months was the busy time for coon hunting with dogs as soon as the fur was good. Early in the evening the boys would start out with their torches of hickory bark, dogs whining, skipping and playing, happy in anticipation of the night's sport. A hound was not considered the best coon dog, as he barked on the track, warning the game, and it would have time to find a large tree, but a cur dog would follow the trail so quietly that he would be on the game, unawares, thereby compelling it to seek and climb the first tree. Both guns and axes were carried and when the coon was "treed" if he could not find a hole in which to hide and it was moonlight he could often be shot, otherwise the tree must be felled. The coon is pretty shrewd, and if not pushed too hard usually found a large tree. If the tree was large and the game could not be seen to get a shot, coats were doffed in a jiffy and the chips were soon flying, the hunters taking turns at chopping. No tree was too large to tackle and sometimes they were the largest white oaks, which at this time, if sawed into finishing lumber, would be valued at a hundred dollars or more. The hunters seldom requested permission of the land owner to cut a tree, for if it was a good rail tree he would split it into rails, if no he did not care for it. When the tree was about ready to fall the boys, with clubs, and the dogs anxious for the fight, would form a circle in the woods out of danger in the direction the tree was to fall, ready for the chase. The coon would usually jump as the tree commenced falling, and when he was spied a grand rush would be made and the dogs would soon have him. A coon is a hard fighter and when tackled by a dog he turns on his back and fights with both teeth and claws. A dog not accustomed to such fighting is knocked out in the first round, but the old hunting dog gets him by the throat and never releases his hold until the game is dead. As coonskins were only worth from fifty to seventy-five cents each, hunting was not very profitable where this investment was divided between three or four boys, but the fun and excitement compensated fully for the financial shortage. In the northwest part of the township there was a great forest called the "Galloway Woods," owned by non-residents, uninhabited and uncultivated before the Civil War. This woods was full of wild game, deer, wild turkeys, raccoons, foxes, minks and squirrels. At times hunters from a distance would come with a pack of hounds and start the deer, while the hunters would follow on horseback. Many times some of us who survive can recall the baying of hounds, and if coming in our direction how we watched for the deer as they bounded through the woods with the pack close in pursuit, taking up the cry of the leader of the pack as they followed in a straight row eagerly chasing the timid frightened animals. It was very exciting; and then came the hunters, guns over their shoulders, and horses on the gallop. Such a scene with the sweet music of the hounds impressed a boy so intensely that it is just as vivid as of yesterday, although three score years have passed. Wild turkeys were still to be found in droves of twenty-five or upwards, fifty years ago. Hunters would follow them carefully during the daytime, getting a shot now and then. About sundown the turkeys would begin to go to roost by flying into the branches of tall trees. The good hunter who understood the game would then, after marking carefully the location, leave the flock. If it was moonlight he would return at midnight or later when the moon was high, and bring down a few turkeys by shots from his trusty rifle, by getting the range so that the turkeys would be seen against the moon. Rifles were all muzzle loaders and the ramrod would extend to the end of the gun barrel. To the end of the ramrod the hunter would attach a glove or mitten so that it hung down three or four inches below the gun barrel when the gun was sighted, then the aim must be so the mitten or glove would drop just below the form of the turkey looking toward the moon, and fire. John Curry, who was the most noted and successful hunter in the vicinity, seldom missed a shot. As I go back in memory I can see him now mounted on his chestnut sorrel hunting horse, "Alex," as he dashed through my father's sugar camp in front of our home at full speed, leaning forward with rifle over his shoulder, on his way to the Galloway Woods on many a winter afternoon. About dusk he would return slowly with one or two large wild turkeys hanging from the pommell of his saddle. He had a great coon dog, "Old Ben," who was sure of his game and never failed treeing a few raccoons and opossums every night he had the opportunity to "take the trail." Ben was the envy of every hunter and hunting dog in the neighborhood. Among the other noted hunters may be named Sardius Ward, David McCune, the Hensils, and, in fact, the boys in almost every family. In the days before the Civil War the hunting and shooting was all with rifles. A man or boy with a shotgun was ridiculed, as a boy fifteen or sixteen years of age was a good shot and could bring down a squirrel from the tallest oak tree with a rifle. There was a great deal of trapping of raccoon, minks, and other small game. Quails were caught in traps, a whole covey at once, and wild turkey were caught by building rail pens and tapering the pen off at the top, only leaving a small opening through which the turkey would fly down to the corn scattered inside the pen. Once inside the pen it was not possible to fly straight up to the escape and they were then easily caught by the trapper. As there were no game laws in those days game of all kinds was shot any time in the year. When the township was first settled bear and wolves were plentiful and wolves' scalps brought $4 each after the county was organized. Colonel James Curry was a member of the legislature, representing the counties of Madison and Delaware in 1820, when the bill was passed for the erection of Union County, so called, as it was from territory of Franklin, Madison and Delaware, therefore a union of counties. Hon. Job Rennick, a prominent citizen of Chillicothe, represented Ross County, and after the bill was passed he remarked to Colonel Curry facetiously that "he now had a county and all it was fit for was wolf traps." Could these grand old men who first settled the county and, by the labor and hardship they endured, blazed the way for civilization, visit Jerome Township with its fine macadamized roads, telephones and automobiles, what a revelation it would be to them.

The last bear killed in Jerome Township was on the farm of James Buck, afterward owned by Perry Buck, and near the banks of Sugar Run. A wounded bear had been chased into the neighborhood by dogs and finally came to bay. A number of dogs were gathered up among the settlers and a great fight was soon in progress. Among the dogs were two or three bear dogs and they knew how to tackle the game by running in behind the bear and snapping at the heels and would then be out of reach before the bear could turn, keeping up this method of attack until the bear was completely tired out, and then the dogs could close in on him. In this pack of dogs two or three were not accustomed to bear-fighting and would rush in front of the animal and one stroke of his great paw would put them out of the fight. In this scrimmage one or two dogs were killed.

Mr. James Buck, who was working in a corn field near, had his hoe in hand during the battle. He became very much incensed at the rough usage of the dogs by the bear and signified his intention of attacking the bear in front with his hoe, but was warned by James Curry, who was an old bear hunter, that he had better keep off at a good distance, as the bear, although wounded, had good use of his forepaws and one stroke would be sufficient to put him out of the fight for good. After the dogs had fought for some time, and to the satisfaction of the onlookers as well, the animal was dispatched by a rifle shot. While the exact date is not known, it was soon after the war of 1812, and some of us have been shown the spot on a little hillside on the east bank of Sugar Run.

Fox hunting was great sport and very exciting when the hunters were mounted. On the day set the hunters would assemble at a time and place agreed upon with all hounds and hunting dogs that could be brought together in the neighborhood. Some of the old hunters would take the advance with the best dog and beat the brush in some locality where the game was likely to be sprung. If there was snow on the ground and it was soft and melting a track was soon struck and would often be followed by sight some distance until the scent would become warm before the dogs were allowed to take the trail. When they did start and were baying on the track it was sweet music to the hunters' ears and they were all off on the gallop, following the hounds through brush, over logs, streams and fences, in a wild race which frequently continued for hours. In some instances the fox would double on the track, dodge the pack, and run through the fields or pastures where there were sheep or cattle and by the time the trail was again found the game would be a mile or two away, heading for the Scioto River or Darby Creek, and often reaching a place of safety in a hole among the rocks. It was great sport and dangerous as well, leaping fences or ditches, but a few bruises were just a part of the game and were not taken into consideration by the hunter if he could only, by a wild and reckless ride, be in at the death. Some of the men who yet survive and have reached the milestone of three score and ten, can feel the flush of youth yet come to their cheeks as they go back in memory to the days when they followed the hounds more than half a century ago.

In addition to the fox hunt, there was some horse racing without the hounds. There were no trotting races ,as that kind of sport was too tame for the boys of those days. The racing was just for sport and there was little betting. There was one track at Plain City, but on the Jerome Township side of the line running north, just west of where the flouring mill now stands. Another track was down on the bottom land near the creek, and just opposite and below the farms of Uncle Zack Noteman and Uncle Levi Taylor.

On the Fourth of July or Saturday afternoons during the summer and fall months, the clans gathered for the sport and some swift runners were usually on the ground with their backers. The distance was usually a quarter or half-mile dash. The jockeying for advantage in the "go" was often long and sharply contested and at times resulted in a clash at the finish between the backers of the rival horses.

On the Post Road toward Dublin, near the Tavern of Uncle Steve Lattimer, was another favorite race track. Here would gather the horsemen from Dublin, Pleasant Valley, and West Jefferson, frequently for an afternoon outing. The races would be fast and furious until toward evening, and usually the day's amusement wound up with an exhibition not on the program, participated in by such actors as Hen Davis, of Dublin, Abe Garabrant and Tom Gregg, of Jefferson, and sometimes the Lattimers and Kilburys would take a hand just as peacemakers. When the racing was subsiding and the arguments commenced, we boys would climb to the top of the stake and rider fence to see the fun, as we could get a better view of the performance, and for another reason it was safer.

In those days the actors were not governed strictly by Queensbury rules; neither did they wear three-ounce gloves, and the rounds were not limited in number, although there was usually but one. That was in ante-bellum days, and after the Civil War Thompson Kilbury fitted up a fine circle half-mile track on his farm, where the horsemen had some very interesting meets.

There were some fine bred running horses in the community, among which the Printer and Lexington stock were the favorites. Running races was the great sport of that period and it was very fascinating. Compared with the baseball and football of the present day, there are nine points out of ten in favor of the race horse.

A boy must indulge in some kind of exciting exercise, and breaking colts or riding wild horses was the favorite sport of the country boy fifty years ago. When a farmer boy arrived at the age of 16 or 17, he was given a colt by his father, and was next given a new saddle and bridle. He was as proud of his outfit as the boy of today who has a rubber-tired buggy or an automobile.

There were many races along the soft, smooth dirt roads by these boys going and returning from town in the evenings, just for the fun and excitement and with no thought of betting. Among them were riders that would make a cowboy riding a bucking broncho green with envy. The racing on the Kilbury track, after the close of the Civil War, was conducted in a very quiet manner. No rowdying was allowed, and it was interesting, clean sport. At this time, the Cone boys, who had some fine horses, took an interest in this sport, as did the Careys,

Taylors, Millikins, McCanns, and Converses around Plain City, all of whom were great horse fanciers, as were their fathers before them.

THE OLD LOG SCHOOLHOUSE.

Until about the year 1852, when the select school building was erected at New California, the schoolhouses were all built of logs. The schoolhouse attended by the children in the vicinity of the village was located in the center of a great woods, about three-quarters of a mile northwest from New California, on the farm of Perry Buck.

There was no cleared ground and the paths leading to the schoolhouse were marked by blazing the trees, and ran through the woods in many directions. The house was built of heavy logs, one room about thirty feet square, fitted with benches without any backs, and the desks consisted of long boards about a foot and a half wide, resting on wooden pins fastened into the logs by an inch and a half auger hole. Windows on three sides, and the front wall, with the one door in the corner, was taken up by the blackboard.

The house was heated by a long, heavy iron box stove. The children from at least twenty families attended this school, and in those days the families were not as small as they are today. I think it is safe to say that there were sixty scholars in the district, and it seems an impossibility, as we go back in memory today, to see how they could all be crowded into a room of that size. Still, we did go to school there and learned something—in fact, the writer and many others never attended any other district school.

The district was in a radius, say commencing with the farm of James Robinson on the Watkins Road, now owned by Mr. Seigman, taking the McCampbells, Woodburns, Mitchells, Gills, Currys, Cones, Beards, Bucks, and Taylors on the Marysville Road.

We had a lot of fun in winter, playing fox and hounds in the snow, running miles through the woods, choosing and having our snowball battles. Base, Black Man, Corner Ball, Town

Ball, Anti-over, and two-ol'-cat and three-ol'-cat were the favorite games. The professional baseball of today was fashioned from the old town ball, played in the early days. The ball was made by unraveling old woolen stockings, winding the thread around a burnt cork, wetting it so that it would shrink and harden, and then covering it with sheepskin. There was a pitcher, a batter and a catcher. The other participants did some desultory outfield work and took their "turns" at places on the infield. Good pitching, batting, catching and running were all developed in town-ball playing, and there was plenty of material to draw from when professional baseball was first organized.

Of other games and sports, there was running and jumping, wrestling, boxing, and now and then a real fight with knuckles, for there were clans and gangs in those days. In the summer time the boys would build play houses out of poles and cover them with green leaves and twigs for the girls, where they had their stores of May-apple blossoms or berries to exchange for Genseng or Snake-root, as that was the usual commodity in trade.

There were spelling schools frequently when the good spellers from surrounding districts would come in for a contest, and the excitement would be up to fever heat as one by one the scholars went down on a hard word. The next week our best spellers would visit other schools, and so it would continue through the winter months.

Among the early teachers of that school were Caroline Buck, Olive Gill, Maria Buck, Rev. I. N. Laughead, Jane Porter, Polly Snodgrass, Emma Dodge, Eliza Gill, Sophia Dodge, Nan McCampbell, Lorinda Wilkins, Dr. D. W. Henderson, Elijah Brown, Charles Green, George Thompson, Milton Roney, and perhaps others whose names I do not now recall.

On Friday afternoons there were declamations by the boys and compositions by the girls. Parents would come in and we had a great time doing examples on the blackboard, parsing grammar lessons, and spelling.

The teachers did not spare the rod, but used it on all occasions, if in his or her opinion it was necessary. It did a boy a lot of good to have the teacher send him out to get a switch to whip a boy he did not like very well. I have a very distinct recollection of a boy getting a good whipping for inducing a little fellow to eat a piece of Indian Turnip, with the result that it burned his mouth seriously. But the greatest disgrace of all was to be "kept in" at recess or after school for some infraction of the rules.

In writing lessons, we used quill pens, and it was a part of the duty of the teacher to make and repair all pens. In the old First Reader in use those days, there was a picture of a cow in a pond. In one of our Friday afternoon exercises I remember of a boy getting up and reciting a verse about the cow which was as follows:

" The cow is in the pond.
The cow gives us milk.
We must not hurt the cow."

That was all he said, and sat down well satisfied with his effort. The boys used to tease him about it until he was a young man. He was a fine young man, and has passed to his reward.

For a number of years the township elections were held in this old log schoolhouse. At these elections many of the voters would spend the entire day at the voting place, and the discussions on political questions between the Whigs and Democrats were often very warm and loud. A club of the "Know-Nothing Party," as it was called, was organized here, a political party opposed to foreigners voting as soon as they set foot on our shores, and was largely recruited from the Whig party. It was only in existence a few years when members of that party and Whig party organized the Republican party. The "Know-Nothing Party" was a secret organization and an amusing story is told about the organization in the old Log Schoolhouse.

The meetings were held there as it was out in the woods, and thought to be a safe place. One night some of the boys of the neighborhood were going home from the village by the path that passed the schoolhouse, and spied a man lurking in the shadows near the door, and heard some discussions inside the room. Approaching the outer guard, which he proved to be, and a young voter, they were informed that the parties on the inside were making "Sugar Wax," and could not be disturbed, as it was a select party. In a few days it leaked out that it was a meeting of the "Know-Nothing Party," and the people of the village were all agog with curiosity. The young man on guard proved to be David O. Taylor, who was afterwards killed in battle during the Civil War.

The merchant of the village of California at that time, was a man by the name of John Robinson, and he had quite a reputation for composing doggerel rhymes hitting on local events. When he heard of this incident, he composed a rhyme, one verse of which is recalled:

" The boys went out the Know-Nothings to find,
The old log schoolhouse they crawled up behind,
As Stephen stood there looking in through the cracks,
The Know-Nothings run with their syrup and wax."

The Stephen referred to in that classic poem was Stephen Cone, who was one of the party of boys.

BARRING THE TEACHER OUT.

In those days, it was the custom in many of the schools to "bar the teachers out" on New Year's morning, and keep them out until they capitulated by agreeing to treat all of the scholars, usually with candy and raisins, as apples and nuts were plentiful and were no rarity for the scholars. New Year's morning some of the older boys would be at the schoolhouse by daybreak, and one of the favorite ways of barring the door, as there were no locks, was to cut down a sapling from the woods near by, about six inches in diameter, put the pole in through a rear window, then cut it off so it would reach from the floor at the rear wall, to the top of the door and there brace it solid. Nail down all the windows but one, which was left so the scholars could be lifted in as they arrived. A fire was started in the stove and a sufficient amount of wood carried in to last through the siege, which would sometimes continue for half a day. The scholars would arrive early, and by the time the teacher arrived all would be ready for the parley, which was generally conducted by the "big boys." Some of the teachers would take it good naturedly, accept the terms dictated, and surrender at once. In that case, the door would be opened and a couple of boys would be dispatched to the village for the treat.

Other teachers would become indignant and at first refuse a conference, and even attempt to smoke the scholars out by climbing up on the roof and covering the chimney with a board. In one instance recalled, sulphur was dropped down the chimney, but the scholars were prepared for such an emergency by having a bucket of water and the fire in the stove was soon put out. Ultimately the teachers came to terms, and all went merry and frequently a half holiday was proclaimed. It was a lot of fun and usually ended in a convivial time for all.

Sleigh riding and skating were the great winter sports. In those days before the streams were ditched, and the trees and bushes were growing along the banks, when the January freshets came the water would not rush in such a torrent. By reason of the logs, drifts and fences, the water would spread out over the low pasture grounds and meadows, and when it would freeze there would be acres of ice.

In the evenings the boys would congregate by the dozen build great fires along the banks, play shinney and other games, often until midnight.

The thick woods along the narrow roads would protect the snow and it was not unusual to have five or six weeks of good sleighing, which was enjoyed by both old and young in sleighing parties and attending singing schol.

MILLING AND OTHER EARLY INDUSTRIES IN JEROME TOWNSHIP.

The first mill erected in the township was by Frederick Sager, who settled on Darby Creek in the early years of 1800. Before this mill was erected, the settlers had to use a pestle

WILLIAM B. LAUGHEAD
96TH O V. I.

and stone mortar, the same as those in use by the Indians. In this manner they would mash the corn and make coarse meal and hominy. At intervals they would place a wooden pack-saddle on the back of a strong horse and load it up with sacks of shelled corn. The pioneer would mount his hunting horse and start on a long and tedious journey to Lancaster or Chillicothe, followed by the packhorse. This trip would consume several days and his return was anxiously awaited by the family and neighbors, as he would not only bring the precious meal, but the capacious leather saddle bags would be filled to full capacity with newspapers and other reading matter, which would be liberally distributed among the settlers.

The site of the old mill erected by Frederick Sager is just above the bridge on the California and Plain City Road, on the east bank near the farm of Samuel H. Ruehlen. The dam was built of logs and brush and this work was very largely done through the volunteer assistance of the settlers. The building was erected in the same manner, as they were all intensely interested in this new enterprise.

The first burrs for this mill were chiseled out of a boulder that Mr. Sager found on the farm of John Taylor. After weeks of tedious work the boulder was split open and the stone dressed ready for use. As soon as the mill was in running order, there was a great rush by the pioneers and also by the Indians, and they came both on foot and horseback from many miles around with their sacks of corn.

For a few years he only ground corn, but there was soon a demand for flour, as the farmers began to raise wheat, and he installed a flouring bolt. For many years the bolting was done by hand. During the dry season the mill could run but little, as there was not sufficient water, but when the creek was not frozen in the winter and spring months, it was a very busy place, as farmers came with their grain from great distances, and when the water power was sufficient the mill ran day and night.

Mr. Sager also erected the first sawmill in the township, attached to his grist mill and run by the same water, thus furnishing the first boards and sawed lumber used in the cabins. Before that date the floors and doors were made of puncheons split out of timber and smoothed by a drawing knife and adz. Mr. F. Heminway finally purchased this mill and it bore the name of the "Heminway Mill" for many years and until it was finally abandoned for want of water power.

The Kahler boys erected a sawmill along in the fifties on Robinsons Run, just above the bridge on the Plain City and California Road, which was run by water power and was the last mill in the township run by water. They also erected a grist mill near the same site run by steam power, which they operated successfully for a number of years.

The above described are the only grist mills that were ever erected in the township, although some of the sawmills have had burrs attached for grinding corn.

Many times a boy sent to the mill horseback on a sack of corn would have to wait all day for his grist. If the fishing was good he did not object, as he always took his hook and line along. The miller did not exchange meal and flour for corn and wheat, as was the custom in later years, but took toll out of the grain—he did not have facilities for weighing the grain and generally took the farmer's word for the amount, that the proper toll could be taken out for grinding.

An anecdote is related of one shrewd farmer who usually tried to get the best part of a bargain with his neighbors. Like the Irishman, he thought it was better to "Chate than to be chated." The story is told that he went to the mill one time with his grain and informed the miller that he had two bushels and a half in his sack. After the toll was taken out, he winked at one of his neighbors and said that he had "two bushels and a half and a peck and a toll dish full." The miller having taken out a toll dish, the sly old farmer got one peck ground free.

A doggerel poem written by a wag was set to music and sung with much glee by the old pioneers at some of their convivial gatherings.

THE OLD MILLER'S WILL.

"There was an old man lived all alone,
He had three sons, big men grown,
And he was about to make his will
All he had was a wet weather mill.

Chorus:

To my hi fal lal, diadle I da

He called unto his youngest son,
Say son, O! son, my life is run,
And if I to you the mill do make,
Pray what is the toll you intend to take?

First Son—

Dad, O! Dad, my name is Breck
And out of a bushel I'll take a peck;
And if a fortune I can make,
That is the toll I intend to take.

You ain't the boy, the old man said,
You ain't the boy that's learned my trade
And unto you the mill I won't give,
For by such toll, no man can live.

Second Son—

Dad, O! Dad, my name is Ralph,
And out of a bushel I'll take half;
If a fortune I can make
That is the toll that I will take.

Third Son—

Father, Father, my name is Paul,
And out of a bushel, I'll take all;
If a fortune I do lack,
Will keep the toll and swear to the sack.

You are the boy, the old miller said,
You are the boy that's learned my trade,
Unto you the mill I give,
For by such toll a miller can live.

The old lady throwed up her hands and cried,
The old miller rolled up his eyes and died;
He died, and died without a will
And the old lady got the mill

To my hi fal lal, diadle I da."

POTTERIES.

Isaac Mason started the first pottery in Jerome Township. His little plant was located on the old Sager farm, on the east bank of Darby Creek, afterward known as the T. T. Kilbury farm, which he operated for a number of years.

TANNERIES.

In the early days the tanning business was quite extensively carried on in the township. William McCune operated a tan yard for many years, just over the line in the township, near Plain City. In those days, in the spring when the sap was coming up, many large white oak trees were cut down and the bark peeled for tanning purposes, and it was always a ready sale on the market. Unless the trees were needed for rail timber, they were frequently allowed to rot.

The tan yard of Asa Converse, located on his farm just west of the David Moss farm on the California and Unionville Road, was perhaps the most extensive tannery of those days. In addition to the tanning business, he ran a boot and shoe manufacturing and repair shop. He employed a number of shoemakers during the winter season, and did quite a large and profitable business.

Mr. Arthur Collier for a number of years carried on the tanning business in Jerome. The country tan yard was so convenient for farmers in either selling hides or having them tanned for their own use, but is now a business of the past and of which the younger generation has little knowledge, as it is largely concentrated in the cities.

ASHERIES.

Asheries for the manufacture of black salts and sometimes saleratus, were quite common. The proprietors had wagons running all over the country buying up the ashes saved by the housewives or by the boys in the springtime when burning logs in the clearing, and it was quite a source of revenue.

Kibourne and Amos Beach operated quite an extensive ashery in the village of Jerome for many years. Peter Beaver was also engaged in that business at New California, but these industries are all abandoned, although in the early days the business was quite profitable.

COOPERAGE.

The manufacture of barrels was engaged in quite extensively in the township by a number of citizens. The McCampbell brothers, John, Joseph, Andrew and Charles, were all coopers by trade, and engaged in that business on their farms during the winter season. Robert B. Curry, John Oliver, James and William Woodburn were also engaged in that line. They made suger barrels, flour barrels and pork barrels, many of which were disposed of in the neighborhood, but the bulk of them were hauled to Columbus. They had great high racks on heavy wagons which were used to transport the barrels to market, and merchandise of all kinds was brought back in return. The loads were immense, and while I have no definite knowledge as to the number of flour barrels that could be loaded in one of those wagons, it seems to me that fifty would be a safe guess.

Tradesmen of all kinds were in the country, and there was scarcely a farmer's family that did not have some member who could do mechanical work, either as shoemaker, harness maker or a wood worker. Nelson Cone was, perhaps, the best all-round mechanic along Sugar Run. He manufactured boots and shoes, harness and saddles. He was also a wood worker and made sleds, ox yokes, plow stocks and all kinds of farm implements.

Among the shoemakers were Perry Buck, the Fleck boys, David Beard, and some of the Germans, a Mr. Myers and others. George Ruehlen, who arrived in Jerome Township direct from Germany, along in the fifties, was an expert workman and erected the first up-to-date cider mill and press in the township. He also operated a sawmill for a number of years.

Nearly every farmer had a good set of tools and made and repaired all kinds of farm implements himself, instead of running to town and to the shop of a carpenter or blacksmith every time it was necessary to have a nail driven or a board sawed. They were especially expert in the manufacture of ax handles out of tough hickory timber, so much in use those days.

The fathers always took a great deal of pains to instruct their boys in the use and care of tools. There was one kind of work along this line that did not appeal to the farmer boy particularly, and that was filing a cross-cut saw. He was well aware that getting the old saw out, in company with a rat-tail file, meant hard work as soon as the saw was sharpened.

If there was one kind of labor harder than any other on a farm, it was for a boy to tackle a saw log about four feet in diameter with a cross-cut saw, for the other fellow was sure to "lay down" on the saw. Did you ever, my old farmer boy friend—now three score and ten—ever know it to be otherwise? I think not.

SOCIAL GATHERINGS AND SINGING SCHOOL.

Before the days of the Civil War, the young people residing along Darby Creek and Sugar Run were noted far and near for musical talent, both vocal and instrumental. Every winter singing schools and literary societies furnished the principal entertainments for all, old and young.

These entertainments were held in the schoolhouses in the neighborhood and on special occasions, such as concerts or literary exhibitions at the close of the schools, they were held in the old Seceder Church at New California, or one of the churches at Jerome.

Until about the year 1850, the old square or "buckwheat" notes were used in the music books. The first singing book that used the round notes was the Carmina Sacra, and the first teacher was a Mr. Maynard. Then came a Mr. Dixon, Pinney Case of Jerome, Mr. Moulton of Boston, Wm. M. Robinson of Marysville, Sireno B. Phipps of Columbus, Samuel Robinson of Darby Township, and Nelson Cone. In later years James Curry, now a Presbyterian minister of Newark, California, taught a few terms.

After the regular terms of the singing schools closed with a day concert in the spring, the teachers would insist that the young people keep up the practice during the spring and summer months. These practices were held in the evenings and Dan Cone, James Curry, and David G. Robinson were usually the leaders, standing up in front, giving the key with a tuning fork, and beating time.

There was great rivalry between the choruses of Jerome and Darby Townships, and there were many concerts and musical contests. In the summer of 1860, the singers of Jerome, Darby and Milford Center held an all-day concert in the grove on the farm of Michael Sager at Unionville. A number of the music teachers were present in the interest of their favorites, and considerable feeling was displayed by the different factions—each chorus claiming the laurels.

Of soprano and alto singers who were prominent in musical affairs in those days, and still residing in the vicinity, only the names of Amanda McCampbell Comstock, Phebe Curry Williams, Susannah Robinson McKittrick, Mary Curry Gill, Nancy Bain Curry, and Jennie Taylor Carson are recalled, and of the young men tenor and bass, not one. The Robinsons, Gowans, Cones, Liggetts, Dodges, Woodburns, McCampbells, Laugheads, Mitchells, Gills, Currys, Flecks, Beards and Bucks are all gone, and but few of that generation survive.

There were few pianos and organs, but violins, flutes, and violin-cellos were the principal musical instruments. Some of the young people were quite talented, and of the Cone family of seven boys, all were violinists.

No public dances were held, but when the young people would meet in the evenings, even at the house of a strict Methodist or Presbyterian, they would indulge in a little social dance—a cotillion, swinging eight, Virginia Reel, or French four, with a jig dance by a few of the boys to the old tune of "Money Musk."

Then there was the apple cuttings, which closed at 9 o'clock sharp, after all the tubs, jars and crocks had been filled with apples, pared, cored and quartered, ready to be strung on cotton cord two or three yards in length and hung to the joists above the fireplace to dry. There was no canned fruit, and the apples and peaches were dried around the open fireplaces or on kilns. The kilns were usually made in the orchard by digging a trench a foot deep, a yard wide, and two or three yards long. This trench was arched over with brick, and at one end a chimney several feet in height was erected. The brick over the trench was then given a thick coat of clay mortar, smoothed down carefully, and soon dried ready for use by building a fire in the kiln. Newspapers or a cloth was spread over the kiln to keep the fruit clean when it was put in, and in this manner apples and peaches were dried for winter use.

When the apples were all pared and cut at these evening gatherings, the floors without carpets were swept up, refreshments were served, and the evening festivities commenced. The old plays were "Snap Up," March to Quebec," and many others. Some of the older persons will recall the old song as the boys and girls would march around the room by couples.

" We're all marching to Quebec
    Where the drums are loudly beating,
  The Americans have gained the day
    And the British are retreating;
  The War's all o'er and we'll turn back
    To the place where first we started,
We'll open the ring and choose a couple in,
    To relieve the broken-hearted."

When a boy or girl was "out" they were assessed a pawn which was usually a handkerchief or a knife. To redeem it the penalty was not very severe, sometimes being a mock-marriage to your sweetheart. Some boy or girl would be blindfolded and the prosecutor would hold the pawn to be redeemed over the head of the judge, saying, "Heavy, heavy hangs over your head." The judge questioning, "Fine or superfine?"—fine if it is a boy and superfine if a girl; then the penalty was pronounced by the judge. When the company was congenial both boys and girls were pleased to be assessed some penalty for the pleasure of redeeming.

There were wood choppings and the young men of the neighborhood would gather at some farmer's home, especially when the father or some of the boys were sick, but frequently just for a visit, chop wood and haul it to the home in long lengths, working all day, and a sufficient amount of wood would be chopped to last for many weeks. On the same day, the girls would assemble at the house and have a quilting party. In the evening a great supper would be spread and all would be merry with songs and plays until the "wee small hours."

Corn huskings were also evenings of amusement and helpfulness among the farmers. There was always some strife among the boys to see who could find the largest number of red ears, as every red ear found entitled him to kiss his best girl. It would even be intimated that a girl would quietly pass a red ear to the right boy, or if a boy had any doubts about finding one, he would place an ear of the right color in a convenient pocket before he started to the "husking bee."

The debating societies furnished entertainment and amusement for many winter evenings at the schoolhouses. These debates were participated in by many of the old settlers who were well versed in current events and were good historians as well. In fact, it may well be doubted if the average citizen of today is as well versed in the early history of the Republic as the pioneers of fifty years ago, and these debates were usually quite interesting.

The best class of farmers usually took two or three weekly

newspapers, one of which was a church paper, and it is recalled that the favorite one was, especially among the Presbyterians, "The Watchman of the Valley," published in Cincinnati. "The Dollar Newspaper," published in Philadelphia, was also a favorite among the farmers, as in addition to all the current news, a continued story by one of the good writers was published, some of which continued for months.

There were no dailies outside of the cities, and the arrival of the weeklies in the Saturday's mail was hailed with great interest.

The writings of some of the standard prose writers and poets were in every household, including Shakespeare, Byron, Burns, Shelley, Scott, Young's Night Tohughts, Josephus, Rollins, and many standard histories. The Bible and hymn book was always on the stand in the living room, and they were both used every day.

CHURCHES.

"Lower Liberty Presbyterian Church" was organized about the year 1807 near Plain City. Services were first held in private houses, then in a schoolhouse on the lot where the first church building was erected. Among the first members were the Ewings, Mitchells, Chapmans, Taylors, Gills, Wingets, Currys, Robinsons and Bucks.

Rev. Samuel Wood was the first pastor, from 1808 to 1815. He was succeeded by the following named ministers: Rev. Wm. Dickey, Archibald Steele, James Hoge, D. D., Elder Hughes and Cable, until 1821, and Rev. James Robinson from that date until 1828, followed by Rev. Davis C. Allen until 1831. Rev. James Dolbear served from 1831 to 1838 and Rev. Wm. Galbreath from 1839 to 1848.

In 1837 the denomination was divided into the old school and new school. Rev. Benjamin D. Evans, Rev. Henry Shedd, Rev. Kuhn. Rev. Uhlfelder afterward supplied the pulpit until 1853, when the society was disorganized and church building abandoned.

The first church building of this society was erected about

1815-1816 on a plat of ground of about four acres, donated by Walter Dun, one mile west from Plain City on the Post Road, in the forks of the road running through the Ricard farm from the east and just across that road from the southeast corner of the old Ewing farm now owned by Harlan Wood. It was a large frame building, not plastered, no chimney, and no way of heating. Therefore, it would not be occupied in the winter season. There were two aisles, one running through the center lengthwise of the building and the other from side to side, crossing the main aisle.

As in the old days the men sat on one side of the church and the women on the other. The seats were ordinary rough benches, supported by legs inserted through inch and a half auger holes. In the year 1836 a large red brick building was erected on the same site, in which services were held until about 1850.

The pulpit was in the front of the church and as a person entered they faced the congregation. The platform of the pulpit was at least six feet high, and only the head and shoulders of the minister could be seen, as the front wall of the pulpit was so high. The seats all had high-board backs and a door next to the aisle had a button to it which was turned as soon as the children were all counted in. In those days families all sat in the same seat and the seat of each family was well known. Strangers and transients were seated in the rear part of the church, unless invited to sit with some family. Sunday school in the morning at 9:30, church at 11, two prayers and sermon an hour in length, then half hour "intermission" for dinner, carried in baskets, and it was a good diner, cold biscuits, cold pork or sausage, doughnuts, "pound cake," and mother's juicy gooseberry or currant pie an inch and a half thick. And what appetites we had! Then up to Uncle Jimmie Ewings, well for a drink out of the real "old oaken bucket," and a little visit, then back to the church for another long sermon.

The music was not classical but there were many good voices and it was a real praise service. The singing was usually led by two of the Elders of the church. As there were not a sufficient number of hymn books for the congregation, the two leaders would stand up in front of the pulpit and "line out" two lines of the hymn, then leading the singing. Jesse Gill and James Robinson were the two leaders for many years, finally Benjamin Fay, who played the flute and was quite a musician, organized a choir of the young people and I recall he would stand up and give the key with his flute. The music was greatly improved and enjoyed under his leadership. Mascal Ewing, who was educated for the ministry and was a fine scholar, would frequently read sermons to the congregation when they had no minister. The "Old Red Brick Church" drew great congregations and in the summer time the church would often be filled to overflowing, as the people would come for many miles, even as far as Milford Center and Fairview, now Ostrander, in wagons, horseback and on foot. When the young people would start home on their prancing horses it would look like a troop of cavalry. The services usually lasted until 2 :00 o'clock. Not one of the members of that old congregation survives and of the young girls who sang in the choir I recall but two who are living, Jane Curry Randall, of Plain City, and Susannah Robinson McKitrick, residing near New California, and of the young men not one. Of the ruling elders I recall the names of James Ewing, T. M. Ewing, John Taylor, Jessie Gill, James Robinson, Stephenson Curry, David Chapman, Abner Chapman. The old church building, after the congregation was disorganized, was abandoned to the birds and bats, the windows knocked out, the yard grown up in weeds and bushes, and so it remained until after the close of the Civil War. In the year 1870 it was torn down and the brick was hauled to Plain City and used in the erection of a Presbyterian church on the site now occupied by the Commodius Church, to which it gave way a few years ago. When that church was erected I was secretary of the building committee and Rev. Wm. H. Galbreath, who was pastor in the old church in 1839, preached the dedicatory sermon. The organizers of the old church were a God-fearing people and while the good old fathers and mothers have gone to their rewards, their seed was sown on fertile ground and has borne good fruit, as evidenced by the fact that many of their descendants are still zealous workers in the vineyard of the good old Presbyterian Church at Plain City and other churches. Some of the descendants of this congregation became ministers of the Presbyterian Church, among whom may be named David G. Robinson, son of James Robinson, and James Curry, son of Stepenson Curry, who has been a prominent minister in the state of California for thirty-seven years and is now located at Newark in that state. David G. Robinson died about the year 1872-73.

THE OLD SECEDER CHURCH, NEW CALIFORNIA.

The Seceder Church, now the United Presbyterian Church, was organized at New California between the years 1835 and 1840. The society was organized by the McCampbells and the Beards, who emigrated from Rockbridge County, Virginia, in 1835, and soon after came the Liggetts. The McCampbells and Beards were connected with the Associate Church of Ebenzer and Timber Ridge congregation, Virginia, before coming to Ohio.

Services were first held at the residence of Wm. McCampbell, Sr., and then in the cooper shop of John McCampbell.

Rev. James Wallace organized the congregation and the first rulings elders ordained and installed were Wm. Bigger and David Beard, with about thirty members.

Rev. Robert Forester, who resided at Reynoldsburg, Ohio, supplied the church the first two years.

Rev. I. N. Laughead was the first pastor installed. He became pastor in April, 1843, and so continued until April, 1864. He was also pastor of the U. P. Church at Unionville Center for the same period. He stated in a letter at one time that his salary at first was $300 per year and never was above $400. Rev. Laughead was also a farmer during his pastorate here and had one of the best improved farms in the neighborhood. He was quite successful as a manager and accumulated considerable property, although it was not by reason of the meager salary he received as a minister.

He also taught school in the winter season and some of the older persons residing now in the community were his pupils. He was a devoted Christian and enterprising citizen, and gave the best of his life ministering to his congregation, composed of earnest, God-fearing people.

Mrs. Laughead was a woman of intelligence, devoted to the interest of the congregation, and reared an interesting family. The oldest son, William Bradford, died in the army during the Civil War and the only daughter, Elizabeth, now Mrs. J. H. Young, resides in Pasadena, California, and two sons, James and Leander, reside in Iowa.

In the spring of 1865 Rev. Laughead and family removed to Washington, Iowa, where he and his good wife were laid to rest several years ago. The first church building erected by the congregation was of logs about the year 1841. The ceiling was very low and some of the benches used as seats did not have any backs. When the minister was in the pulpit his head reached almost to the joists, which were heavy enough for a railroad bridge. The congregation worshiped in this building until 1852, when the old frame building now used as a township house was erected on the same site now occupied by the church building erected in 1904.

Of the old families who were members of this great congregation may be named McCampbells, Liggetts, Beards, Robinsons, Mitchells, Woodburns, Gowans, McDowells, Biggers, McCrorys, Taylors, McCulloughs, and Bains

I do not recall but one of that old generation who organized the church seventy-eight years ago who survives—Martha Robinson Beard, widow of Andrew Beard, now living with her daughter, Martha Williams, in Cleveland, Ohio. But few of the younger generation reside in Jerome Township, and of the McCampbells, Amanda Comstock and Dell McCampbell, and of the McDowells, Porter and Leander; the Liggetts, Mrs. Clement Evans; the Taylors, Mrs. S. H. Carson.

Rev. James A. Taylor succeeded Rev. Laughead in April,

1865, to November 19th, 1867. From that date until Rev. John Gilmore was installed September 12th, 1871, there was no regular pastor. He was followed by Rev. D. M. Gordon in January, 1875, and Rev. Ebenezer E. Cleland succeeded in April, 1878, to September, 1895. Rev. B. E. Dobbins, September, 1897, to April, 1902. Rev. R. C. Finney, July, 1903, to August, 1909. Rev. E. H. Thompson, the present pastor, July, 1911.

The good influence of this congregation in the community for three-quarters of a century has not only been for the spiritual welfare of its membership, but for the spiritual and moral welfare of all the people. While at this time the membership is greatly reduced as compared with that of fifty years ago, yet their influence for all that is good in society and the high regard and reverence that still obtains for the Sabbath day and the ceremonies of the church is all in the interest of good citizenship. If we had more such churches in our country there would not be need for so many prisons.

In the early days, soon after the select schoolhouse was erected, a class was organized by the Methodist denomination. Rev. Merrill, who afterward became a distinguished Bishop in that church and an eloquent speaker, was the first minister. Nelson Cone, Judah Dodge (who was an exhorter in the church for many years), James B. Dort, John Ruehlen, John Nonnemaker, James Ketch, and a number of the other old families were active members of the church. Services were held in the Select School building or township house, at California.

A Sunday School was organized and flourished with a good attendance for a number of years. In time some of the active members died and others affiliated with churches at Plain City or Jerome, and the organization was abandoned.

About the year 1854 a number of German families, including the Kimberlies, Ruehlens, Housers, Myers, Masts and others, came direct from the Fatherland and settled in the vicinity. They held services frequently in the township house, but did not have any regular minister. Many of the young people of the neighborhood attended these meetings, and while they could not understand the sermon, they enjoyed the singing, as there were some splendid voices among these good German people.

When the U. P. Church was at the zenith of its prosperity they had great congregations. They came in wagons, buggies, on horseback and a-foot, and from the number of horses hitched to the trees in the woods near the church it resembled a Camp Meeting or County Fair. Like the services in the old Red Brick Presbyterian Church near Plain City, they continued all day, with two sermons and a half hour for lunch. The singing was usually led by Moderwell and Hunter Robinson, by reading two lines of the Psalm, then leading in the singing.

PLAIN CITY.

The population of Plain City at this time is about 1,500, and of that number 400 reside in Jerome Township. The flouring mill, owned and operated by U. D. Beard, is located on the west bank of Darby Creek in Jerome Township. The mill was erected by Dr. W. I. Ballinger and Richard Woodruff in 1873, and has always done a good business, handling a large amount of grain.

The Plain City M. E. Church is located in Jerome Township. The church building is beautiful and commodious, the congregation numbering about 500, with a large and flourishing Sunday School. The Church Society of Pleasant Valley was organized in the cabin of Andrew Noteman about the year 1812, and has been in existence continuously, the majority of the congregation residing in Madison County. Rev. S. A. Stephan is the minister in charge at this time.

Pastime Park, joining the village on the north, is located on the old farm owned in the early days by William McCune, who also operated quite an extensive tannery. The park contains 27 acres of ground, and has a fine race-track for matinee races and training horses. The grove of natural forest trees is beautiful, and a great pleasure resort. Chautauqua meetings are held in the park every year. The "City of Tents"

ROBERT L. WOODBURN
86th O. V. I.

MAJOR LLEWELLYN B. CURRY
Paymaster U. S. Navy.

CAPTAIN JAMES CUTLER
2nd U. S. I., 1st O. V. C., Civil War·
Mexican War.

DUNALLEN M. WOODBURN
58th O. V. I.

CAPTAIN JAMES A. CURRY
War of 1812.

during these meetings is quite large and the attendance is numbered by thousands.

Many picnics and Fourth of July celebrations were held on these grounds before the Civil War. Some of the older citizens recall these celebrations held every year in Pleasant Valley, and in those days the meetings were patriotic indeed. Usually one good speaker, the reading of the Declaration of Independence, a few patriotic songs, music by a good martial band, made a day of real enjoyment. Long tables were erected, filled with the substantial "fat of the land," and a free dinner for all.

In the year 1833 Otway Curry, who resided in a log house on the exact spot where now stands the residence of Charles M. Jones, composed a poem especially for the Fourth of July celebration. It was set to the music of Pleyel's Hymn Second, and sung July 4th, 1833, in Bigelow's Grove, Pleasant Valley, under the leadership of Nelson Cone. The poem will be herewith published as a part of the early history of Pleasant Valley, frequently referred to by the newspapers of today.

> "God of the high and boundless   heaven,
>   We call upon Thy name;
> We tread the soil that Thou hast given
>   To Freedom and to fame.
> Around us on the ocean waves
>   Our starry banners sweep,
> Around us in their lowly graves
>   Our patriot fathers sleep.
>
> With fearless hearts and stalwart hands
>   They bore the eagle high
> O'er serried arms and battle brands
>   Careering in the sky;
> For Freedom, in her darkest day,
>   Their life-blood bathed the plain;
> Their mouldering tombs shall pass away,
>   Their glory shall remain.

4

God of the Free, Thy children bless,
   With joy their labor crown;
Let their domain be limitless,
   And endless their renown.
Proclaim the morn of Freedom's birth
   O'er every land and sea,
Till her pure spirit fill the earth,
   Wide as the heavens are free."

The farm which Mr. Charles M. Jones owns and on which
he resides, adjoins Plain City on the north and was purchased
by his father, Thomas Jones, in 1856, who was the first man
to introduce Norman horses in this section of the State. He
also dealt largely in thoroughbred cattle and Plain City became
noted throughout the State for fine horses and cattle.

Charles M. Jones, on his "Pleasant Valley Stock Farm"
as it is still called, deals largely in horses and keeps up the
reputation established by his father more than half a century
ago as a breeder of fine stock.

There are citizens yet living in the vicinity who can remember the days when there were but two general stores in
the village, George Hill, proprietor of one, and Joseph and
Peter Guitner of the other, and "Old Dad Marshall" kept the
grocery, where he dispensed ginger-snaps, blind-robbins, and
red-striped peppermint candy. The merchants of the town
at this time have a large and flourishing trade. Good churches,
goods schools, and the citizens are progressive, prosperous, and
happy.

VILLAGE OF JEROME.

The village of Jerome, also known as Beachtown, Pleasant
Hill, and Frankfort, was platted in the year 1846 by William
Irwin, County Surveyor, for Henry Beach, and the Beach family was the only family residing there. It is pleasantly situated and in the early days was a thriving business town, but
like other inland villages, while it is still a good business town,
it has not increased greatly in population. The Beaches and
the majority of the old inhabitants have passed away, but the

village and vicinity have always been noted for good substantial citizenship, a thriving farming community, and the merchants do a good business in all lines, and at all times.

The first merchants of the village were Amos and Kilburn Beach, and the first tavern keeper was William Case. Other merchants who have been prominent business men in the village are H. B. Seely, Lattimer & Hamilton, George Dixon, Oliver Asbury. The merchants now doing business are Daniel Landecker and H. B. Seely Company.

Herrick B. Seely was for many years a merchant in the village, and also served as Postmaster. He was a fine business man and stood high in the community and among wholesale merchants as a man of strict integrity. At his death the business descended to his sons, one of whom still continues in business in the village in general merchandise, under the firm name of H. B. Seely Co. The firm does a large and profitable business, and are in every way worthy successors of their father, who laid the foundation for long-continued mercantile business by the family.

The first Methodist Church was organized at Jerome in the year 1835 and services were first held at the residence of Henry Beach. Among the early members were the Beaches, Stones, Hallecks, Wells and Frederick families.

A log church was erected in 1842, which was occupied as a church until a short time before the outbreak of the Civil War. A frame church was erected and dedicated April 15th, 1860, by a Rev. Dr. Warner as pastor. Among the ministers who have served as pastors of the congregation are: Rev. Chase, Rev. Hathaway, Rev. John E. Moore, Rev. Edward Rudesill, Rev. J. Shoop, Rev. Thurston, Rev. Ferris, Rev. Pierman, Rev. Abernathy, Rev. J. K. Argo, Rev. Pryor, Rev. Theodore Crayton, Rev. A. Holcomb, Rev. A. L. Rogers, Rev. B. J. Judd, Rev. Tubbs, Rev. Thomas Ricketts, Rev. Thomas Wakefield, Rev. J. H. Middling, Rev. A. Plum, Rev. John Gordon.

The Jerome Presbyterian Church was organized December 16th, 1853, and Rev. William Brinkerhoff was the first pastor.

Templeton Liggett and John Fleck were the first Ruling Elders. Rev. Brinkerhoff served as pastor of the church until the congregation decided to become a Congregational Church, on November 2d, 1862, and he then resigned as pastor. Afterward Rev. Hawn, an old-school Presbyterian, became pastor, followed by Rev. C. N. Coulter in 1866. In 1867 the denomination was again changed to the new-school Presbyterian, and Rev. A. N. Hamlin became pastor, followed by Rev. Stevenson, Rev. Mason, Rev. Hill, Rev. Crow, Rev. Thomas, Rev. Christ, Rev. Henry Shedd. About the year 1898 the Presbyterian and Methodist congregations united and the Presbyterian Society was abandoned. The Methodists now have a good, strong congregation under the pastorate of Rev. John Gordon.

SCHOOLS.

The educational privileges have always compared favorably in the schools of the village with other schools in the township, which is noted in the county for its excellent schools. Under the present efficient Superintendent, Professor Homer E. Cahall, the Special High School ranks among the best in the county.

The new school building, known as the Ryan Memorial School, Jerome Special High School, is modern in every respect and speaks volumns for the community in which it is located. The district, with the help of Mr. Ryan, erected this spacious and beautiful structure, and the school and community owe to Mr. Ryan, the great benefactor, a debt of gratitude for his untiring energy and efforts in their behalf. The School Board and all progressive citizens are entitled to great credit for their support toward securing a new building, and thus advancing the cause of education in this community.

The building is a model as regards beauty and convenience, and cost approximately $11,000. It is a four-room building, and includes library room, office of the School Board and the superintendent, together with a spacious auditorium in the basement, which seats about 300 people. Nothing has been spared that might add to the comfort of the pupils, and the library is up-to-date and contains about 400 volumes. Through the efforts of the superintendent and the School Board the school was placed in the list of second-grade high schools of the State. The school is equipped with a fine apparatus for Physics, Agriculture, and Botany, and the present corps of teachers are very efficient.

The Primary Department is in charge of Miss Marie Pounds, who is an excellent instructor for that grade. Mr. Lon McMillan is in charge of the Intermediate grades, while Professor H. E. Cahall has charge of the High School Department. Mr. McMillan has been a student both at Delaware and Ada Universities, and Professor Cahall is a graduate of Miami University, Oxford, Ohio.

There are about 100 pupils attending the school this year. The district has been centralized, the pupils being conveyed to school in modern vehicles. With a progressive superintendent and well-trained, competent teachers, and with an awakened and thoroughly Christianized community, the school will no doubt prosper in the future as it has in the past.

As the Jerome school of today is much further advanced than the school of fifty years ago, so we may feel confident that fifty years hence the school will, in the onward march of progress, by far surpass the school of today. In the language of the historian, "The Past has taught its lesson, the Present has its duty, and the Future has its hope."

PHYSICIANS.

Of the physicians who have practiced in Jerome may be named Drs. Converse, Asberry, Holland, John E. Herriott, Dr. P. F. Beverly (who served as surgeon of the 30th Regiment, O. V. I.), Dr. Henry, Dr. Bargar, and Dr. Kirbey.

The following named citizens have served as postmasters: Horace Beach, Isaac Wells, George Leasure, Hurd Lewis, Dr. Converse, S. H. Brake, William O'Hara, John Latham, Joseph Brobeck, James Linn, W. Wells, H. B. Seeley, George Dixon,

Olliver Asbury, Lattimer & Hamilton, and Pearl E. Hyland. The mail is now received R. F. D. from Plain City.

Among the old and prominent families who settled in the eastern section of the township in the early days were the Stones, Donaldsons, Norrises, Colliers, Hoberts, Fredericks, Pattersons, Dorts, Cases, Beaches, Wells, Bishops, Evans, Moss, Hudsons, Brobecks, Williams, McCrorys, Herriotts, Magills, Hills, Jacksons, Neils, Langstaffs, Stuarts, Frys, Brakes, O'Harra, Ashbaughs, Perrys, Seeleys, Temples, Bowersmiths, McKitricks, Foxes, Brinkerhoffs, Durboroughs, and many others who came later. There were but few of these families who had members that were eligible to military service who were not represented in the Union Army.

There was quite a military spirit abounding in the village in the ante-bellum days. Some of us who took part in the Civil War can recall the days in the late years of 1840 when the muster and training days of the "Corn-Stalk Militia" on the farms of James A. and Robert Curry were looked forward to by the boys as the great events of the year. When Captain Kilburn Beach, in gorgeous regimentals, cockade and flowing plumes, drilled the Militia, the rattling of the drums and the shrill notes of the fife was the signal for all the boys in the neighborhood to assemble at the place of muster to hear the music and witness the drill.

This recalls the poem in the old Second Reader of that day:

> "Was you ne'er a Schoolboy
>   And did you never train,
> And feel the swelling of your heart,
>   You ne'er shall feel again;
> We charged upon a flock of geese
>   And put them all to flight,
> Except one sturdy gander
>   Who thought he'd show us fight;
> But oh! we knew a thing or two,
>   Our Captain wheeled the van,
> We scouted them, we routed them,
>   Nor lost a single man."

Little did the boys of this neighborhood, when reading or reciting this old poem, think they would, in a few years, have the opportunity to charge upon an enemy in real war, in some of the greatest battles of modern times.

Isaac Wells, a prominent citizen of Jerome, was Orderly Sergeant, and some of us remember about the men lying around on the grass answering to their names as he called the roll at the close of the day's arduous drill. The patriotic and military spirit instilled in the boys by the training and muster days, in which they were too young to take part, was aroused to fever heat when war was declared in April, 1861. At the time when the first company for three months was being organized at New California, I recall that several of us attended a war meeting at Jerome. It was held in the Presbyterian Church and Rev. William Brinkerhoff, pastor of the church, made an eloquent address, of which I remember one sentence distinctly. The drums were on the pulpit platform, to which he called attention by saying: "Munitions of war and the Bible are side by side in the House of the Lord."

The only full company organized in the township was at Jerome. This company was organized in August, 1861, and the officers at organization were: Captain, Elijah Warner; First Lieutenant, Henry Brinkerhoff; Second Lieutenant, Henry Hensel.

One hundred and two soldiers served in the company during the war, and thirty-two died in the service. The company was assigned as Company E, 30th Regiment, O. V. I. Captain Warner was promoted to Major of the Regiment; Lieutenant Brinkerhoff was promoted to Lieutenant Colonel of the 2nd Mississippi, U. S. C. T., and James D. Bain was promoted to the Captaincy of the company.

Lieutenant Colonel Brinkerhoff remained in the Regular Army after the close of the Civil War, and was retired a few years ago with the rank of Colonel. Major Warner, Captain Bain and Lieutenant Hensel are all dead. As I recall, Sergeant James C. Collier, who had a long and honorable service from August 19th, 1861, to August 13th, 1865, is the last survivor of that company of 102 brave Jerome Township boys residing in the vicinity at this time.

The company had a remarkable service and the losses were appalling, as almost one-third of their number were killed or died in the service, and scarcely a man in the company escaped some casualty, either by wounds or by being captured as a prisoner of war.

THE VILLAGE OF NEW CALIFORNIA.

The village of New California was platted in 1853 and the first general store was opened by S. B. Woodburn and Dr. Albert Chapman. Soon after the platt was made, Samuel Ressler of Marysville, Ohio, erected a two-story frame building on the southwest corner of the square for a tavern, and did quite a thriving business for a number of years. He also had a small grocery in the same building. This soon became the great center for the stock business in the southern part of the county. Stock scales were erected and hundreds of hogs would be driven in by the farmers in one day. They were then driven to Pleasant Valley or Worthington to be shipped by rail to New York. Some droves would number three or four hundred and many boys in the neighborhood were employed at 50 cents a day to drive them, often through mud and rain. As there were no bridges spanning the small streams, and the water at times being solidly frozen, it would be the work of hours to force the great droves of hogs across the ice, and the boys well earned the half-dollar a day.

The Ressler Tavern was quite a favorite hostelry in its day, as there was a great deal of travel on the State Road, running from Pleasant Valley to Delaware, and also on the road leading from Marysville to Columbus. Many were the yarns spun in the old barroom as travelers, drovers, and others gathered around the old open-front wood fire Franklin stove, smoking their pipes and "stogies" furnished by the genial landlord. The first mails, once a week, were carried on horseback from Dublin in those ante-bellum days. Still, the arrival of the mail, carried in large saddle-bags, was quite an import-

ant event, as it brought the weekly papers, and all were eager
to hear the latest news—but a week old.

Among the merchants who "kept store" and kept the post-
office in the village the following named are recalled: S. B.
Woodburn, Perry Buck, John Liggett, John Robinson, H.
Benton, George Stokes, William Thompson, Robert Thomp-
son, Otway, John W. and W. L. Curry, Fred Fleck, Robert
Hager, Albert Allen, H. M. Dort, Jesse Curry, and Grant E.
Herriott.

Mr. Grant E. Herriott, the present merchant, has been in
business in the village several years. He is an energetic, progressive young man, has a good trade, is doing a flourishing
business in general merchandise. He takes a deep interest in
the schools, is treasurer of the School Board, is active in all
the business affairs of the township, and is up-to-date.

The first physician who practiced in the village was Dr.
Culver, and in succession Drs. Milo Lawrence, Thomas J.
Haynes, James Cutler, B. F. McGlade, J. S. Howland, Dr.
Merriam, Dr. Vigor, the present physician, has a large and
lucrative practice.

Some of the characters of the village were quite interesting, and had some traits that would have made David Harum
green with envy. The village blacksmith was John Walley,
which recalls the poem:

> " Under a spreading chestnut tree,
>   The village smithy stands;
> The smith, a mighty man is he,
>   With large and sinewy hands;
> And the muscles of his brawny arms
>   Are strong as iron bands."

In his shop the schoolboys congregated at the noon hour
to watch the sparks fly from the red-hot iron, as the swarthy
smith hammered the horseshoes into shape and nailed them to
the hoofs of many wild and vicious horses.

John was a great story teller, and it was claimed that he
had great imagination and at times "used the truth with parsi-
monious frugality." He claimed to have invented a magnify-

ing glass, through which he could look into the earth three miles. With this glass he located several gold and silver mines in the neighborhood, but they were never developed for lack of funds, He never would allow anyone to see the glass, as he claimed he did let one man look through it and it magnified so strong that it killed him.

He was also a great skater and one of his stories was that one time when he lived in Dublin, Ohio, he skated to Columbus and back, twenty-four miles, before breakfast, and cut ten acres of wheat with a cradle the same day. He did not let the seasons spoil a good story. The tales of the Arabian Knights vanished into nothingness beside the wonderful stories of the blacksmith, and it is but little wonder that the schoolboys stood with eyes distended and mouths agape as they listened to his wonderful tales.

The Gowan boys also erected quite a pretentious blacksmith and wagon-shop and for many years did a thriving business. Others recalled in the same line were Wilson Martin and John Hickman. Both of the latter were queer and interesting characters, and many amusing stories could be related of their peculiarities.

Martin was quite a nimrod and usually kept his rifle handy in the shop for any emergency, if game was reported in the vicinity. One day he was busily engaged shoeing a horse for a farmer when a boy came into his shop and reported a flock of wild turkeys in the woods near by. Martin dropped the horse's foot, seized his rifle, bullet pouch and powder horn and made for the designated quarry on the double quick, leaving the horse half shod. In about two hours he returned, groaning under the load of three sleek, fat, brown turkeys on his back. All the villagers assembled to see the game and congratulated Martin on his wonderful prowess as a hunter. He, like many other great hunters, was no doubt drawing on his imagination a little by relating how he had driven these wild turkeys, that were swifter on foot than the fastest deer-hound in the country, to cover and how he had brought them down from the highest oak trees with his good and unerring rifle, "Black Bess." It was a thrilling story and the villagers were much enthused. But soon a damper was to come, as a neighboring farmer appeared on the scene after a man who had been killing his flock of tame turkeys. Martin was very much crestfallen when he learned the truth, and the farmer, a very liberal man, presented Martin with the turkeys and bade him "sin no more." But the blacksmith never heard the last of it from the village boys, who teased him about not knowing the difference between a tame and a wild turkey.

THE LITTLE BROWN SCHOOLHOUSE.

The old schoolhouse standing on the northeast corner of the square at New California is one among the last of the old landmarks left in that village of buildings erected more than half a century ago.

The house was very substantially built, as was the custom in those early days, otherwise it would not have stood intact for three score years. The frame is of heavy hewn oak, doors, windows, casing, weather-boarding and shingles walnut, all worked out by hand. As you enter the front door there is a small room on the right about twelve or fourteen feet square, used for a hat and cloak room, and a similar room on the left, used for election purposes. The main room will seat about seventy-five persons, and was heated by a big box-wood stove, standing in the center of the room. It is undoubtedly the oldest schoolhouse in the county at this date, and according to the recollection of the "oldest inhabitants" it has received but one coat of brown paint since it was erected.

This house was erected in 1852 and the first "Select School" was taught by Llewellyn B. Curry in the winter of 1582-3.

By the kindness of my two old schoolmates, Robert Mc-Crory and R. L. Woodburn, a photograph of the old schoolhouse, as it now appears with broken windows and weather-beaten by the blistering suns of summer and the blasting storms of more than fifty winters, was placed in my hands.

As we look at that photograph, what memories of the days

of more than half a century ago come trooping thick and fast, some sweet memories and some sad. Sweet memories, as the old song goes, of

> "School days, school days,
> Good old Golden Rule days,
> Reading, and writing, and 'rithmetic,
> Taught to the tune of a hickory stick."

Pleasant days to think about now, but not all so pleasant when the "schoolmaster" used the rod with a heavy hand, as he was wont to do on frequent occasions, but usually not amiss.

Then there are the sad memories when we recall the great majority who, with us, pored over the hard examples in Ray's Arithmetic and parsed, with the thirty-five rules of the old Kirkham Grammar,, Gray's "Elegy" and "Hamlet's Soliloquy," who have crossed the dark river. No other period in the life of man is so fraught with unalloyed happiness as the good old school days.

The citizens of that day who by their enterprise and with a view of raising the standard of the common schools, erected the building have all passed to their reward, but their work has borne good fruit. Among the many old settlers who were interested and assisted both by work and contributions may be named Jesse Gill, John, Alfred, Samuel, David and Andrew McCampbell, Samuel B. and John Woodburn, John, William, Templeton and Henry Liggett, James A. Stephenson, Robert and John Curry, Nelson Cone, Jesse and David Mitchell, Dixon, Thomas, James, Moderwell and Mitchell Robinson, Walter Gowans, John McDowell, Rev. I. N. Lauhead, Perry Buck, Judah Dodge, James and David Dort, Jame Ketch, William Bigger, William Taylor, Anthony Wise, Elijah, Ira and Henry Fox, Landon Bishop, John Ruehlen and John Nonnemaker.

Many other citizens in the township whose names might be mentioned were interested, but the names given are of the old settlers within a radius of two miles who took an active part in this advanced movement in educational matters.

The building fund was secured by private subscription, excepting $50 donated by the township, with the proviso that it could be used for elections and township meetings.

As there was no other public hall in the village, it was used not only for elections, but for all kinds of political, religious, Sunday School, singing schools and public meetings as long as it was occupied for school purposes and served the public well for nearly half a century.

The original idea in erecting the building was for the sole purpose of establishing a "Select School" where the higher branches were taught to prepare students for teaching or to enter college. The teachers were, with few exceptions, college graduates, and the branches taught included higher mathematics and the languages. A literary society was organized and was continued from year to year as long as the Select School was kept up, which was for a period of about forty years and until a graded district school was established in the village.

The school was largely attended and at one time it was shown by the records of certificates issued by the Board of School Examiners that there was a sufficient number of teachers in Jerome Township to supply all the schools in the county.

Many young men and women who attended this school received, through encouragement from these high-grade teachers, their first incentive to secure a collegiate education. A large number of them did enter college and were graduated with honors and are now successful business or professional men and attribute their success largely to the educational advantages in this school.

Among the teachers were Llewellyn B. Curry, Rev. I. N. Laughead, Rev. Isaac Winters, Olive Gill, David Cochran, Samuel Graham, Mr. Johnson, Thomas Evans, R. L. Woodburn, George Ruehlen, Mr. McCharahan, Leroy Welsh, James Curry, John Stockton, E. L. Liggett, Calvin Robinson, David H. Cross and J. W. Baughman.

Of these teachers the following named have died:

Llewellyn B. Curry, Rev. I. N. Laughead, Rev. Isaac

Winters, David Cochran, Samuel Graham, E. L. Liggett, Olive Gill Mitchell, Leroy Welsh, and R. L. Woodburn.

The names and residences of the survivors so far as known are: Thomas Evans, in Decatur, Illinois; Colonel George Ruehlen, Quartermaster U. S. Army, Washington, D. C.; Rev. James Curry, Newark, California; Calvin Robinson, Hartington, Nebraska; D. H. Cross, Pasco, Texas, and J. W. Baughman.

Of the other named teachers the addresses are not known, if they still survive.

The descendants of 'the old settlers named as taking an active part in organizing this school were all pupils of the school, numbering from three to perhaps six in each family, and in all several hundred during the forty school years. The school term only extended over the late autumn and fall months and did not interfere with the public schools of the winter, and many of the students taught country schools during the winter and "boarded around" among the scholars.

They are now of the third generation, counting from the first settlers of the county in 1798. Many of that generation have reached the allotted age of three score years and ten, and those who survive are scattered all over the continent, from the Atlantic to the Pacific.

Many pleasant incidents are recalled of those good old days, and as the classes of boys and girls were about equally divided, in the parlance of today it would be known as a Co-ed School.

A beautiful woods of sugar and other forest trees, the property of James A. Curry, adjoined the schoolhouse lot. This was the favorite trysting place of the boys and girls ranging from 16 to 18 years of age. At the noon hour many of these pupils could be seen walking under the shade of the grand old forest trees and perhaps late in the fall gathering hickory-nuts, which were usually in abundance. No doubt some of these joyous-hearted girls and boys, as they strolled along the shady paths, or, seated on the trunk of a fallen tree, plighted their friendship — perhaps love — talked not only of the present but of the future. Can any of the old pupils, whose hair may now be sprinkled with the gray tints of the autumn of life, recall such a scene? Some of these joyous hopes were destined to be rudely broken by the cruel fate of war. Family ties were to be severed; sad hearts of mothers, sisters and sweethearts were to linger prayerfully in the old farmhouses along "Sugar Run" waiting for the loved ones who would never return.

The fall term of 1860 ended the school days of many of those farmer boys forever, and they were to play an important part in that great drama of Civil War.

Already the bark of the war dogs could be heard sounding nearer and nearer.

The writer, with several other students who had attended this "Select School," had just entered upon a college course at Otterbein University, but in the spring of 1861 our books were packed, and so ended our school days for all time.

NEW CALIFORNIA SCHOOLS OF TODAY.

The school building is a substantial frame erected about three years ago, with five rooms and thoroughly modern, with all conveniences for the comfort of the pupils. To those of us who were pupils here almost three-score years ago, it is a great pleasure to witness the marked progress in educational facilities, although the school here at that early date was considered among the best in the county. The erection of the old frame schoolhouse which still stands on the corner of the square, marked the first advance in higher education in this community. While all the old families of enterprising and Christian citizenship who first inaugurated this movement have passed away, still their descendants have kept up their interest in education matters, and it is pleasing to note that some of them are now members of the School Board and join hand in hand with the newcomers in all matters pertaining to good citizenship.

Professor J. B. Hughes is the present Superintendent, assisted by a corps of competent teachers, all of whom rank among the best qualified teachers of the county: Mr. Henry Stewart, Principal; Miss Margaret Strapp and Miss Ada May, Primary Department; Miss Leo D. Wise, Intermediate; Miss Lelon Neill, Grammar; Miss Nora Mulcahy, Assistant High School Principal. The grand total of pupils in attendance is 196; graduates in 1913, 10; and 39 pupils in the different grades in High School, with three courses: Latin, English, and Commercial, all adapted to the needs of pupils who aspire to a college or university course.

The Board of Education is now planning to erect a high school building of four rooms during the ensuing year. The following named progressive citizens compose the Board of Education at this time: J. W. Mitchell, J. M. Curry, G. W. Carson, John Gugle, John McKittrick, Dr. W. C. Vigor (Clerk), Grant E. Herriott (Treasurer). Under the management of this board, with Professor Hughes and the competent teachers, this school holds an enviable place among the schools of the county and in all matters connected with the school in its onward progress the citizens of the community take a great pride.

With comfortable covered conveyances in which all the pupils are carried from their homes and returned safely, it is certainly a joy to be permitted to attend such a school, as compared with the conditions fifty years ago, when the pupils were compelled to wade through mud or snow up to their knees in the winter season, and but few comforts and conveniences in the schoolhouses.

What a transformation! Only two centralized schools in the township at this time, and before the system was changed at least ten district. Graduation from these high schools prepares the farmer boy for business or entry into college.

Of the many school-teachers of Jerome Township of continuous service for a long period, C. L. Curry is no doubt entitled to the credit and stands at the head of the list. He taught every year from the winter of 1868 to 1884 inclusive, a period of seventeen years, with no interval — a total of nineteen terms, or seventy months.

SERGEANT ROBERT A. LIGGETT
96th O. V. I.

ROBERT McCRORY
30th O. V. I.

WILLIAM M. LIGGETT
96th O. V. I.

CAPTAIN WILLIAM McCRORY
7th Ohio Independent Sharpshooters.

CAPTAIN ANDREW GOWANS
94th O. V. I.

SERGEANT JAMES E. GOWANS
46th O. V. I.

ALEXANDER D. GOWANS
96th O. V. I.

THOMPSON O. COLE
96th O. V. I.

Olive Gill, Emma and Sophia Dodge, Nancy McCampbell and many other teachers of long service might be named.

Mr. Curry has always taken a deep interest in educational matters, not only in the township, but in the county and State, and still keeps up his interest and is always ready to lend a helping hand for advancement along progressive lines in the public schools.

THE VILLAGE OF ARNOLD.

The village of Arnold is located on the Toledo and Ohio Central Railroad at the crossing of the gravel road leading from Plain City to New California.

The railway station was located and the village platted on the land of Mrs. George Arnold, for whom the town is named, in the fall of 1893. The station was first named New California, until application was made for a postoffice, and the name was then changed, as there was a postoffice at New California.

Mr. James Arnold, who established the first grocery in the village, was appointed Postmaster. He discontinued business and the office was abandoned. Fred Smith was commissioned Postmaster in 1896, but never performed the duties, as he sold his business just at the time his commission arrived. Mrs. Carrie Fleck was then appointed to the position, and she, with her husband, Perry Fleck, established a general store in the village in the fall of 1896.

Mrs. Fleck continued as Postmistress until the office was discontinued, March 1st, 1910, by reason of establishing free mail delivery, and mail is now received from Plain City, R. R. No. 3. Mr. and Mrs. Fleck have built up a good trade in groceries and drygoods, and deal largely in produce by having a wagon run on a number of routes through the country, and deliver their produce in Columbus every week.

There is one grocery, of which J. W. Cunningham is proprietor; an ax-handle factory, and two warehouses, both owned by J. R. Herriott, at the Station. Quite a large amount of goods—coal and other freight—is received at the Station,

5

and a great deal of timber and sawed lumber is shipped from this point. There are twenty-four dwelling houses and the village has a population of about one hundred, the children attending the Central School at New California.

JEROME TOWNSHIP CITIZENS WHO HAVE SERVED AS STATE, COUNTY, AND TOWNSHIP OFFICIALS.

Four Jerome Township citizens have served as members of the Ohio Legislature.

James Curry represented the counties of Delaware and Madison before Union County was organized, for the years 1812, 1813, 1814, 1815; also for the years 1819, 1820, and was a member of the Legislature when the law was enacted for the erection of Union County, so named as territory was taken from the counties of Delaware, Franklin, Logan and Madison.

Otway Curry represented the counties of Crawford, Marion and Union in 1837 and 1838.

Robert L. Woodburn represented Union County in 1904-1908.

Charles D. Brown was elected in 1912 and is the present Representative.

COUNTY OFFICERS.

ASSOCIATE JUDGE
James Curry 1825-1827

PROBATE JUDGES
James McCampbell.............................1894-1900
Dudley E. Thornton............................1906-1913

PROSECUTING ATTORNEYS
Otway Curry 1848-1853
Robert L. Woodburn............................1877-1881

COUNTY TREASURER
William M. Liggett...............................1879-1883

COUNTY AUDITORS
Clark Provin 1821-1823
W. L. Curry...1875-1882

CLERK OF THE COURT

Robert McCrory 1888-1892

COUNTY RECORDER

Edward H. Hatton................................1905-1911

SHERIFF

James Ewing 1823-1828

Charles M. Robinson................................1862-1864

J. Ed. Robinson................................1896-1900

COUNTY COMMISSIONERS

Jesse Gill 1844

Nelson Cone 1853

John K. Dodge................................ 1878

TOWNSHIP OFFICIALS.

JUSTICES OF THE PEACE

Clark Provin	1821	Perry Buck	1854
John McCune	1823	Templeton Liggett	1855
James Ewing	1824	I. N. Wells	1855
James Buck	1825	James Ketch	1856
Henry Sager	1827	Samuel B. Woodburn	1858
James Buck	1828	I. N. Wells	1858
William Long	1832	James Ketch	1859
John McCampbell	1837	I. N. Wells	1867
Caleb Converse	1838	S. B. Woodburn	1867
S. Snodgrass	1839	Nelson Cone	1869
Thomas Wason	1839	S. B. Woodburn	1870
Thomas M. Ewing	1841	S. W. H. Durboraw	1870
Thomas Mason	1842	Nelson Cone	1872
Joseph Button	1842	S. B. Woodburn	1873
Thomas M. Ewing	1847	S. W. H. Durboraw	1873
Perry Buck	1848	J. P. McDowell	1875
Kilbourn Beach	1848	James Ketch	1876
James B. Dort	1850	S. W. H. Durboraw	1876
Thomas M. Ewing	1850	James Robinson	1878
Perry Buck	1851	Nelson Cone	1879
I. N. Wells	1852	Robert McCrory	1879
Leroy F. Hager	1853	Perry Buck	1882

Robert McCrory 1882
J. P. McDowell.................. 1882
Benjamin W. Evans...1884-87
J. P. McDowell.............1885-88
Robert McCrory 1885-88
H. S. Gillespie.................1887-90
William Stone 1888-91
H. S. Gillespie.................1890-93
Benjamin W. Evans...1891-94
William H. Stone.........1891-94
J. P. McDowell.............1891-94
R. S. Fry.............................1894-97
S. W. H. Durboraw...1894-97

J. P. McDowell.............1894-97
R. S. Fry.....................1897-1900
Samuel L. Neil........1897-1900
J. P. McDowell.........1897-1900
J. P. McDowell.............1900-03
R. S. Fry.............................1900-03
Henry Brobeck 1901-04
J. P. McDowell.............1903-06
D. J. Landaker.............1905-08
J. P. McDowell.............1906-09
J. P. McDowell.............1908-12
Pearl Hyland 1910-14
J. P. McDowell.............1912-16

J. P. McDowell has served many years longer than any other Justice of the Peace — a period of thirty-three years, should he be spared to serve out his present term.

TOWNSHIP OFFICIALS — 1913.

TRUSTEES—George Grewell, J. J. Mayberry, C. L. Koerner.
TOWNSHIP TREASURER—Grant E. Herriott.
TOWNSHIP CLERK—W. C. Vigor.

All of the township officials were very much interested in the Soldiers' Monument, and rendered efficient service in the erection and dedication of the monument.

The number of votes cast in the township at the election in November, 1912, was 445, and the total population, as near as can be ascertained, is 2,200, an increase of 2125 since the organization of the township in the year 1821.

DEDICATION OF SOLDIERS' MONUMENT.

Services were held May 30, 1913, in the old United Presbyterian Church, where the first war meeting was held April 24th, 1861.

Following is the program of exercises for the day:

Hon. J. L. Cameron...President of the Day
Song—America.
Invocation...Rev. James Curry
Introducing President of the Day.....................Thomas J. Dodge

Song, "The Little White Church in the Wildwood,"
School Children.
Address ....Hon. Frank B. Willis
Song, "Battle Hymn of the Republic"..............School Children
Flag Drill...Twelve Little Girls
Recitation, "The Loyal Legion"...........................Miss Mary Gill
Marshal of the Day...George C. Edwards
Aid...Prof. Homer E. Cahall
Aid...Ney Fleck

PARADE.

Marysville Drum Corps.
Soldiers.
School Children.
March to the Monument.
Song, "Columbia the Gem of the Ocean"...........School Children
Unveiling of Monument—By Children
Ruth Woodburn Sharer, Mabel Kahler, Will Thompson,
William Curry Jeannot.
Historical Address................................Colonel W. L. Curry
Presentation of deed to Township Trustees by Monument
Committee.
Response on behalf of Trustees and Citizens of the Town-
ship accepting the Monument............Hon. Charles D. Brown
Song, "Star-Spangled Banner"........................School Children
Doxology.
Benediction...Rev. John Gordon
Decorating Graves.

COMMITTEES.

General Committee.

C. L. Curry	David Wise	Joseph Kahler
G. E. Herriott	Arthur Collier	Jasper Converse
T. J. Dodge	J. C. Collier	Delmore Snodgrass
S. H. Carson	J. P. McDowell	Robert McCrory
	George C. Edwards.	

Music.

Prof. J. B. Hughes   Mrs. Dell McCampbell

Mrs. W. C. Vigor   Ruth Evans   Jesse Mitchell
                    Mrs. William Fry.
                    Decoration.
Dr. W. C. Vigor   Sanford Stewart   Andrew Gill
        Malcolm McCampbell   Mrs. Ed. Hinderer
Harrold Fry   Mrs. J. M. Curry   Mrs. T. R. Dodge
                    Flowers.
Mary Hooper   Alice Ish   Mrs. Walker Carson
        Maggie Patch   Emma Comstock   Helen Fry
                Bernice McDowell   Hazel Herriott.
                    Flag Drill.
Leo Wise   May Williams   Cecil Dodge   Alma Hopper

On the four sides of the Monument, just above the foundation, are the names of battles of Gettysburg, Chickamauga, Vicksburg, and Appomattax. On the four large dies are the names of the soldiers. On the two upper dies are two inscriptions:

1861   OUR JEROME TOWNSHIP HEROES.   1913

In honor of the men who served in the Army of the Union. Those who fought and lived and those who fought and died. May this shaft ever call to memory the story of the glory of the men who wore the Blue.

> Bright upon historic page,
>   Enrolled their names shall ever shine,
> With peerless luster, age on age,
>   Through bright'ning realm of coming time.

Portrait of Lincoln is on one of the dies, and the names of soldiers on the remaining one.

The committee has secured from Fort Monroe, Va., a siege gun 10 feet 5 inches long, weighing 16,000 pounds, and eighty 8-inch shells. These are to be placed on the monument lot and around the lot will be erected an iron fence. The lot and Monument have been deeded to the Trustees of Jerome Township, and will be carefully preserved as a sacred trust for all time.

An interesting account of the services of unveiling and the

dedication of the Monument was published in the Marysville Tribune, from which the following extracts are taken:

"Jerome Township's enduring tribute to its soldier dead, a monument of White Bronze, costing $1,500, was dedicated Memorial Day, with exercises of a particularly fitting nature.

"Practically all of the citizens of the township, and many from the adjoining neighborhoods, were gathered at New California to witness the unveiling of the beautiful shaft, and participate in the program of dedicating the memorial to future generations.

"Distinguished sons of the township who have spent their later years in other localities were present in large numbers to join in this memorial and loving devotion to the comrades and associates of their boyhood days, also to decorate the graves of comrades who lie buried in the peaceful and quiet little cemetery—

"Under the sod and the dew,
Waiting the judgment day,

and to renew on this hallowed soil of their youth the many friendships that have been left uncultivated, but not forgotten, through years of separation and absence from the old-time scenes.

"The Monument at New California is a magnificent shaft of white bronze, 21 feet 4 inches high, with an heroic figure of an infantryman at the summit. In addition to bearing the names of 400 Jerome Township soldiers, cast on the monument, inside the base of the shaft are the following historical papers: Roster of all soldiers who enlisted from Jerome Township; names of committee which had charge of its erection; photographs of sixty Civil War veterans; names of school children of the township; names of subscribers to the Monument Fund; copies of songs sung by the school children at the dedication, with program of the ceremonies."

Extract from a letter published in the Tribune, signed "L. A. D." from New California, is quite interesting and appropriate:

"The patriotic people of Jerome Township crowded the

high-pressure mark on Decoration Day. The occasion was the unveiling of a monument at New California in memory and recognition of the sacrifices and heroism of her brave soldier boys from the Revolution down to and including the Spanish-American War.

"Decoration Day dawned bright and warm, and long before the hour for the unveiling exercises the streets of the little village were filled with people from all quarters, including Marysville, Plain City, and some far-distant points.

"New California had never had so large a gathering on its hands and was completely taken by surprise."

HISTORICAL ADDRESS DELIVERED AT THE UNVEILING OF JEROME SOLDIERS' MONUMENT BY COLONEL W. L. CURRY.

"The citizens of this township may well take a just pride in the history of its citizenship, both civil, military, and religious, from the first settlement one hundred and fifteen years ago. To this township belongs the credit of having the first white settlers within the territory now composing Union county. The first cabin was erected by Joshua and James Ewing on the west bank of Darby Creek, one mile from Plain City, in the year 1798.

"You have assembled today on historic ground. This land, known as the Virginia Military District, was ceded by the State of Virginia to the United States, with the stipulation that it was to be given to her soldiers for services rendered during the War of the Revolution.

"The patent for the land on which you stand today was signed by President Andrew Jackson in favor of a soldier of the Revolution.

"When the War of 1812 was declared, almost every man then a citizen of the township between the ages of 21 and 50 served in some capacity during the war, and names of eleven

---

Note.—A page or two of this address was copied from the township history appearing in this volume, therefore published in duplicate, as it could not be abbreviated without marring the historical connection.

of these soldiers are engraved on this monument. A company was organized at Plain City, largely recruited from Jerome Township. The Captain of the company was Jonathan Alder, who had been a captive among the Indians for many years. This company marched by order of the Governor to a point about three miles north of Marysville, where they erected a blockhouse on the west bank of Mill Creek, which they garrisoned for a short time. This was done for the protection of the settlers along Darby Creek and Sugar Run.

"Captain Alder, who had lived among the Indians for many years and knew their mode of warfare, claimed that they would not attack the blockhouse but would murder the women and children in the settlements. Therefore, on his advice the company returned to their homes. This is the only fort erected within the territory of Union County. No attack was made on the settlers during that war, but there were many alarms and the women and children who were left without protection were kept in constant fear of an outbreak, as visits were made to the settlements frequently by roving bands of Indians who claimed to be friendly.

"How appropriate it is that this beautiful and substantial monument should be erected on this spot of sacred memory— erected on land given to a soldier of the Revolution for his services in fighting for liberty during that war and to perpetuate the memory of the heroic deeds of our ancestors. Also in memory of their sons in the War of 1812, who protected the land so dearly bought, as well as the soldiers of the war with Mexico, the soldiers of the Civil War, who saved the government established by their forefathers, and the soldiers of the war with Spain, who fought to free an oppressed people. All worthy sons of worthy sires. Your ancestors of the Revolution, the War of 1812, the Civil War, and of all our wars, have left you a noble heritage of a Republic founded and perpetuated by their valor.

"The story of the inception, the progress and the completion of this monument which you dedicate today, is one of patriotic service by the citizens not only residing in this community, but of many friends and relatives of these soldiers residing in other States who have given substantial assistance.

"To Robert L. Woodburn, whose generous bequest made it possible to erect this memorial, is due the credit in a larger degree than to any other person. He was born and his boyhood days were passed within sight of this spot. His early school days in the old log schoolhouse in the woods, and next in the Little Brown Schoolhouse still standing yonder, a silent witness of this scene. Graduating at Wesleyan College, Delaware, as is well known, he became a successful lawyer and business man, and represented the county in the State Legislature with credit. His many generous deeds are well remembered, but it was not that charity paraded before the world, but the true charity when 'the left hand knoweth not what the right hand doeth.'

"During all of his busy life he never tired of talking of the old home, old associates, and school days. A few years ago, in conversation with Robert McCrory and myself, he suggested that he would be pleased if I would write a brief history of the services of the soldiers who enlisted from the township, while some of the old landmarks and buildings were still standing. It was then agreed that they would have photographs of the old church and the old schoolhouse taken, and I was assigned to the historical part of the work. The erection of a monument was taken up for consideration after the historical work had been commenced.

"In due time the photographs were produced and from that day, some four years ago, I have been endeavoring to fulfill my part of the contract. Before starting on his European tour Mr. Woodburn visited me and stated that he had left a bequest in his will for this memorial. I never saw him in life again, but he was true to his promise, and with the enthusiastic support of the citizens and zealous work of your committee, you see before you the result of their laudable efforts.

"To secure subscriptions and to look after all the details leading up to the completion and erection of this memorial has been no easy task. The committee has worked untiringly and the patriotic citizens have responded cheerfully and generously to every call financially and by helpful assistance in arranging for this patriotic service.

"In the sealed receptacle inside of the monument is deposited the name and service of every soldier who enlisted from the township, the name of every subscriber to the Monument Fund, the names of the school children of the township, photographs of upward of sixty soldiers of the Civil War, a copy of the program of the day, with songs, and the names of the committees who have had charge of all matters pertaining to the erection of the monument.

"You all have an interest in this memorial, and some day in the far future, perhaps one hundred years hence, this receptacle will be unsealed and your names will be read by your decendants.

"Fifty-two years ago—April 24, 1861—the first war meeting was held in this church, and the older citizens, Presbyterians and Methodists, were prominent in this meeting. Rev. B. D. Evans, a Presbyterian minister, made an enthusiastic patriotic speech, and although three-score years of age, he afterward enlisted as one of the minute men and went to Cincinnati to assist in repelling the invasion of the Confederate army into Ohio.

"The Bible and the munitions of war were side by side on the old pulpit. Much enthusiasm was manifested, and David O. Taylor, the first to enlist, was killed on the battlefield at Dallas, Ga., on the 27th of May, 1864.

"Dr. James Cutler, a young physician of this village who had served in the Regular Army during the Mexican war, was elected Captain of the company. The company commenced at once to drill in the fields and meadows surrounding this village, and the shrill fife and the rattling drum were heard two or three times each week.

"The busy hands of mothers and sisters in a few days furnished the first uniforms, consisting of red jackets and black caps. Young ladies of the neighborhood purchased silk in Columbus and made a large silk flag which was presented to the company down on the square July 4, 1861. Before the company was recruited to the required number a call was made for three years' service and this company did not enter the field as an organization, yet every one of them enlisted in the three years' service in many different regiments.

"These boys marched gayly away to the wild music of war-drums, the blare of trumpets, with bright banners and uniforms, fathers, mothers, sisters and brothers cheering them on; but they did not all return. Three-score and ten of your boys sleep on the battlefields of the South. Those who did return, came with banners blackened with the smoke of battle, faded uniforms, and sun-bronzed heroes of many battles. They served in forty-two different regiments, batteries, and other organizations.

"Some of your boys, my fellow citizens, fought on almost every great battlefield of the war. They were at Gettysburg, where 41,000 boys of the North and South fell in two days; they were at Chickamauga, where 35,000 boys fell in two days; they were at Shiloh, Stone River, Cheat Mountain, Port Republic, Antietam, Vicksburg, and many of the battlefields of Virginia; they were in the 'One Hundred Days under fire from Chattanooga to Atlanta'; some of them marched with Sherman to the sea, and others were at Appomattox at the surrender of Lee's army. This is the true story of the services of the soldiers of this township to whom you pay tribute today by this ceremony of dedicating this monument and the strewing of flowers.

"Three score and ten died for you and me that we might live and enjoy the many blessings of a free and united nation.

"Upward of 2,600,000 soldiers served in the Union Army during the Civil War. Of that number Ohio furnished 313,180, and the losses, killed and those who died of wounds, were 35,475. Union County sent to the battlefield 3,000 soldiers, one-tenth of whom enlisted in this township. Upward of 500 who enlisted from the county were killed or died of wounds and disease in the service, and the total casualties were 1,035.

About one-eighth of that number were from Jerome Township.

"We had no officers of high rank in the Civil War. One reached the rank of Colonel, one Major, five of Captain, but the rank and file who carried the musket, the carbine and knapsack did the fighting and won the battles that saved the nation.

"The erection of monuments and memorials to commemorate the sacrifices, sufferings and deeds of the fallen heroes of all our wars is very commendable. How appropriate the inscription on your monument, which reads as follows:

> " *'In honor of the men who served in the Army of the Union. Those who fought and lived and those who fought and died. May this shaft ever call to memory the story of the glory of the men who wore the blue.'*

"This inscription should be memorized by every pupil in your schools, for the erection of memorials arouses the patriotic enthusiasm of the youth of our land and instills in their minds loyalty to our flag and all that it implies.

"The public school is the nursery of patriotism. Its best fruits are true Americans and the making of loyal and intelligent citizens. Then how appropriate it is that they should take part in these patriotic ceremonies. It will be an ominous day in the history of any family when it no longer remembers with gratitude the worthy deeds of its ancestors, and there is no cause, except religion, holier than the service to country or state.

"First comes the cross, then the flag, for Christianity and patriotism go hand in hand.

"One word more, my old neighbors and friends: always keep in mind and teach your children that this is the most sacred and pathetic of all American holidays; let it not become a day of noise and a gala day. Remember the religious sentiment of honoring the dead and perpetuating their deeds of valor in the beautiful ceremonies which make the day more sacred and nobler than any other holiday.

"In the 'brave days of old' each year on the anniversary

of the battle of Marathon, the Greek sires would take their boys to the battlefield of Marathon, show them the monument erected to the heroes who there fell in defense of their land, and exalt the example of those who sacrificed life and limb for their country.

"So should we, the friends and descendants of these brave men and heroes of all our wars, from Lexington in the War of the Revolution to Appomattox, kindle the fires of patriotism in our boys by holding up to them the imperishable deeds of our soldiers on all of our battlefields.

"My fellow citizens, when the last survivor who enlisted here has answered his last roll call on earth, we can see with prophetic eye the descendants of these heroes gathered about this monument, reciting to their children and children's children the heroic deeds of their ancestors on the battlefield.

"The victories were not all won by the soldiers at the front, for there was a loyal battle line in our homes in the North. There were heroes and heroines in the old homesteads who were not permitted to go to the front during the dark days of the war. Some citizens with families, others physically disabled, but all through those long and weary years their patriotism never faltered and they were ever ready to open their purses for payment of bounties and to care for families of the soldiers on the battle lines.

"Then there were the mothers, the wives, the sisters, and the sweethearts—it has been truly said that there was one line that was never broken during the war; that was the line of the loyal women. Some of them are here today who cheered father, brother or sweetheart as he marched away to the music of the war-drums in 1861-1865. You waited anxiously for many of them who did not return.

"You loved them better than life, but you could only hope and pray. Your hearts were on the battle line at the front for your dear one was there and you would have scorned him had he failed in his duty to home and country. Your love and prayers followed him on the march and in the carnage of battle, and he could not have been otherwise than brave.

"Through all the long and weary years of the war you did not lose faith; you wrote messages of cheer, suffered for every shot that pierced a loved one, and those who were spared returned victorious to receive your blessing. Of the many bright and happy girls who with their willing hands made and presented the silk flag to your boys within a stone's throw of this spot, July 4th, 1861, not more than half a dozen reside in this community today.

"The fathers and mothers of that day have all passed away and the boys and girls of 1861 are now of the older generation. There are some sad hearts here today—widows of soldier husbands who have passed to the other shore, there awaiting the happy reunion, perhaps but a few years hence.

"But to you, with all its sadness, you rejoice that your loved ones—husband or father—fought the good fight and is so highly honored today by this patriotic service and memorial.

"And where are the boys who drilled and marched over the meadows and along the streets of this village fifty-two years ago? Were the First Sergeants of the forty-two organizations in which these boys served here today and would give the command, 'Attention to roll call!' they would not all answer 'Here.' But on parade he could report to the Adjutant: 'Sir, all present or accounted for.' Three score and ten died with honor on the field, two hundred sleep in the cemeteries of the North, only a remnant of the old guard survives, but 'all present or accounted for' would be the answer.

"One parting word, comrades of the Great March. You are not only veterans in service, but veterans in age now. Your heads are graying, your steps are halting, but you are young in heart—steadily marching behind the great recruiting officer, Death. The ranks are thinning—one hundred going down each day. We will not all meet on this historic ground again, but there are some here today who may live to see the Memorial Day when there will not be a veteran of the great war on earth.

"There will be eloquent words spoken; there will be patriotic songs by the children; there will be strewing of the sweetest flowers of springtime over the graves of your departed heroes, but not one will answer 'here' when the roll is called. My comrades, when we have all been mustered out by the Great Commander, when we have heard the bugle sounding reveille, for the last time calling us to duty, when 'taps' and 'lights out' have been sounded for the last time, let us be ready to join our comrades on the other shore. It will be 'good night' here and 'good morning' over there. Salute the flag! Break ranks! Farewell!"

WAR HISTORY OF JEROME TOWNSHIP.

At the first election held in Jerome Township, May 10th, 1821, the total number of votes cast was fifteen. In the year 1861, at the breaking out of the War of the Rebellion, the population of the township was 1398, and the total number of voters was 216, the number of voters having increased 201 in forty years.

The number of soldiers enlisting from the township during the war was 151 in excess of the number of voters in the township, or more than one-fourth of the total population of men, women and children. This is a most remarkable record of enlistment and challenges comparison with any township of like population in the State.

It is shown by the official records that the average age of the soldiers who fought the battles of the Rebellion was less than 20 years. A number of Jerome Township boys were under 16 years of age at enlistment and at least one was but 14.

The following table, compiled from official records, will be of interest to all students of war history:

Total enlistments in the Union Army—

At the age of 10 and under	25
At the age of 12 and under	225
At the age of 14 and under	1,523
At the age of 16 and under	844,891
At the age of 18 and under	1,151,438
At the age of 21 and under	2,159,798
22 years of age and over	618,511

JAMES C. CONE
121st O. V. I.

DANIEL R. CONE
U. S. Navy.

CORPORAL STEPHENSON B. CONE
121st O. V. I.

OTWAY B. CONE
121st O. V. I.

WILLIAM McCAMPBELL
86th O. V. I.

JASPER CONVERSE
18th U. S. I.

ADDISON T. McCAMPBELL
187th O. V. I.

SERGEANT AMMON P. CONVERSE
46th O. V. I.

Adding the number under 21 and over 22—that is, 2,159,-798 and 618,511—the total enrollment was 2,778,309. Never before was a nation saved by youths in their teens.

LOSSES.

One hundred and ten thousand were killed in battle or died of wounds. Two hundred and forty-nine thousand, four hundred and fifty-eight died of disease and other causes, and two hundred and eighty thousand were wounded.

Ohio furnished 313,180 soldiers and the losses in killed, died of wounds and disease were 35,124. Of this number 3,000 enlisted from Union County, 533 were killed or died of wounds or disease, 360 were wounded, 143 were prisoners of war, and the total casualties were 1,035. The contribution of Jerome Township to this great army was 367, and 75 were killed or died in the service.

WAR OF THE REBELLION — 1861-1865.

There was no more patriotic community in Union County than Jerome Township, and every call for troops from April 15th, 1861, to the close of the war, the quota was filled by volunteers and there was no draft made in the township.

During the war, with scarcely an exception every boy who attended the Select School at New California enlisted in the army.

They were intelligent farmer boys, lithe of limb and with strong healthy bodies. Accustomed to hard work on the farm, and handling wild and vicious horses, they were ideal cavalrymen.

They were also trained marksmen with the rifle and were used to the chase in hunting wild turkeys and all kinds of small game. This was the class of boys who enlisted in that community to fight for the preservation of the Union.

The ancestors of many of these boys had fought for liberty during the War of the Revolution and had left their descendants a noble heritage in which they took an honest pride.

It has been turly said that "It is the mass of character that

6

determines human conditions and decides national destiny; whoever leads a good life, sets a good example, establishes a well-conducted family, worthily rears children, honestly pursues a respectable calling, who is frugal and industrious, makes the most precious contribution to his kind."

Thus had lived these hardy pioneers who came with the Bible, the ax and the rifle, praying, working and watching. Though far removed in kinship, blood will tell for successive generations when opportunity comes, and that they sway and guide us after death of the ancestor is an accepted truth of history.

The warm blood of patriotism and heroism which flowed in the veins of the men of '76 does not become cold by the lapse of years in the veins of their descendants.

The spirit which led them to battle for liberty inspired their descendants to fight the battles of all our wars, in which they have taken so prominent a part, in the War of 1812, war with Mexico, the War of the Rebellion, and the Spanish-American War.

Therefore, at the breaking out of the War of the Rebellion these boys, inspired by the deeds of their forefathers, of which they had heard through their parents from early childhood, were ready to respond to the call to arms before the smoke had cleared from the battered walls of Fort Sumter.

On the evening of the 24th of April, 1861, in response to the call for the first 75,000 volunteers, a war meeting was held in the old Seceder Church at New California. Patriotic speeches were made by many of the old citizens, and among others the Rev. B. D. Evans and Llewellyn Curry. Volunteers were called for, and the first young man to enroll his name and offer his services was David O. Taylor, who soon after joined the Thirteenth Ohio Regiment, and after serving his country for three years with honor, was killed on the battlefield of Dallas, Georgia, on the 27th day of May, 1864. About forty of the young men of the neighborhood volunteered that evening.

Dr. James Cutler was a young practitioner, residing in the

village, and as he had served two years in the Regular Army during the Mexican War, all eyes were turned toward him as a leader. He was an intelligent and progressive young man with a good practice and in whom the fathers and mothers had great faith.

They were, therefore, extremely anxious that he should enter the service and command the company in which their boys enlisted. But he did not need any prompting, as he was enthusiastic and was among the first to sign the enlistment roll. He was elected Captain and gave the company their first drill in the old Scott tactics.

W. L. Curry was elected First Lieutenant and D. R. Cone Second Lieutenant.

Among the first to volunteer was Walter Gowans, a patriotic Scotchman upward of 60 years of age, and in honor to him the company was named the "Gowans Guards." The company began drilling immediately at New California. The busy hands of mothers and sisters in a few days furnished uniforms, consisting of red jackets and black caps. The young ladies of the neighborhood made a large silk flag, which was presented to the company.

The company soon numbered sixty volunteers, but before it was recruited to the required number to enter the service the call was made for three years' troops, and many of the boys becoming impatient to be off for the seat of war, began to enlist in companies that were being recruited more rapidly in the larger towns. The organization never entered the service, as their ranks were rapidly decimated by these enlistments in other organizations. All but two or three of this company soon enlisted and seventeen of them died in the service.

The following list of names composes about a complete roster of the company which has been submitted to other members of the company for verification and correction: James Cutler, Captain; W. L. Curry, First Lieutenant; D. R. Cone, Second Lieutenant; J. D. Bain, David Bain, William Beaver, W. J. Conklin, Otway Curry, W. W. Curry, David Curry, James A. Curry, James Curry, J. C. Cone, S. B. Cone, O. B.

Cone, William Channell, W. H. H. Fleck, T. S. Fleck, Walter
Gowans, Sr., Andrew Gowans, Alexander Gowans, William
Gowans, James Gowans, S. W. Gowans, Lewis Hoffner, James
Hill, L. J. Ketch, Lewis Ketch, John Liggett, R. A. Liggett,
B. F. Lucas, William B. Laughead, John Morford, James R.
Mitchell, George Mitchell, David McIntire, J. L. McCampbell,
Jeff Mahaffey, Jacob Nonnemaker, D. G. Robinson, Delmore
Robinson, C. L. Robinson, J. B. Robinson, George Ruehlen,
David Shinneman, James Smith, George Stokes, Atlas Perkins,
David O. Taylor, Daniel Taylor, David Wise, William Wise
and Samuel Wise.

In this company were twenty-seven who had been students
at the Select School. Seventeen of the original members were
killed or died of wounds or disease, and of those who lost their
lives in the service nine were students in the Select School.

A company was organized at Plain City, Ohio, for the first
three months' service, in which twenty-nine Jerome Township
soldiers served. The company was assigned as Company G,
17th Ohio Volunteer Infantry. At the expiration of their
term of service, every one of them re-enlisted in other regiments, as did those who served in the 13th Ohio Volunteer
Infantry, first three months' service. The first and only full
company recruited in the township was organized at the village
of Jerome, under the first call for three years' service, and
went into camp in August, 1861. The company was assigned
as Company E, 30th Regiment, Ohio Volunteer Infantry.
Other detachments enlisting in the first call for three years'
service were assigned in the First Ohio Cavalry, the 13th,
32nd, 40th, 46th, 54th, and 66th Ohio Volunteer Infantry.
During the years 1862, 1863, 1864, and until the close of the
war, every quota assigned to the township was filled, and they
served in the following designated organizations:

Cavalry Regiments.

1st Ohio Volunteer Cavalry.. 2
12th Ohio Volunteer Cavalry. ....

Infantry Regiments.

13th, 17th, 30th, 32nd, 34th, 40th, 46th, 54th,
58th, 63rd, 66th, 82nd, 85th, 86th, 88th, 94th,
95th, 96th, 110th, 113th, 121st, 128th, 129th,
133rd, 136th, 145th, 174th, 186th, 187th, 181st,
197th, 27th U. S. C. T., 18th U. S. I........................   33
47th U. S. C. T.

7th Ohio Independent Sharpshooters.................   1
10th Ohio Battery, Light Artillery......................   1
U. S. Signal Corps...   1
9th Minnesota Infantry.......................................   1
Indiana Infantry   1
United States Navy...   1
Squirrel Hunters ....   1—   7

A total of..   42

In the year 1864 an organization was formed of prominent
citizens who were not eligible, by reason of age or disability,
for military service, to pay bounties to the boys who were
willing to enter the service. A large amount of money was
contributed voluntarily for that purpose, and in some instances
several hundred dollars were paid to each volunteer. Samuel
B. Woodburn was treasurer of the association, and among
other prominent members were A. H. McCampbell, John Mc-
Campbell, John K. Dodge, Thomas Jones, James Roney, Wm.
Thompson, Joseph Cole, John Curry, Albert Chapman, James
Mitchell, and many others. There was scarcely a family in the
township that did not have someone in the Army of the Union,
and there was continuous recruiting. The people thought,
talked, and read of but little else than the means of prosecut-
ing the war to a successful end.

To write the history of the services of the soldiers of
Jerome Township who served in forty-two regiments and
other organizations, would be to write the history of every
great campaign along the battle lines from the Atlantic Ocean
to the Mississippi River, for some of them participated in
almost every great battle of the war. As an evidence of that

fact the reader has only to peruse the brief history of each organization in this volume. They fought at Gettysburg, and Chickamauga, the two greatest battles of the war. Some of them were at Aantietam, Vicksburg, Shiloh, the Wilderness, Stone River, Port Republic, Seven Pines, Lookout Mountain. One hundred days under fire, from Chattanooga to Atlanta. They marched with General Sherman's Army to the Sea. They were in the greatest cavalry expedition of the war, under General James H. Wilson, through Alabama and Georgia. Were in the saddle when the war closed.

Those in the navy were at Fort Henry and Fort Donaldson. Some of them participated in the great review at Washington.

But a brief history can be given in the limited space in this little volume of each organization, and much time has been devoted to securing the data for enlistment, discharge or death of each soldier. Only the time and place of muster-in of each of the different organizations, with a short history of their campaigns, battles, losses and date of muster-out, is given. Great pains have been taken to get correct dates and statistics as to the true history of the service of each organization. The regiments of long service and hard campaigns made more history and are entitled to more extended notice, but the members of all organizations are entitled to full credit, for they all did their duty in whatever capacity they served. The majority of them were boys and usually enlisted at the first opportunity, not knowing where or what the service of the organization to which they were assigned would be. It was only "their's to obey."

THE BOYS OF '61.

BY W. L. CURRY.

At the call of their country our boys of Jerome
Marched away to the sound of the bugle and drum;
In the flush of their youth went the manly and brave,
To stand by the banner our forefathers gave;
How many? Three hundred—*our* heroes in blue,

They showed to the world how their hearts could be true.
Did they all come back from the dark battle lines?
Nay—four score are sleeping 'neath the shade of the pines.

Go look for their deeds on the 'scutcheon of fame;
Go read in the sunlight each glorious name;
Old Round Top is crowned with their glory today,
And Shiloh's invested with splendor for aye;
Where bravely they struggled and died for the free,
Chickamauga flows on with a song to the sea;
And other proud fields have extended a crown
To the boys of Jerome—*our* sons of renown.

They came from the battle all shattered and torn,
Not as they went forth in the flush of the morn;
Their standards were riddled with shot and with shell,
But their war-drums had sounded rebellion's death-knell.
Their ranks were depleted, their comrades afar
Slept peacefully under the Southern star;
But proudly erect marched the immortal few—
Our heroes, each man in his garments of blue.

Who hailed them? A nation they'd saved by their might,
And planted fore'er on the ramparts of Right.
The welcome was great that came after the strife—
The kiss of the mother, the sweetheart, the wife;
The drum became silent, the bugle was still,
They echoed no more on the red battle hill;
And the Angel of Peace, with her pinions outspread,
Looked down on the living and wept for the dead.

The land that we love honors still every son
Who rushed to its aid at the flash of the gun;
On many a field seeks the column the sky,
Enriched with a record that never can die;
So long as our banner invincible waves,
Memorials will rise to the worth of our braves;
And ever the country to which we are true
Will laurel the brow of our soldiers in blue.

FIRST OHIO VOLUNTEER CAVALRY — THREE
YEARS' SERVICE.

A company of the First Ohio Cavalry was recruited at
Plain City, Ohio, under the first call for three years' troops,
and was assigned as Company K of that regiment, organized
at Camp Chase, Ohio, in the summer of 1861. Twelve Jerome
Township soldiers served in this company, three of whom died
in the service — James S. Ewing, Presley E. Goff, and Benjamin F. Lucas; and five — James Cutler, W. L. Curry, Sanford P. Clark, Presley E. Goff, and Alanson Sessler — were
prisoners of war.

As the writer served in this regiment and has personal
knowledge of the campaigns and battles in which they participated, it is hoped that the reader may have charity and
overlook any seeming overestimated distinguished services of
the regiment. It is a hard task to condense in a page or two
the record of the services of a regiment which served four
years and participated in many decisive battles.

The company left Plain City September 8th, 1861, going
across the country in carriages and wagons, to Camp Chase.
A few days later the election for commissioned officers was
held and Dr. T. W. Forshee of Madison County was elected
Captain; Dr. James Cutler of Jerome Township, First Lieutenant; A. H. McCurdy of Morrow County, Second Lieutenant; and W. L. Curry was appointed Orderly Sergeant.

The regiment was fully equipped and mustered into the
U. S. service October 5th, 1861, with twelve companies, under
Colonel Orin P. Ransom, an officer of the Regular Army;
Lieutenant Colonel T. C. H. Smith, and Major Minor Millikin.

The regiments that were so fortunate as to get a Regular
officer for a Colonel were usually well organized, and that was
the case in the First Ohio. We had a great contempt for our
Colonel in the beginning, as he was a regular martinet, but
when we got into the field we had a very high regard for him,
as he at once inaugurated strict military discipline, and, as the
boys said, "brought the officers to time," organized an officers'
school, and looked after the smallest details of clothing, ra-

tions and all things that pertained to the comfort of his men; systematically examined for himself all clothing, equipments and food before allowing them to be issued, and whatever was poor in quality or short in quantity he rejected with good round oaths and with a savage threat of arrest to the quartermaster or commissary.

Of the commissioned officers of the regiment, four attained the grade of Colonel, five of Lieutenant Colonel, sixteen of Major, four of Surgeon, two Assistant Surgeon, one Chaplain, forty-six of Captain, and one hundred and twenty-nine of Lieutenant, making in all two hundred and seven commissions. There being originally twelve Captains, thirty-four Lieutenants were promoted to the rank of Captain. There were but four officers in the regiment at the close of the war that were commissioned at the organization, all the other officers remaining in the regiment at the close of the war having been promoted from the ranks. Of the Colonels of the regiment, Ransom resigned, Millikin was killed at Stone River, Smith was promoted to Brigadier-General, and Eggleston was also promoted to Brigadier-General. Colonel Cupp was killed at Chickamauga, Major Moore and Lieutenant Condit were killed at Stone River. Captain Emery and Captain Scott were killed in action, as was Lieutenant Allen. Although we denounced Colonel Ransom as an "old martinet and tyrant," we soon learned to respect him as a disciplinarian, and before the end of our service, blessed his memory for the strict discipline inaugurated when we first went into camp.

The large per cent of the boys recruited in the regiment were farmers, and as in that day a great deal of horseback riding was done, many of our men were, as the saying goes, "raised on a horse's back" and were fine horsemen. To be an accomplished rider it must be learned when the person is young and at the age when he has a certain amount of recklessness and has no fear. A person that is timid and has no confidence in his ability to control his horse can never become a good rider.

The men were accustomed to caring for horses and understood feeding, grooming and saddling, and did not have these duties to learn after enlisting. Many of the men brought their own horses to camp and owned them throughout the war and received 40 cents a day from the Government for their service. The men who owned their own mounts usually had the best horses and cared for them best, as they had a pecuniary interest and also understood the care of horses.

While no soldier can become a good cavalryman unless he is a good horseman, we soon learned that the service of a cavalryman, with all its many attractions, was at all times laborious, and while he might be a good rider he had many other duties to learn and perform.

The trooper has his carbine to care for and keep in order, which evens him up with the infantryman in care of arms and equipments, and in addition to this he has his revolver, saber and horse equipments to keep in order, and his horse to water, feed and groom every day, and the soldier who enlists in the cavalry service expecting a "soft snap" will soon learn, to his sorrow, that he has been laboring under a grievous mistake.

On a campaign or march in good weather, when it is not necessary to pitch tents at night, the infantry stack arms, get supper, and are soon at rest or asleep; but not so with the cavalryman. The company must first put up the picket rope, and then the horses must be watered, fed and groomed. If there is no forage for his horse in the wagon train he must hunt for it, and perhaps go a mile or two in the search. Then he unsaddles, gets his coffee, grooms his horse, and is ready to lie down an hour after the infantryman is asleep. In the morning, if the cavalry are to move at the same hour as the infantry are to march, they must have reveille an hour earlier than the infantry, to have time to feed, groom and water the horses; and while he has the advantage on the march, it would not be considered by the average citizen a very easy task to march forty, fifty or even sixty miles a day mounted, which was a usual occurrence on our scouts and raids.

Captain Forshee and Lieutenant McCurdy both resigned in

June, 1862, when the command of the company devolved upon Lieutenant James Cutler.

On the 9th day of December, 1861, the regiment broke camp, marched through the capital and embarked on their first campaign, from which many comrades were destined never again to return. Arrived at Cincinnati at daybreak the next morning, the regiment took boats and reached Louisville, Ky., on the morning of the 11th, the first regiment of cavalry to enter that department save Wolford's Kentucky regiment, and, quoting from Reid's history: "The First Ohio was the nucleus of that host of cavalry which, under the leadership of Stanley, Crook, Mitchell, McCook, Kilpatrick, Long, Minty, Millikin and Wilson, achieved such triumphs for the country and fame for themselves."

"The history of the cavalry of the Southwest—its fearless rides, its daring raids, its bloody charges, its long nights of weary marching, as it carried desolation and destruction into the very heart of treason—is a record of heroic achievements unsurpassed in the annals of that service."

The regiment remained in camp at Louisville until January 16th, 1862, then marched to Lebanon, Ky., and was in camp at Lebanon and Bardstown until about the last of February. During all the winter months the regiment was busy drilling and scouting, and had a few skirmishes with General John Morgan's cavalry.

About the last of February the regiment marched to Louisville and embarked on steamers for Nashville, Tenn. March 14th they made a dash in the night as the advance of General Buell's army to save the bridge across Duck River at Columbia. They marched with Buell's army through rain and mud to the relief of General Grant's army at Pittsburg Landing, arriving opposite the battlefield on the Tennessee River the evening the battle closed, but too late to take part in the battle fought April 6th and 7th, 1862.

From April 8th to May 30th, during the siege of Corinth, Mississippi, the regiment was constantly on picket, scouting and skirmishing duty in front of the Confederate Army, and this was the first real hard service. After Corinth was evacuated, we followed the Confederate Army up, had some brisk fights and took many prisoners.

In June, moved east along the Memphis & Charleston Railroad with Buell's army, toward Chattanooga, and participated in the great countermarch of the army through Tennessee and Kentucky to Louisville. They participated in the battle of Perrysville, Ky., October 8th; was in the advance to Nashville and the Stone River campaign.

In the battle of Stone River, Tenn., December 31st, 1862, in making a saber charge Colonel Minor Millikin, Major D. A. B. Moore and Lieutenant Condit were killed. Adjutant William Scott and Captain S. W. Fordyce were wounded, and the regiment lost heavily. From the battle of Stone River until June, 1863, the regiment was employed in scouting and patroling, watching the movements of the enemy. Captain Cutler having resigned, W. L. Curry, a prisoner of war, was promoted to a Lieutenancy and had command of Company K. The regiment advanced from Murfreesboro with General Rosecran's army June 24th, and had some shart fights in driving the enemy through the mountain passes to Chattanooga. In August Lieutenant Curry was transferred to the command of Company M.

In•the advance on Chattanooga the First Ohio, under command of Lieutenant Colonel Cupp, crossed the Tennessee River September 2nd, and was conspicuous in the expedition under General Stanley in the attempt to cut the railroad south of Chattanooga. After a severe encounter with a large force of the enemy near Lafayette, Ga., it passed up the Chattanooga Valley, reached the battlefield of Chickamauga early on the morning of September 20th, and lost heavily in the engagement of that day. Colonel Cupp was killed while forming the regiment for a charge. Of the 900 men composing the Second Brigade, 134 were killed and wounded.

After falling back to Chattanooga, the troops were allowed no rest, but on the 26th of September started on the famous raid driving Wheeler's cavalry from Washington, Tenn., to

Muscle Shoals, Ala., taking more than 1,000 prisoners and several pieces of artillery.

The regiment then returned to Chattanooga and took part in the assault on Mission Ridge, where William Johnson of Company K was killed. After the battle of Mission Ridge the First moved to the relief of Burnsides, at Knoxville, being the first regiment to reach that city, having several skirmishes on the way and capturing many prisoners.

On the 16th of December a detachment of the regiment made a brilliant charge at Calhoun upon a rebel brigade commanded by General Wheeler, sweeping them from the field and taking many prisoners.

January 4th, 1864, about 400 members of the regiment reënlisted at Pulaski, Tenn., as veterans for "three years, or during the war," and were given a furlough for thirty days.

After the veteran furlough, during which time many recruits joined the regiment, we were remounted at Nashville, Tenn., and May 22nd started on the march to join General Sherman's army and arrived at Rome, Ga., about the first of June, after having had several skirmishes while marching on the flank of the 17th Army Corps.

The regiment participated in the "One Hundred Days under fire from Chattanooga to Atlanta," was continuously scouting and raiding, and was a part of the two divisions of cavalry commanded by General Kilpatrick which made a raid around the Confederate Army during the siege of Atlanta in August, 1864.

After the surrender of Atlanta, September 1st, and while General Sherman was organizing for his "March to the Sea," the regiment was ordered to Louisville, Ky., was remounted and joined the army of General George H. Thomas at Nashville, Tenn. After the victory at Nashville the cavalry corps under General James H. Wilson rendezvoused at Gravelly Springs, Alabama, until March, 1865. General Wilson, having organized a cavalry corps of 12,000 veteran cavalrymen, cut his way down through Alabama and Georgia, capturing the fortified city of Selma, Alabama, April 2nd, 1865, with 2,700 prisoners, including 150 officers, and in addition 2,000 cavalry horses, 72 siege guns, 26 field guns, and 66,000 rounds of artillery ammunition, gaining a complete victory over General Forrest's forces.

The last fight of the regiment was at Columbus, Ga., which was taken by a saber charge April 15th, 1865.

A detachment of the First Cavalry, under command of Captain J. O. Yeoman, was with the command that captured the President of the Confederacy.

The regiment garrisoned Georgia and South Carolina from April to September, then returned to Ohio and was mustered out at Camp Chase on the 28th of September, 1865, after four years' hard service, Company K having lost twelve who died in hospital, nine killed, twelve wounded, and ten taken prisoner —making a total loss of forty-three.

The First Ohio Cavalry carried on its muster rolls nearly 1,800 names and mustered out at Camp Chase 701 men. The regiment marched 11,490 miles and fought in the States of Kentucky, Tennessee, Mississippi, Alabama, Georgia and North Carolina. The losses in killed, died of wounds and disease were 204. Upward of 200 were wounded, 130 were prisoners of war, and the total casualties were five hundred and thirty-five.

As shown by the official records, the regiment participated in fifty-one battles, fights and skirmishes.

TWELFTH OHIO VOLUNTEER CAVALRY — THREE
YEARS' SERVICE. *

The order for raising this regiment was issued August 20th, 1863. The companies, recruited in many counties in the State, rendezvoused at Camp Taylor, Cleveland, Ohio, and the regiment was mustered into the United States service November 24th, 1863, under Colonel Robert W. Ratliff, Lieutenant Colonel Robert H. Bentley, both of whom were brevetted Brigadier Generals.

Five boys of Jerome Township were in this regiment —

* Contributed by Jesse L. Cameron, who served in the regiment.

Nelson E. Adams, Wm. S. Channel, Isaac Carey, Philip Hawn and Daniel Heath. Channel and Heath both died in the service.

While the organization was yet incomplete six companies were called to Johnson's Island to guard prisoners and meet, if need be, the threatened invasion of rebels from Canada, intent on releasing the 3,000 imprisoned rebel officers there. The companies thus employed were A, C, D, F, I, and L. The other companies were quartered at Camp Chase until February, 1864, when the whole regiment was brought together at Camp Dennison. Here it was mounted, armed and vigorously drilled until the 27th day of March, when it started to the front and entered upon its memorable career.

Its first duty was to assist General Burbridge in breaking up the armed bands of guerillas and bushwhackers in Kentucky. Scattering itself over that State, it soon became a terror to marauders and rebel sympathizers, dispersed the guerrillas and restored order.

This task accomplished with commendable promptness, the Twelfth joined in an expedition against Saltville, Va. But after a toilsome journey of several days it was halted and turned about to make one of the most rapid marches known to warfare, traveling over 180 miles in fifty hours. It struck the rebel forces at Mt. Sterling, Ky., on the 9th of June, 1864, and gallantly led the charge. In this battle the regiment fought many times its number, but never for a moment wavered. At one time sixty men of the Third Battalion, mostly from Company C, fought a rebel regiment for thirty minutes, losing many precious lives, but holding its ground until help came. Of this devoted little band Union County furnished Joseph Smith, Hylas S. Moore and J. L. Cameron.

For its gallantry the Twelfth was complimented at the close of the fight by General Burbridge, who remarked that it had saved the day for him. These laurels were dearly bought, for the loss of the regiment, all told, was 197 men.

The battle lasted all day, and at night the regiment remained on the battlefield. Company C, chosen for special guard duty, got no rest. Three days' and nights' marching and fighting was now to be followed by a gallop of thirty-three miles to Lexington on the 10th; fresh horses drawn, and on to Paris, Ky., on the 11th. Waiting here for supplies and ammunition until evening, the regiment again mounted and moved forward for a night's march to Cynthiana. Early on the morning of the 12th of June, while darkness was yet so dense that the lurid jets of powder flame blazed from the carbines, the regiment was leading the charge again in battle, sustaining itself heroically, and gaining a complete victory in this engagement. On the 14th of June the regiment received the thanks and congratulations of President Lincoln and the Secretary of War, and was again complimented for its gallantry by the Commanding General.

Again breaking into detachments, the Twelfth scattered over Kentucky, dispersing marauders and keeping order, until the month of September, when it concentrated at Mount Sterling and again started with General Burbridge's expedition to Saltville, Va.

The expedition led over 300 miles without provision trains, tents or ambulances, was cause of much privation, and on the 2nd of October was again at its accustomed place leading the advance into one of the most hotly contested battles of the war.

The rebel fortifications were in the deep mountain gorges and rendered operations by mounted men impossible, yet, dismounted, the Twelfth made again and again its famous carbine charges and reaching well up to the enemy's works. All day long the battle raged in the mountain fastness, but toward the close of the day ammunition was exhausted and the rebel forces reinforced by 5,000 of General Early's fresh troops, and General Burbridge was compelled to abandon the expedition. A rapid retreat began, and as it still had ammunition, Company C was detailed a special guard for the rear, and many times during that disastrous night and the following day did this devoted little band halt in the mountain passes and hold the pursuing foe in check while the retreating column hurried on.

ROBERT McDOWELL
32nd O. V. I.

JESSE B. McDOWELL
40th O. V. I.

JOHN P. McDOWELL
32nd O. V. I.

EDGAR G. MAGILL
96th O. V. I.

LEWIS J. KETCH
121st O. V. I.

EDWARD G. ADAMS
136th O. V. I.

JAMES F. CHAPMAN
136th O. V. I.

CORPORAL JOHN Q. ADAMS
136th O. V. I.

Forty-nine men of the Twelfth lay dead or wounded on the field of battle on this eventful day. Returning to Lexington, the regiment reorganized, drew fresh horses and supplies, and on the 10th of November was again in the saddle marching toward Cumberland Gap.

Reaching that point on the 26th, scattering again, it was engaged for a short time destroying bands of marauders around Bean Station and Rodgersville. General Stoneman now took command, and being joined with General Gillem, the whole force, including the Twelfth, was, in the earlier part of December, marching in a third expedition against Saltville. On the morning of December 15th Kingsford was reached and a strong rebel force appeared on the opposite banks of the river. Halting his column, Stoneman sent Gillem to cross above and prepare for battle. The impatience of the Twelfth knew no bounds when in sight of the gray uniforms and eagerly they awaited the bugle sound to charge. That coming, with a wild yell they galloped through the water, which was up to the horses' joints, to the opposite bank. Opening a fire from carbines, and revolvers at short range, the enemy was for a moment confused, and General Gillem then coming up aided to complete the rout.

Pursuit was given, and many of the enemy lay dead along the road as the Twelfth poured into their fleeing ranks volley after volley from their carbines. Hurrying forward, Bristol was reached just before day. The Yankees dashed in, and less than half an hour afterward Bristol, with all its immense stores, was ours. Halting to complete the destruction of the rebel supplies and tearing up the railroad, the column again pushed forward to Abington. At Abington Company F of the Twelfth, a special escort of General Burbridge, led the charge, the regiment following, and that place was taken, with a large number of prisoners and immense military supplies.

Pushing on, the column struck the army of the rebels under General Vaughn, which soon broke in confusion, and the boys of the regiment joined in a headlong chase of five miles, with drawn sabers. Many pieces of artillery were taken here.

7

Without halting the troops pushed on, and on the 12th the regiment had the grim satisfaction of leading the charge into Saltville, capturing the place where so many prisoners were lost a few months previous. Every vestige of the place was destroyed. At the close of the day, on the 17th, a desperate battle was fought with the troops of Breckenridge and Vaughn, near Marion.

Returning from this raid, the regiment collected at Lexington to draw fresh horses and close up the broken ranks. Scattering again, it was a short time doing general patrol duty and looking after rebel sympathizers and bushrangers in Kentucky. Coming together again the last of February at Louisville, Ky., the whole joined Stoneman's command and embarked for Nashville by river. On through to Murfreesboro and thence to Knoxville, where a veteran brigade was formed by uniting the Twelfth Ohio, Fifteenth Pennsylvania, and Tenth Michigan Cavalries. On the 20th of March this brigade was in motion marching out to Strawberry Plains, then on through Bulls Gap, Jonesboro to Yakin River. The stream was badly swollen, and several comrades drowned. Uriah Jolly was rescued here by Comrade Cameron.

Pausing a short time to close up the ranks, the forces swept on, galloping through Jacksonville, on the line of the Virginia & Tennessee Railroad at Christiansbury. This road was torn up and destroyed for many miles. Sweeping down into North Carolina, the Danville & Richmond Railroad was struck and destroyed for a great distance.

Hastening on, the troops brought up before Salisbury. A rebel force under Pemberton, with several pieces of artillery, came out to defend the town. Scarcely halting, the Twelfth led the charge, and in spite of all opposition Salisbury was soon in flames, many Union prisoners released, and immense quantities of military stores consigned to the flames. On the 17th of April the regiment marched on to Lincolnton, which place was captured by a charge led by Company C of the Twelfth, under Lieutenant Stewart. Two hundred picked men, under Major Moderwell, were now chosen to march eighty miles to the Catawba River crossing and destroy the bridge of the Charlotte & South Carolina Railroad. On the morning of the 30th they came across the forces of Vaughn and Duke. Sweeping down upon them, they cut their way through, captured thirty-five prisoners, a large quantity of small arms and two pieces of cannon and some seven officers and 223 men. Paroling the prisoners on the spot, the command returned to Dallas, Company C having some wounded, but not fatally. On the 23rd the regiment started for Knoxville, but learning that President Lincoln had been assassinated they joined in a headlong chase after Davis. They finally returned to Sweetwater, Tenn., thence on to McMinnville, thence to Nashville, and on the 24th of November the regiment was discharged. Of 1,462 men, only 628 remained. As shown by the official records, the losses in the regiment, killed, died of wounds and disease, were one hundred and sixty-four.

THIRTEENTH REGIMENT, O. V. I.— THREE MONTHS AND THREE YEARS.

The Thirteenth Ohio was organized at Camp Jackson, Columbus, Ohio, in April, 1861, for the first three months' service, under the command of A. S. Piatt as Colonel; C. B. Mason, Lieutenant Colonel, and J. G. Hawkins, Major. Colonel Piatt was soon succeeded by Colonel W. S. Smith, who was appointed Brigadier-General of Volunteers in May, 1862, and Colonel J. G. Hawkins of Union County assumed command of the regiment.

The regiment was reorganized at Camp Dennison, Ohio, for three years' service, in May and June, 1861, before leaving the State.

The months of May and June were spent in drill and discipline at Camp Dennison, and in July the regiment joined General McClellan's forces, then operating in Western Virginia. In the battle at Carnifex Ferry, September 10th, its courage and discipline were tested and not found wanting.

On the 13th of December it joined General Buell's army in

Kentucky, where it remained in camp until February, 1862. It formed the advance of Buell's forces on Nashville.

On the 10th of March the regiment was ordered to report to General Crittenden. On the 19th Companies A and G were detached to assist in repairing bridges on the Alabama and Tennessee Rivers, and on April 2nd the remaining companies, under command of Lieutenant Colonel Hawkins, joined the column on the march to reënforce General Grant at Pittsburg Landing.

The scene of action was reached on the 6th, and the regiment immediately moved forward to meet the foe. In a desperate struggle with the Washington Battery of New Orleans the Thirteenth captured it entire. The enemy, having retreated, the Thirteenth joined in the investment of Corinth, and after the evacuation moved with Buell's army to Chattanooga.

In the meantime Bragg had left Chattanooga and was on his way to Louisville, Ky., with designs on Ohio and Indiana. Then commenced the "never-to-be-forgotten" march of the Army of the Ohio. From this time until the advance on Murfreesboro the regiment was constantly employed in foraging, picket duty and skirmishing.

On the 26th day of December the advance commenced and arrived at Stone River on the evening of the 29th. On Wednesday, December 31st, the Thirteenth, under Colonel J. G. Hawkins, assisted in the rescue of a train that was about to be captured by the rebel cavalry. A few hours later the terrible but brief struggle commenced with cost the regiment 142 officers and men killed, wounded and missing. It was in this engagement that Colonel Hawkins was killed. On January 2nd, 1863, the Thirteenth again participated in the fighting, and on the morning of the 3rd, Murfreesboro was evacuated and the enemy retreating. During this series of battles the regiment lost 185 officers and men.

On June 24th the line of march was resumed, and the army moved southward. It took an active part in the battle of Chickamauga, on the 19th and 20th. It joined the advance to the relief of Knoxville and pursued the enemy across the Holstein River to Dandridge, twenty-five miles from the North Carolina line, then returned to Knoxville. In January, 1864, about three-fourths of the Thirteenth reënlisted for another three years, and after the furlough home promptly reassembled at Camp Chase and returned in a body to Chattanooga.

In May, 1864, the regiment entered upon the Atlanta campaign, and after some hard skirmishing gained possession of Tunnel Hill, Rocky Face Ridge and Dalton, driving the enemy into the fortifications at Resaca. In the assault upon Lost Mountain on the 27th of May the Thirteenth took a prominent part.

The forces, unable to make any impression on the enemy's works, were withdrawn, the regiment losing on this occasion fifty killed, wounded and prisoners. On the 9th of June it went into camp at Acworth, keeping up a continuous skirmish with the retreating enemy.

About this time the term of enlistment of the non-veterans expired. The veterans of the regiment were consolidated into a battalion of four companies, to be called the Thirteenth Ohio Volunteer Infantry Battalion. It participated in the engagements at Kenesaw, Atlanta, Jonesboro and Lovejoy, then went into camp six miles north of Atlanta. On the 4th of October the battalion joined in the pursuit of Hood into Tennessee. Encountering the enemy at Franklin, a severe struggle ensued, in which the National troops were again successful. On December 3rd the Thirteenth Battalion entered Nashville, and from this time until the battles of the 15th and 16th, in a charge made by the Third Brigade, the Thirteenth was among the first over the works and assisted in the capture of four guns. After the defeat at Nashville the Confederate Army retreated rapidly and the battalion remained quietly in camp at Huntsville, Ala.

On the 16th of June, 1865, the Thirteenth, with the Fourteenth Corps, was ordered to Texas, where it remained in service until December 5th, 1865. Returning to Ohio, it was discharged at Columbus January 17th, 1866, having served four years and nine months and participated in many decisive battles. Colonel Joseph G. Hawkins of Union County, a brave and distinguished officer, was killed at the battle of Stone River, Tennessee, December 31st, 1862.

One company of the 13th was recruited in Union County for the three months' service, of which Joseph Hawkins was the first Captain, and James D. Bain and Harvey S. Wood of Jerome Township served in that company, assigned as Company F. On reorganization for three years' service Captain Hawkins was promoted to Major and J. D. Smith and Jeremiah Slocum both served as Captains of this company.

Captain Reason R. Henderson of Union County was severely wounded in the battle of Shiloh, Tenn., April 7th, 1862, and was discharged by reason of his wounds September 10th. In the new regiments being organized there was a great demand for experienced soldiers to officer these organizations. Captain Henderson was immediately appointed Major of the 121st Regiment, O. V. I. He was a good disciplinarian, a fine drill master, and rendered efficient service until again compelled to leave the army on account of his wounds.

David O. Taylor of Jerome Township was killed at the battle of Dallas, Ga., May 27th, 1864, and the total loss in the regiment, killed and died of wounds and disease, was 221. Of the 160 men who enlisted in this regiment from Union County the loss in killed and wounded or by disease was forty-five.

SEVENTEENTH OHIO VOLUNTEER INFANTRY.
THREE MONTHS.

The 17th Ohio Volunteer Infantry three months' service was organized at Camp Anderson, Lancaster, Ohio, and was mustered into the U. S. service April 27th, 1861, under command of Colonel John McConnell.

The regiment was immediately ordered to Virginia and up to July had some skirmishing with guerillas and was employed guarding provision trains in the vicinity of Buckhannon and Sutton. On the 3rd of July they were ordered to Zanesville,

Ohio, and were mustered out of the U. S. service August 15th, 1861, at Camp Goddard. During their service the loss was three men—one by drowning and two by disease. As shown by the official record, twenty-nine Jerome Township soldiers served in Company G of this regiment, organized at Plain City and commanded by Captain Thomas J. Haynes.

It was one of the first regiments to respond to the call of President Lincoln for 75,000 men. Every soldier of Jerome Township who served in this regiment reënlisted in the three years' service and a number of them were killed or died in the army. Jerome Township furnished her full quota under the first call, and every call thereafter. The 17th Regiment organized for three years had a distinguished service and served in the Army of the Cumberland throughout the war, participating in many decisive battles, but it seems that no Jerome Township soldiers served in that regiment. The losses by death were 232 in the three years' service.

THIRTIETH OHIO VOLUNTEER INFANTRY.
THREE YEARS' SERVICE.

The 30th Ohio Volunteer Infantry is named as one of the three hundred fighting regiments, and is well entitled to that honor for distinguished service.

Company E of the 30th Ohio Infantry was organized by Captain Elijah Warner at Jerome, Union County, Ohio, in the month of August, 1861, and marched thence to Camp Chase, a distance of twenty miles, where it arrived on the 19th day of August. On the 29th the company was mustered into the United States service, with the following commissioned officers: Elijah Warner, Captain; Henry R. Brinkerhoff, First Lieutenant, and Henry Hensel, Second Lieutenant.

On the 30th the regiment was ordered into the field, and on the 2nd of September arrived at Clarksburg, W. Va., then moved forward to Weston, where it received its first outfit of camp and garrison equipage. On September 6th the regiment joined General Rosecrans at Sutton Heights, leaving four companies—D, F, G, and I—at this place and two—C and E—at

Big Birch Bottom. The remainder of the regiment moved forward and on the evening of the 10th discerned the enemy near Gawley River, at Carnifex Ferry, where a sharp encounter ensued. Night coming on, ended the battle. Early on the following morning it was discovered that the enemy had evacuated their position and retraced across the river.

Colonel Ewing was the first man to enter the deserted fortifications. He found, amid a multitude of camp and garrison spoils, two fine French dress swords, one bearing the coat of arms of Napoleon I, and a stand of colors bearing the following inscription:

" Floyd's Brigade."

" *The Price of Liberty is the Blood of the Brave.*"

The regiment was mustered into the United States service at Camp Chase, Ohio, on the 28th day of August, 1861, for three years, under Colonel John Groesbeck, who was soon succeeded by Colonel Hugh Ewing. The regiment served in West Virginia in detachments until August, 1862. On the 16th of that month the regiment started to join the army in Eastern Virginia. The right wing reported for duty at General Pope's headquarters on the 26th, and after the engagement at Centerville the left wing joined the right, having been under fire but not engaged with the musketry in the battle at this place.

On the 2nd of September the regiment was relieved from duty at General Pope's headquarters and joined its brigade— the First—at Upton Hills. On the 7th it moved to Frederick City, Md., and on the 14th arrived at South Mountain, where a severe struggle with the enemy took place, with a loss of eighteen men killed and forty-eight wounded. In this engagement Company E suffered most severely, having one killed and six wounded.

In the battle of Antietam the Thirtieth, lacking proper support, was thrown back into slight confusion and compelled to fall back. It lost three officers killed and two wounded, eight men killed and thirty-seven wounded. The National colors were torn in fourteen places by the enemy's balls, and two color-bearers, Sergeants Carter and Nathan J. White, fell dead on the field. A stand of colors was rescued on this occasion by David McKim of Company E.

On the 10th of October the Thirtieth moved into West Virginia, and on the 13th of November went into camp near Cannelton. A few weeks later it started on a march into Logan County, returning with seventeen prisoners and seventy-five horses. In January, 1863, it moved down the Ohio and Mississippi to join General Grant's army, and on arriving at Helena, Ark., was assigned to the Third Brigade, Second Division of the Fifteenth Army Corps. On the 21st it landed at Young's Point, and for a few weeks worked on the canal at that place. In March it moved to the relief of a gunboat in Steel's Bayou, returning to Young's Point on the 28th.

On the 29th of April the regiment embarked on the R. B. Hamilton, and with other troops engaged in a demonstration on Haines' Bluffs. In May it joined in the movement upon Vicksburg, and from the 20th until the surrender of this stronghold the regiment was constantly engaged either in fatigue or picket duty or in assaulting the enemy's works. The loss of the Thirtieth during the siege was one commissioned officer killed and six wounded, six men killed and forty-eight wounded. After the surrender of Vicksburg the regiment pursued Johnson to Jackson, and upon the evacuation of that place returned and went into camp at Black River.

On the 26th of September it moved with Sherman via Memphis to Chattanooga, and on the 25th of October participated in the assault upon Mission Ridge, losing thirty-nine men killed and wounded.

In November the Thirtieth followed in pursuit of the retreating rebels, returning to Bridgeport, Ala., on the 19th of December. During this time the men were compelled to subsist off the country, with the exception of two days' rations issued on the 29th day of November.

In January, 1864, the regiment reënlisted, and after the furlough home joined Sherman's forces at Kingston, Ga., on the 20th day of May. On the 23rd it started on the march through Dallas and Acworth, and on the 19th of June arrived at the foot of Kenesaw Mountain. During this march the Thirtieth was almost continuously under fire. It took an active part in the battle on the 26th, losing thirty-five men killed and wounded. On July 2nd the regiment moved toward Atlanta, and on the 22nd was attacked and thrown into some confusion at first, but soon rallied and succeeded in repulsing the enemy, not, however, without considerable loss. On the 28th the regiment gallantly stood its ground and resisted four successive attacks of the enemy, losing thirty men killed and wounded. Under its fire the foe forsook a stand of colors and in its immediate front 105 dead rebels were found.

The Thirtieth was transferred to the First Brigade on the 5th of August, and on the 29th the non-veterans were mustered out. On the 31st the rebels attacked the line of the First Brigade, but were repulsed, the Thirtieth losing in this encounter twenty-five men killed and wounded.

On the 2nd of September Jonesboro was evacuated by the enemy, the regiment pursuing them to Lovejoy's Station. After spending several weeks in camp at East Point, the Thirtieth followed in pursuit of Hood's army into Alabama, returned to Atlanta, then marched to Fort McAllister and took part in the successful assault on that place.

After the fall of Savannah the regiment passed through the Carolinas, having a sharp engagement with Johnson at Bentonville, and frequent skirmishes with the enemy. It arrived at Goldsboro March 24th, 1865; then proceeded to Raleigh on the 14th of April, and aided in the capture of Johnson's army.

The Thirtieth marched to Washington via Richmond, and after passing in review, moved to Louisville, Ky., and thence to Little Rock, Ark. Here the regiment remained in camp until mustered out August 21st, 1865, having participated in twenty engagements and having its colors shot in almost every battle.

The regiment had a most remarkable service, as it participated in great battles in the States of Virginia, Mississippi, Georgia, Tennessee, Maryland and North Carolina. They marched and were transported by water and railroads several thousand miles.

Of the commanders of the regiment, Colonel John Groesbeck was transferred to the 39th O. V. I.; Colonel Hugh Ewing and Colonel Theodore Jones were both promoted to Brigadier-Generals; Lieutenant Henry Brinkerhoff was promoted to Lieutenant Colonel of the Second Mississippi Regiment, U. S. C. T. He remained in the Regular Army after the close of the war, had a long and honorable service, and was retired with the rank of Colonel but a few years ago.

Captain Elijah Warner was promoted to Major and James D. Bain was promoted to the Captaincy of Company E.

The total losses in the regiment, killed, died of wounds and disease, as shown by the official record, were two hundred and seventy-seven.

One hundred and two soldiers served in Company E of Jerome Township, and the loss, killed and died of wounds and disease, was thirty-two, or about 33 per cent of the total enlistments. Many others were wounded and a number were prisoners of war.

32ND REGIMENT, OHIO VOLUNTEER INFANTRY.
THREE YEARS' SERVICE.

The 32nd Ohio Infantry was organized during the summer of 1861, under Colonel T. C. Ford, and was one of the first regiments to answer the call of the President for three years' service.

Company B of this regiment was recruited in Union and Champaign Counties, and was mustered into the service at Camp Chase August 9th, 1861, with the following commissioned officers: W. A. Palmer, Captain; A. B. Parmeter, First Lieutenant, and J. B. Whelpley, Second Lieutenant. It joined the regiment at Camp Bartley, near Mansfield.

Four soldiers of Jerome Township served in Company B of this regiment — John P. McDowell, Robert N. McDowell, John B. Robinson and Henry M. Converse. Robert N. McDowell died in the service, and John P. McDowell and John

B. Robinson reënlisted as veterans and served until July 20th, 1865, participating in all the campaigns and battles of the regiment for four years and until the last shot was fired.

After remaining a short time at Camp Bartley the regiment was transferred to Camp Dennison, where it was equipped, armed and ordered to the front, joining the Union forces at Cheat Mountain Summit, West Virginia, on the 3rd of October. In December it accompanied General Milroy in the movement on Camp Alleghany, losing on this occasion four killed and fourteen wounded. After this expedition the regiment spent the winter in camp at Beverly, and in the spring of 1862 took part in the actions against Camp Alleghany, Huntsville and McDowell. In the engagement at Bull Pasture Mountain, on the 8th of May, when the Union Army fell back to Franklin, closely followed by the enemy, the 32nd was the last regiment to leave the field, and lost on this occasion six killed and fifty-three wounded. While at Franklin it was transferred to General Schenck's brigade, and was with General Fremont in the Shenandoah Valley and shared in the engagements at Cross Keys and Port Republic on the 8th and 9th of June. Returning up the valley it remained at Winchester, Va., until September 1st, then moved to Harpers Ferry, losing 150 men in the engagement on the 14th.

In January, 1863, the regiment was ordered South, joined the army at Memphis, Tenn., and was with the army under Grant in his advance in the rear of Vicksburg, taking part in the action at Port Gibson and in the battles of Raymond, Jackson and Champion Hills. In the last-named engagement it made a bayonet charge and captured the First Mississippi rebel battery. For this feat of gallantry the battery was turned over to Company F of this regiment, which became the 26th Ohio Battery.

In the assault upon Vicksburg, in May, 1863, the regiment was in the front line of the forces operating against that rebel stronghold, and it, with the Fourth Division, Seventeenth Corps, General J. A. Logan commanding, was detailed to take possession at the surrender.

The 32nd lost in this campaign and siege 225 men. In July, 1863, the regiment moved with Stevenson to Monroe, La., and in October accompanied McPherson to Brownsville, Miss. In February, 1864, it operated under Sherman at Meridian, then returned to Vicksburg, reënlisted, and after the furlough home joined Sherman's army at Acworth, Ga., on the 10th of June. It was in the assault on Kenesaw Mountain, on the 27th of June, and at Nicojack Creek on the 10th of July. In the fighting around Atlanta on the 20th, 21st, 22nd and 28th the 32nd took an active part, losing more than half its numbers.

After the fall of Atlanta the regiment joined in the pursuit of Hood, marched with Sherman to the sea, and through the Carolinas, and on the 20th and 21st of March, 1865, took part in the engagement at Bentonville, then moved with the National forces to Raleigh, and was present at Johnston's surrender. Marched through Richmond to Washington and took part in the grand review before the President and his cabinet. After which it moved to Louisville, Ky., was mustered out of the service July 20th, then proceeded to Columbus, Ohio, where the men received their final discharge on the 25th day of July, 1865.

It is claimed that the 32nd Regiment lost and received more men than any other from Ohio. Company B entered the field in September, 1861, 108 strong, and during the war received sixty-eight recruits, making the total enlistments 176. The company lost, while in the field, ten killed and died of wounds, eleven wounded, seventeen died of disease, and seven taken prisoners.

Russell B. Bennett, Chaplain of the 32nd, was known in the Seventeenth Army Corps as the "Fighting Chaplain." He not only believed in the efficacy of prayer, but also believed in the efficacy of shot and shell, and instead of remaining in the rear during an engagement, he was always up in the front line, not only to minister to the wounded and dying, but, with gun in hand, taking his place in the ranks and encouraging the soldiers by his coolness and bravery.

Of the many instances in which he rendered good services during a battle we give one as related by the boys of the regiment:

On the day the brave and gallant McPherson fell (July 22nd, 1864), the Seventeenth Corps was hotly engaged. The 32nd Regiment was flanked on all sides and was compelled to change front several times, not knowing in what direction to next look for the enemy.

At one time, during a few moments' lull in the battle, the 32nd was lying down in the edge of a cornfield waiting for the next attack. The Chaplain, cautioning the boys to lie very still and protect themselves as best they could, advanced into the cornfield to make a reconnoissance, and, mounting a stump some forty or fifty yards in front of the line, discovered the battle line of the enemy rapidly advancing, and moving back to his regiment passed the word along the line that the enemy was close upon them. Then, taking the musket of William B. Mitchell of Company B — brother to John and James Mitchell of Marysville (both deceased) — he fired on the advancing line. Mitchell, lying upon the ground, would rapidly reload the gun, and again Bennett would fire, and all the time exhorting the boys to "lie low" until the enemy were close upon them, then to "fire low."

All this time he stood erect, not seeming to have any thought of his own safety, but only solicitous for the soldiers of the regiment, whom he loved so dearly. Mitchell was killed as he lay on the ground, and his body falling into the hands of the enemy, was never recovered. Bennett was universally respected and loved by all the officers and soldiers of the regiment, and today the boys all have a good word for Chaplain Bennett, who died a few years ago.

The regiment has to its credit twenty-two important battles, besides many skirmishes. More than 2,500 soldiers served in the regiment and 560 were mustered out at the close of the war, and the loss in killed and died of wounds and disease was two hundred and forty-nine.

34TH REGIMENT, OHIO VOLUNTEER INFANTRY.
THREE YEARS' SERVICE.

This regiment was organized at Camp Lucas, Clermont County, in the summer of 1861, under Colonel Abraham S. Piatt. About September 1st it moved to Camp Dennison, Ohio. The regiment was equipped and the men uniformed in light blue Zouave dress and was called the Piatt Zouaves, and was ordered to West Virginia in September. The baptism of fire was with a Virginia regiment at Chapmanville, Va., September 25th, in which the loss was one killed and eight wounded.

During the fall and winter months the regiment was on picket duty and scouting, and had some skirmishing with guerillas. In the month of May, 1862, the regiment had a sharp fight with the rebel forces under Humphry Marshall, near Princeton. In an engagement near Fayettesville, Va., September 10th, the regiment lost 134 killed, wounded and missing, and the loss in officers was very heavy. After this fight they fell back to Point Pleasant, Va. The regiment was on garrison duty until May, 1863. In that month the regiment was mounted and their next engagement was at Wythesville, where Colonel Toland of the 34th was killed.

In January, 1864, a large number of the regiment reënlisted as veterans. After the veteran furlough the regiment was engaged in raiding and destroying railroads, during the months of May and June, and was engaged in the great Lynchburg raid under General Hunter. They saw some hard service and the losses were heavy.

In a fight near Winchester, July 20th, the loss was thirty killed and wounded, and Lieutenant Colonel Shaw of the 34th was mortally wounded. In the battle of Winchester, September 19th, they were hotly engaged and six men of the color guard were killed, the total loss being sixty.

In the fall of 1864 and the winter of 1865 the regiment was on garrison duty the greater part of the time at Beverly. The regiment was very much reduced in numbers and at Cumberland, Md., the survivors were consolidated with the 36th Ohio

Volunteer Infantry. It was afterward known as the 36th Regiment, Ohio Veteran Volunteer Infantry.

The regiment was in thirty-three battles, fights and skirmishes, and the loss in killed and died of wounds and disease was two hundred and sixty. The first Colonel, A. S. Piatt, was promoted to Brigadier-General and two commanders of the regiment were killed on the field.

40TH REGIMENT, OHIO VOLUNTEER INFANTRY. THREE YEARS' SERVICE.

This regiment was organized at Camp Chase, Ohio, in the summer and fall of 1861, and was mustered in as a regiment December 11th under Colonel Jonathan Cranor. Eight soldiers of the regiment were credited to Jerome Township, one of whom, Jesse V. McDowell, died in the service.

The regiment served throughout the war in the Army of the Cumberland and participated in a number of decisive battles, including Chickamauga, where it came on the field in Granger's Corps and Steadman's Division just at the critical time Sunday afternoon, September 20th, 1863, fought under General George H. Thomas, "The Rock of Chickamauga," and was a part of the Union Army that saved the day in that bloody battle. They lost heavily, and among the wounded was Dell Snodgrass of Jerome Township.

The regiment left Camp Chase, Ohio, for the front December 11th, 1861, was ordered to northeastern Kentucky and was soon actively engaged in scouting and skirmishing on the Big Sandy River with the Confederate Army under Humphrey Marshall.

In January, 1862, it took an active part in the battle of Middle Creek; then went into camp at Paintville. It operated in Kentucky and Virginia until February, 1863, when it moved to Nashville, Tenn., and was assigned to the First Brigade, First Division, Reserve Corps, then at Franklin.

While at this place the Fortieth repulsed an attack made by Van Dorn with a large mounted force. On the 2nd of June it moved to Triune, and on the 23rd joined Rosecrans' army in

ESLEY PATCH
121st O. V. I.

WILLIAM N. KILE
17th O. V. I.

SERGEANT MARION STEVENS
54th O. V. I.

HARMON PATCH
121st O. V. I.

SERGEANT JAMES C. COLLIER
30th O. V. I.

GEORGE C. EDWARDS
174th O. V. I.

DAVID EDWARDS
96th O. V. I.

FESTUS EDWARDS
187th O. V. I.

the movement upon Shelbyville, Wartrace and Tullahoma. It remained at Wartrace and Tullahoma until September 7th, when it moved forward in the advance on Chattanooga and took an active part in the battle of Chickamauga. Soon after this engagement the regiment went into camp at Shellmound, where four of its companies reënlisted. In the battle of Lookout Mountain, November 24th, the Fortieth took a prominent part. In January, 1864, in went into camp near Cleveland, Tennessee, and in May entered upon the Atlanta campaign, participating in nearly all the battles through to the end.

In the battle of Lookout Mountain, November 24th, 1863, the regiment fought with conspicuous bravery and was highly complimented in general orders. The regiment lost heavily on the Atlanta campaign, and among the killed were Captain C. F. Snodgrass, Captain Charles Converse and Major Thomas Acton died of wounds.

Captain James Watson was promoted to Lieutenant Colonel and commanded the regiment at the close of the war. The regiment participated in seventeen battles and fights, besides many skirmishes, and the losses by death—killed, died of wounds and disease—were two hundred and thirty-seven. The regiment had a service in which the survivors may well take a just pride.

At Pine Knob, Georgia, on the 7th of October, Companies A, B, C, and D were mustered out, and the remainder of the regiment moved with the Fourth Corps, sharing in the pursuit of Hood and in the retreat before Hood from Pulaski.

In December, 1864, at Nashville, Tenn., the non-veterans were mustered out, and the veterans consolidated with the Fifty-first Ohio Infantry. The combined regiment was then transferred with the Fourth Corps to Texas, where it performed guard duty until mustered out December 3, 1865. About forty men from Union County were members of Company D of this regiment, four of whom were killed, six died in the hospital, two were drowned, and three were wounded.

8

46TH REGIMENT, OHIO VOLUNTEER INFANTRY.
THREE YEARS' SERVICE.

This regiment was organized at Worthington, Ohio, in the fall of 1861 and was mustered into the United States service October 16th, 1861, under Colonel Thomas Worthington and Lieutenant Colonel Charles C. Walcutt. Colonel Worthington resigned November 21st, 1862, and Lieutenant Colonel Walcutt was promoted to Colonel and commanded the regiment with marked ability through many of the hard and decisive battles in which it participated.

Colonel Walcutt was promoted to Brigadier General for distinguished service on the field. He was severely wounded twice, and was one of General Grant's most trusted young officers in the Army of the Tennessee.

Nine soldiers of this regiment, of whom Sergeant James Gowan was one, served from Jerome Township. Sergeant Gowan was killed at the battle of Mission Ridge, Tenn., November 25th, 1863, and William Hudson and Thomas Wray died in the service. To have served in this regiment through its many campaigns and battles was a distinguished honor. The other six names are: William B. Herriott, David M. Pence, John P. Williams, Charles C. Comstock, Ammon P. Converse and Edward R. Buckley.

The regiment joined General Sherman's army at Paducah, Kentucky, in February, 1862, and participated in the bloody battle of Shiloh, Tenn., April 6th and 7th, 1862. The loss was 295 killed, wounded and captured.

In April the regiment moved with the army upon Corinth. The summer of 1862 was spent at Memphis, and in November the Forty-sixth started on a campaign through Mississippi under General Grant. In June, 1863, it participated in the siege of Vicksburg, and after the surrender moved upon Jackson. In October the regiment, under Sherman, embarked for Memphis and Chattanooga. It took part in the assault on Mission Ridge, sustaining a heavy loss; then marched to the relief of Knoxville.

At Resaca, New Hope Church, Kenesaw, and the various

battles and skirmishes of the Atlanta campaign, the Forty-sixth was ever at the front. At Ezra Church the regiment especially distinguished itself in repelling the attacking rebels and capturing the colors of the Thirtieth Louisiana. After the fall of Atlanta, the regiment pursued Hood into northern Alabama and Tennessee. In November it marched with Sherman to the sea, participating in a sharp encounter at Griswoldsville and in the skirmishing around Savannah. From Savannah it moved to Bentonville, where it was complimented for gallant conduct in the battle at that place.

The Forty-sixth moved through the Carolinas, on to Washington, and after the grand review proceeded to Louisville, Ky., where it was mustered out on the 22nd of July, 1865.

The regiment has to its record eighteen battles, as shown by the official records, with many skirmishes; marched many hundreds of miles, was on the firing line when the war closed, and fought in the last battle of General Sherman's at Bentonville, N. C., March 19th, 1865. The losses, killed, died of wounds and disease, were 290, and the total casualties as shown by the official record were seven hundred and twenty-five.

54TH REGIMENT, OHIO VOLUNTEER INFANTRY.
THREE YEARS' SERVICE.

This regiment was organized at Camp Dennison, Ohio, in the summer and fall of 1861, under Colonel Thomas Kirby Smith, who was promoted to a Brigadier-General August 11th, 1863.

Fourteen Jerome Township soldiers are credited to the regiment, of whom James Clark and David Kent died in the service. The regiment was ordered to Kentucky in February, 1862, and arrived at Paducah on the 20th of that month, where it was assigned to the division of General W. T. Sherman. The regiment was among the first troops to arrive by steamer, going up the Tennessee River, at Pittsburg Landing, early in March.

It was on outpost duty continuously through the month

of March, and when the battle of Shiloh commenced it held the Union lines on the extreme left. It participated in that bloody battle, April 6th and 7th, with a loss in killed, wounded and missing of about two hundren men. During the siege of Corinth the regiment was on the front line the greater part of the time until the evacuation of that stronghold by the Confederates, May 30th, and had a number of skirmishes and minor engagements.

Soon after the evacuation of Corinth the regiment moved with the Division to LaGrange, Tenn., and then on to Holly Springs, Miss. In July the regiment marched to Memphis, Tenn., and from here was on several scouting and reconnoitering expeditions, and was with the advance of Sherman's army on the first expedition against Vicksburg.

In the engagement at Chickasaw Bayou, on the 28th and 29th of December, the regiment lost twenty men killed and wounded. In January, 1863, it took part in the assault and capture of Arkansas Post.

From this place the Fifty-fourth proceeded to Young's Point, La., and for a time was employed in digging a canal; then marched to the rescue of a fleet of gunboats which were about to be destroyed. In May it moved with Grant's army to the rear of Vicksburg, was engaged in the battles of Champion Hills and Big Black Bridge, and on the 19th and 22nd of May took an active part in the assault upon the enemy's works, losing in the two days forty-seven men killed and wounded.

In October the regiment proceeded to Memphis and thence to Chattanooga, taking part in the assault on Mission Ridge, November 26th. The following day it marched to the relief of Knoxville and after pursuing the enemy through Tennessee into North Carolina returned to Chattanooga, and from there proceeded to Larkinsville, Ala. On the 22nd of January, 1864, the Fifty-fourth reënlisted, and after the furlough to Ohio, returned to the Army with 200 recruits.

In May it joined Sherman's Atlanta campaign, and participated in the engagements at Resaca, Dallas and New Hope

Church. In the assault upon Kenesaw Mountain, June 27th, the regiment lost twenty-eight killed and wounded. At Nicojack Creek, July 3rd, thirteen were killed, wounded and missing; in the battles on the east side of Atlanta, July 21st and 22nd, ninety-four were killed, wounded and missing; and at Ezra Chapel, on the 28th, eight more were added to the list of killed and wounded.

From this time until the 27th of August the Fifty-fourth was continually engaged in the works before Atlanta. It took a prominent part in the engagement at Jonesboro, pursued Hood northward, returned and marched to the sea, taking part in the capture of Fort McAllister on the 15th of December. It moved through the Carolinas, participating in many skirmishes, and in the last battle of the war at Bentonville, N. C., March 21st, 1865.

The regiment moved to Richmond, Va., and from there to Washington City. After passing in review it moved to Louisville, Ky., thence to Little Rock, Ark., and there performed garrison duty until mustered out, August 15th, 1865.

The regiment marched upward of 3,500 miles, participated in seventeen hard-fought battles and many skirmishes. The losses in killed, wounded, died of disease and missing were five hundred and six. It fought in the States of Tennessee, Mississippi, Arkansas, Georgia, and North Carolina.

FIFTY-EIGHTH OHIO VOLUNTEER INFANTRY.
THREE YEARS' SERVICE.

This regiment was organized at Camp Chase, Ohio, in the winter of 1862, under the call of the President for 300,000 troops, under Colonel Val Bausenwein, and was largely composed of Germans, both officers and men of the ranks.

Colonel Bausenwein resigned and Lieutenant Colonel Peter Dister commanded the regiment. He was killed December 29th, 1862, in a fight on the Yazoo River, Mississippi, and the regiment lost in killed, wounded and missing upward of forty per cent of the number engaged.

It saw its first hard battle at Fort Donelson, and its next at

Pittsburg Landing. It took part in the siege of Corinth, then moved to Memphis, where it was ordered to Arkansas. In January, 1863, it shared in the capture of Arkansas Post, and in April joined Grant's Vicksburg campaign. It participated in the engagements of Deer Creek and of Grand Gulf.

On the surrender of Fort Donelson the Fifty-eighth was the first regiment to enter the Fort, February 16th, 1862, and Lieutenant Colonel Rempel, commanding the regiment, hauled down the Confederate flag. The regiment was hotly engaged in the battle of Shiloh, April 7th, with a loss of nine killed and forty-three wounded.

During the summer of 1863 the companies of the regiment were transferred to ironclads and flotillas and saw some hard service in running the blockades of the rebel batteries at Vicksburg, and in the battle of Grand Gulf the regiment lost heavily. The regiment has to its credit twelve battles, many skirmishes, and the losses in killed died of wounds and disease totaled three hundred and five.

The service of this German regiment was long and honorable, and the members of the regiment have left to their families a noble heritage of devotion to the flag of their adopted country. The regiment was discharged at Columbus, Ohio, January 14th, 1865.

Dunallen M. Woodburn was the only soldier of Jerome Township who served in this regiment. He left home without the consent of his paretns, which was a very usual occurrence in those war days. He was but 14 years of age, and enlisted January 16th, 1862, serving continuously until the regiment was discharged. He reënlisted as a veteran, and was promoted to Drum-Major of the 47th Regiment, U. S. C. T.

He had a remarkable service for a boy of 14, and now after a lapse of more than fifty years I recall an incident of the battle of Shiloh. Knowing that the 58th Regiment was in the battle and that his parents, John and Maria Curry Woodburn, would be anxious about him, the day after the battle, April 7th, 1862, I mounted my horse and after a search of several hours on the battlefield, strewn with the dead of both armies, I found "Dun," as we called him, as happy and unconcerned as if he had been at his home. I sought and found Colonel Bausenwein, who, in his Fez cap, was enjoying his pipe, and requested that Dun accompany me to our bivouac, to which he readily consented.

I took him on my horse and we made our way to my regiment. We had no tents and it rained almost continuously for two or three days, but I shared my blankets and rubber poncho with him. All around were dead artillery horses and ambulances were busy gathering up our own boys in the dense woods, and no doubt he will recall this incident vividly.

SIXTY-THIRD OHIO VOLUNTEER INFANTRY.
THREE YEARS' SERVICE.

This regiment was organized at Worthington and Marietta, Ohio, by the consolidation of two battalions, known as the Twenty-second and Sixty-third. It was organized in February, 1862, under Colonel John W. Sprague, and immediately joined the Army of the Mississippi under General Pope, and was engaged in all the movements which resulted in the capture of Island No. 10, and in the siege of Corinth.

It took part in the battles of Iuka and Corinth under Rosecrans. After operating in Alabama and Tennessee until October, 1863, the Sixty-third joined the Army of the Cumberland, and participated in the battles of the Atlanta campaign, the march to the sea, and through the Carolinas. It took part in the review at Washington, then moved to Louisville, where it was mustered out July 8th, 1865.

In the battle of Corinth, Miss., October 4th, 1862, the regiment captured in a charge one gun of a battery, with the Captain commanding, and a number of prisoners. The loss in this battle was almost fifty per cent in killed and wounded. Sergeant Eli Casey, the only Jerome Township soldier who served in the 63rd, was killed in this battle.

A large number of the regiment reënlisted as veterans January 2nd, 1864, at Prospect, Tenn. They were in the last battle of any importance participated in by General Sherman's army, at Bentonville, N. C., March 19th, and their last skirmish was March 31st, near Newbern.

The regiment was engaged in fifteen battles, besides many skirmishes, and the loss by death was three hundred and sixty-seven, as shown by the official records.

SIXTY-SIXTH OHIO VOLUNTEER INFANTRY.
THREE YEARS' SERVICE.

Seven Jerome Township soldiers served in this regiment, two of whom, Corporal Delmore Robinson and David Shineman, died in the service.

The Sixty-sixth Ohio was organized at Camp McArthur, Urbana, Ohio, October 1st, 1861, under Colonel Charles Candy, and on the 17th of January, 1862, moved to West Virginia and reported to General Lander at New Creek, where the first field camp was made. General Shields soon succeeded General Lander, and the Sixty-sixth, for a few weeks, was stationed as provost guard at Martinsburg, Winchester and Strasburg; then crossed the Blue Ridge to Fredericksburg, where it was assigned to the Third Brigade under General E. B. Tyler. Orders were soon received to countermarch for the relief of General Banks in the Shenandoah Valley and for the protection of Washington, then threatened by Stonewall Jackson.

In the battle of Port Republic, June 9th, the regiment took an active and prominent part in defending a battery of seven guns. The enemy had possession of these guns at three different times, and as many times were compelled to abandon them by the regiment. After fighting for five hours against overwhelming numbers, General Tyler withdrew his command. The regiment lost on this occasion 196 of the 400 men engaged.

The Second Division, under command of General Banks, opened the battle at Cedar Mountain, and in the desperate struggle which ensued the regiment lost eighty-seven killed and wounded of the 200 men in arms. Its battleflag had one shell and nineteen bullet holes made through it, and one Sergeant and five Corporals were shot down in succession while carrying it. The regiment was again actively engaged at Antietam on the 17th and 18th of September. On the 27th of December, 1862, General Stewart, with 2,000 rebel cavalry, made an attack on Dumfries, a small town garrisoned by the Fifty-seventh and Sixty-sixth Ohio Regiments, about 700 troops in all. After fighting fiercely for several hours, the enemy was forced to retreat.

After participating in the battle of Gettysburg, the Sixty-sixth pursued Lee to the Rappahonnock; and in August, 1863, proceeded to New York to enforce the draft. In September it was transferred to the Army of the Cumberland, near Chattanooga, and in November took part in the battles of Lookout Mountain, Mission Ridge, and Ringgold. On the 15th of December the regiment reënlisted, and at the end of veteran furlough returned to Bridgeport, Ala., where it remained in camp about three months. In May, 1864, it moved with the First Brigade, Second Division, Twentieth Corps, on the Atlanta campaign.

At Resaca the Sixty-sixth was actively engaged, but with slight loss. On the 25th of May it took part in the engagement near Pumpkin Vine Creek, and for eight days kept up a continuous musketry fire with the enemy. On the 15th of June the regiment led the advance on Pine Mountain, and in the battles of Kenesaw, Marietta and Peach Tree Creek fought with conspicuous gallantry. After the capture of Atlanta the Sixty-sixth remained on duty in that city until Sherman started on his "march to the sea." From Savannah it moved northward through the Carolinas and on to Washington, passing over the old battlefield of Chancellorsville, thus making the entire circuit of the Southern States.

The regiment marched and was transported by rail upward of 11,000 miles; participated in sixteen hard-fought battles; a score of fights and skirmishes, and served in twelve States. The losses in killed, died of wounds and disease were two hundred and forty-five, and the total casualties were upward of five hundred. The regiment was discharged at Columbus, Ohio, July 19th, 1865.

Company F, organized in Union County, and the one in which the Jerome Township soldiers served, lost forty-one by death, thirty-four wounded, and eight were taken prisoners of war. To have served in this regiment, participating in its marches, campaigns and many battles, is sufficient honor for any soldier who served in the armies of the Union. But a remnant of that fighting regiment survives to tell the story of Gettysburg and of the many other bloody fields on which they fought.

82ND REGIMENT, OHIO VOLUNTEER INFANTRY.
THREE YEARS' SERVICE.

This regiment was organized at Kenton, Ohio, in the fall of 1861, and was mustered into service under Colonel James Cantwell, December 31st, 1861. It was ordered to Fetterman, Va., in January, 1862, and that winter was devoted to drilling and equipping. In March it was assigned to Gen. Robert Schenk's Brigade and the baptism of fire was the attack on Bull Pasture Mountain.

On the 25th of May it moved with the army under General Fremont to Cross Keys, and followed Stonewall Jackson's forces to the Shenandoah. In the organization of the army of Virginia, under General Pope, the Eighty-second was assigned to an independent brigade under Milroy, of the First Corps, Sigel's command.

In August it was again engaged with Jackson at Cedar Mountain. A few days later the two armies met on the opposite banks of the Rappahannock River, and for more than a week kept up an incessant skirmishing, the enemy making many attempts to gain Waterloo Bridge, which was defended by Milroy's Brigade. When orders were received for the destruction of the bridge, the work was intrusted to the Eighty-second. Then followed the second Bull Run battle, in which the regiment fought with conspicuous gallantry, losing heavily.

In this engagement Colonel Cantwell was killed and Colonel James S. Robinson assumed command.

It participated in the advance on Fredericksburg, and in December went into winter quarters at Stafford C. H. General Howard succeeded General Sigel in command of the Eleventh Corps; and the Eighty-second having been relieved from duty at headquarters, reported to General Schurz, its division commander, and by him was designated as a battalion of sharpshooters for the division. In the movement upon Chancellorsville on the 2nd of May, the Eighty-second performed good service, and from this time until the 7th, was engaged in the trenches or on the picket line.

When the army fell back the regiment returned to Stafford and remained quietly in its old camp until the 10th of June. Then, having been assigned to the Second Brigade of the Third Division, it moved on the Gettysburg campaign, and so severe was its loss in this sanguinary battle that only ninety-two of the 258 men who went into the action remained to guard its colors.

The Eleventh Corps followed in pursuit of the retreating enemy as far as Warrenton Junction. At Hagerstown the Eighty-second had been assigned to the First Brigade of the Third Division, and when the Third Division was ordered to guard the Orange and Alexandria Railroad, it was placed at Catlett's Station, where it performed guard and patrol duty until September. On the 25th, the regiment, with the Eleventh Corps, was transferred to the Army of the Cumberland, and participated in the battle of Wauhatchie, October 28th, and in the assaults upon Lookout Mountain and Mission Ridge.

On January 1st, 1864, the Eighty-second reënlisted for another three years' service; on the 10th started to Ohio on veteran furlough; on the 23rd of February reassembled at Columbus, Ohio, with 200 recruits, and, on the 3rd of March, joined its brigade at Bridgeport, Ala. Here the Eleventh and Twelfth Corps were consolidated, forming the Twentieth, and the Eighty-second was assigned to the Third Brigade, First Division of this corps.

On the 30th of April marching orders were received and the regiment entered upon the Atlanta campaign, moving toward Resaca. On the 14th of May it assisted the Fourth Corps in repulsing an attack by the rebels on Dalton Road, and in the engagement of the next day held an important position with but slight loss.

At Dallas the regiment took an active part, holding the center of the line. The entire brigade was exposed to a heavy fire; by sunset almost every cartridge was gone, and it was only by searching the cartridge boxes of the dead and wounded that a straggling fire was kept uptil night, when the brigade was relieved.

On the 20th of July it crossed Peach Tree Creek and found the rebels in the woods about four miles from Atlanta. The regiment lost in this affair, seventy-five killed and wounded. During the siege of Atlanta the Eighty-second occupied an important but exposed position. On one occasion the regimental colors were carried away and torn to shreds by a cannon ball. On the 20th of August it was removed to a position on the Chattahoochie, and General Slocum assumed command of the corps. On the 2nd of September the National forces took possession of Atlanta, and the regiment went into camp in the suburbs. On the 15th of November it moved with Sherman's army to the sea—a detachment taking part in the encounter with Wheeler's cavalry at Buffalo Creek. From Savannah it marched through the Carolinas.

The regiment took a prominent part in the engagement at Averysboro, losing two officers and eight men wounded, and was again actively engaged in the last battle of the war at Bentonville, in which it lost two officers and nine men wounded and fourteen men missing. From Bentonville it moved to Goldsboro, and on the 9th of April was consolidated with the Sixty-first Ohio, the new organization being denominated the Eighty-second. After the surrender of Johnston at Raleigh, the regiment marched to Washington, and having participated in the grand review on the 24th of May, went into camp near Fort Lincoln.

On the 15th of June it moved to Louisville, Ky., where it remained until the 25th of July, then proceeded to Columbus, Ohio, and was discharged July 29th, 1865.

The Eighty-second Regiment fought in five different states, and participated in twenty-four battles. The loss in killed, died of wounds and disease, was two hundred and fifty-seven. The service of this regiment was most distinguished, it having participated in many decisive battles, and was on the firing line when the war ended.

86TH REGIMENT, OHIO VOLUNTEER INFANTRY.
THREE MONTHS' SERVICE.

Under the call for 75,000 volunteers by the President, in May, 1862, the quota assigned to Union County was one hundred men. In response to that call, a company was recruited in the county by Captain W. H. Robb, and was assigned as Company E, 86th O. V. I.

Twelve soldiers of Jerome Township served in this regiment, which was organized at Camp Chase, Ohio, in May and June, 1862, under Colonel Barnabas Burns. It was immediately ordered to West Virginia, and was on garrison duty at Clarksburg and Grafton until about the last of July guarding the railroads and supply trains.

July 27th Companies A, C, H and I were detailed under command of Lieutenant Colonel Hunter, and were ordered to Parkersburg to watch the movements of the enemy in that section, as it had been reported that a rebel force under Jenkins was advancing on Clarksburg for the purpose of destroying the railroad and capturing supplies. The rebel force did not succeed in reaching Clarksburg, but attacked the garrison at Buckhannon, destroying the railroad and burning supplies.

The balance of the term of service of the regiment was employed in guard duty. At the expiration of the term of service the regiment was ordered to Delaware, Ohio, and was discharged September 25th, 1862. The loss by death was two. Immediately after discharge many members of the regiment reënlisted in long-term organizations.

85TH REGIMENT, OHIO VOLUNTEER INFANTRY.
THREE MONTHS' SERVICE.

The companies recruited for this regiment in the summer of 1862, rendezvoused at Camp Chase, Ohio, were mustered in under Colonel Charles W. Allison, an attorney of high character of Bellefontaine. A large number of rebel prisoners were confined at Camp Chase and the services of the regiment were required to guard these prisoners.

Colonel Allison was assigned to the command of the post and the regiment was retained on garrison duty during the summer. The duties were very arduous and Colonel Allison proved to be a competent commander. He was anxious to go to the front, but was retained on duty by request of the Governor, as it was important to have vigilant and competent officers in command of the camp and prison.

Some of the companies were sent as escorts to prisoners at different times but did not have any active service in the field. But one soldier of Jerome Township served in this regiment.

The regiment was mustered in June 10th, 1862, and was mustered out September 23rd, 1862. The loss by death was ten.

86TH REGIMENT, OHIO VOLUNTEER INFANTRY.
SIX MONTHS' SERVICE.

The Eighty-sixth Regiment for the six months' service was organized at Cleveland, Ohio, in the summer of 1863, and was mustered in under Colonel Wilson C. Lemert, who had served as a Major in the 86th O. V. I. three months' service, and a number of other officers of the same regiment also served in this new organization.

A company of this regiment was recruited in Union County by Captain James W. Fields, and was assigned as Company B when the regiment was organized and mustered into the U. S. service at Camp Chase in July, 1863.

Fifteen Jerome Township soldiers served in this company, two of whom, James A. Curry and William Wise, died in the service.

The rebel General, John Morgan, was then making a raid through Ohio and the regiment took an active part in pursuit of Morgan and rendered most excellent service under the command of Colonell Shackleford, making hard marches on foot and at other times a part of the command impressing horses. They were continuously making efforts to intercept detachments of the enemy, who were making rapid marches to make their escape across the Ohio River, and were present at the surrender of Morgan's command at Salineville, Ohio.

After the pursuit of Morgan's forces, the regiment returned to Camp Todd, Columbus, Ohio, for a few days, and about the first of August was ordered to Camp Nelson, Kentucky, and having joined the forces under Colonel D. E. Courcy, marched to Cumberland Gap, arriving about the first of September.

General Burnsides arrived a few days later on the opposite side of the Gap, thus investing the Confederate forces. The 86th was stationed on the Harlem Road and formed a line of battle ready for action, and a section of Captain Henry M. Neil's Ohio Battery was stationed on the left. The command of Colonel De Courcy was composed of the 86th Ohio, 129th Ohio, the 9th and 11th East Tennessee Cavalry, and Captain Neil's 22nd Ohio Battery. A peremptory demand was then made for an unconditional surrender of the Confederate forces under General Frazier, who at once accepted the terms without firing a shot. The 86th Ohio was then accorded the honor of marching into the Fort, hauling down the rebel flag, and raising the Stars and Stripes. General Frazier surrendered nearly 3,000 men, 5,000 stands of small arms, thirteen pieces of artillery, with commissary and quartermaster stores.

Company B of the 86th was detailed to assist in guarding the prisoners to Lexington, Ky., and then returned to the Gap and remained on duty until the term of service expired. James A. Curry took sick on this march and died at Crab Orchard, Kentucky, October 2nd. As forage was very scarce, many expeditions were sent out to gather grain and other supplies, and they had many skirmishes with the rebel cavalry.

This regiment saw a great deal of hard service, beginning with the campaign after Gen. John Morgan in July, 1863. Then the winter campaign at Cumberland Gap, participating in the siege and marching back and forth from the Gap to Lexington and Camp Nelson, they were continuously on the move in all kinds of weather. Many regiments that had a much longer service did not experience the severe campaigning that this regiment did, even in six months, as it was rushed to the front as soon as mustered into the service.

The regiment left the Gap for home January 16th and was mustered out at Cleveland, Ohio, February 10th, 1864, after a very strenuous, active service of six months. The loss by death was thirty-eight.

88TH REGIMENT, OHIO VOLUNTEER INFANTRY.
THREE YEARS' SERVICE.

A battalion of four companies of this regiment was organized at Camp Chase, Ohio, under Major Peter Zinn in the summer of 1862, but the regiment was not fully recruited and mustered in until July, 1863, under Colonel George W. Neff.

Ten soldiers of Jerome Township served in this regiment. William Fulk and George F. McIntyre died in the service.

A large number of rebel prisoners were confined at Camp Chase and the regiment was assigned to duty guarding the prisoners. This duty was very strenuous and the men were kept on duty continuously. Before the regiment was fully recruited a battalion of the regiment was ordered to Cincinnati, in September, 1862, to assist in repelling the invasion of the rebel army under command of Kirby Smith. It crossed the Ohio River into Kentucky and was in line of battle some days under command of General Lew Wallace. Manning the fortifications around Covington, they were very highly complimented for their efficient service in front of the enemy by the commanding officer.

As soon as the regiment was mustered Colonel Neff, who had served as Lieutenant Colonel of the Second Kentucky Infantry and had considerable experience in the field, inaugu-

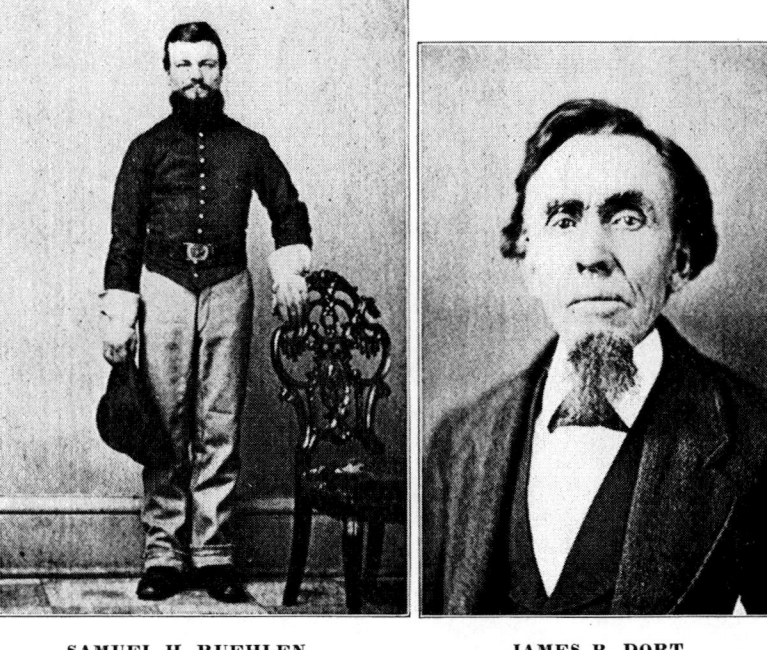

SAMUEL H. RUEHLEN
1st O. V. C.

JAMES B. DORT
Minute Man.

GEORGE RUEHLEN
96th O. V. I.

SAMUEL B. BEARD
95th O. V. I.

WILLIAM H. WILLIAMS
96th O. V. I.

JOHN P. WILLIAMS
95th O. V. I.

DAVID WILLIAMS
18th U. S. I.

WILLIAM BANCROFT
40th O. V. I.

rated the strictest discipline and the regiment under his command became one of the best drilled regiments that had been been organized in the state.

Both officers and men were anxious to go to the front and a few companies were sent to West Virginia and to Maryland for a short time on duty, but were soon ordered back, as General Morgan and his bold riders were making a raid through Ohio in July, 1863.

A part of the regiment was ordered to Camp Dennison and, under Colonel Neff, was deployed ready to resist an attack from Morgan's forces. Trees were felled across the roads leading to Camp Dennison and the obstructions were such that Morgan's column made a detour and did not attack the Post.

After the passing and capture of a large part of Morgan's forces, the regiment was again ordered to Camp Chase and was on duty there until October. Colonel Neff made application to go to the front again, and finally the regiment was ordered to Cincinnati for provost duty. Camp Chase was then garrisoned by a detachment of convalescents and the Veteran Reserve Corps. The men of these detachments being absent from their regular commands, being dissatisfied and discipline lax, there was great danger that prisoners would escape. By request of the commanding officer, the 88th was ordered back to Camp Chase, much to the disgust of both officers and men. The regiment remained on duty at Camp Chase until mustered out July 3rd, 1865.

This regiment was composed of good material, was well drilled, and had the opportunity been given, it would have rendered good service on the firing line. The loss during the service of the regiment was eighty by death.

94TH REGIMENT, OHIO VOLUNTEER INFANTRY.
THREE YEARS' SERVICE.

The 94th Regiment was organized at Piqua, Ohio, in the summer of 1862, and was mustered into the service August 24th, under Colonel Joseph W. Frizell. Captain Andrew Gowan of Jerome Township served in Company H of this

9

regiment and was in the service continuously from August 7th, 1862, to June 5th, 1865, participating in all of its battles. The regiment was immediately ordered to Kentucky before it was armed and fully equipped, and with no experience in discipline or drill. Proceeding by rail to Lexington, on their arrival they found many stragglers from the battlefield of Richmond passing through the town.

The regiment was ordered to Yates Ford on the Kentucky River. This was the first march of the new regiment and on arriving at the Ford about dusk the regiment had their first war experience in a skirmish with the pickets of the enemy, losing two men killed and several wounded. The next morning a large force of rebels advanced on the regiment by shelling the woods with a battery.

The regiment, under orders, fell back slowly to Lexington and on to Louisville with the army. The dusty roads and scarcity of water caused many of the men to become completely exhausted, as they had been marching night and day since arriving at Lexington, August 31st, the day after the fight at Richmond, Kentucky.

This was the introduction of the regiment to the many campaigns and battles in which they were destined to participate, and is referred to by members of the regiment as one of their hardest campaigns.

The regiment remained at Louisville until October 1st. Their next service was in the battle of Perrysville, in which they were actively engaged. They served in the Army of the Cumberland, participating in many decisive battles, including Stone River, Chickamauga, and all the battles around Chattanooga. They served in General Sherman's army on the Atlanta campaign in the summer of 1864, and marched to the sea.

Marching from Savannah through the Carolinas, they participated in the battle of Bentonville, N. C., March 19th, 1865, then marched to Washington and was in the Grand Review.

The regiment participated in nineteen battles, the loss by death was one hundred and ninety-nine, and it was mustered out at Washington, D. C., June 6th, 1865. The regiment was on the firing line in all the battles of the Army of the Cumberland, and was one of the fighting regiments of that splendid army.

95TH REGIMENT, OHIO VOLUNTEER INFANTRY. THREE YEARS' SERVICE.

The 95th Regiment was organized at Urbana, Ohio, and mustered into the service at Camp Chase, August 19th, 1862, under Colonel Wm. L. McMillen. Eleven Jerome Township soldiers served in this regiment and Samuel B. Beard died in the service.

The regiment was immediately ordered to Kentucky, before it had any opportunity to drill, and within ten days after muster it participated in the battle of Richmond, Ky., August 30th, 1862. The regiment arrived at Lexington by rail, and was ordered toward Richmond on a forced march to meet and repel General Kirby Smith's Veteran Confederate army, largely outnumbering the Union forces. On the morning of August 30th the rebels advanced in strong force and the 95th was soon engaged in heavy skirmishing.

A detachment of the 95th under the Lieutenant Colonel contested the advance stubbornly after the Union Army was driven from the field until they were surrounded and upward of one hundred, with the commanding officer, taken prisoners. The other companies of the regiment having fallen back, another effort was made to stem the tide of the heavy Confederate force, but they were soon driven back and about six hundred were taken prisoners, eight men were killed and forty-seven wounded.

The prisoners were paroled and were allowed to make their way back toward the Ohio River as best they could. The 95th was the only Ohio regiment in this battle, and while it was very disastrous to the Union forces, it may well be doubted if even Veterans, under the conditions, could have held the field against such an overwhelming number. While it was a discouraging introduction in their baptism of fire, as soon as the regiment was exchanged strict discipline and drill were inaugurated and during the war it made a record which is recognized as one among the best in Ohio organizations.

In May, 1863, they were again ordered to the field and served through the Vicksburg campaign in the spring and summer. The regiment participated in the campaign on Big Black River, the capture of Jackson, Miss., and in the charge against the rebel fortifications at Vicksburg, May 22nd. After the surrender of Vicksburg they were continuously scouting, raiding and destroying railroads during the summer months, and went into winter quarters at Memphis in the fall. The regiment had been attached to the Fifteenth Corps up to this time, but during the winter was attached to the Sixteenth Corps. In June, 1864, the regiment participated in the disastrous campaign against Tupelo, Miss., under command of General Sturgis, and in the battle of Guntown, January 10th, lost heavily in men and officers.

They were in the second campaign against Tupelo under General A. J. Smith, in July, in which the rebels under General Forrest were defeated. After Sherman had started on his march to the sea the regiment, with the forces under General A. J. Smith, were ordered to Nashville, Tenn. In the battle of Nashville, fought December 15th and 16th, under command of General George H. Thomas, the regiment was hotly engaged both days, storming the rebel breastworks, capturing artillery and many prisoners, but losing heavily. The regiment was then ordered to New Orleans and served under General Canby until the close of the war.

The regiment participated in sixteen battles, many skirmishes, and, as shown by the official records, the losses in killed, died of wounds and disease, were two hundred and seventy-six. The regiment was mustered out at Camp Chase, Ohio, August 14th, 1865.

96TH REGIMENT, OHIO VOLUNTEER INFANTRY.
THREE YEARS' SERVICE.

This regiment was organized at Delaware, Ohio, in the summer of 1862. It was recruited in the counties of Delaware, Knox, Logan, Morrow, and Marion. Company K was recruited in Union County and twenty-three soldiers of Jerome Township served in this company, seven of whom died in the service.

The regiment was mustered into the service August 19th, 1862, under Colonel Joseph W. Vance, who was killed in the battle of Sabine Cross Roads, La., April 8th, 1864. After the death of Colonel Vance, Lieutenant Colonel Albert H. Brown commanded the regiment with distinguished ability until the close of the war. Dr. David H. Henderson of Marysville, Ohio, was surgeon of the regiment. Of the 115 soldiers who served in Company K of the regiment from Union County, 43 were killed or died of wounds or disease, ten were wounded, and six were made prisoners of war. Thomas L. Evans, who served in this company and was promoted to a Captaincy, taught a select school in the little brown schoolhouse still standing on the corner of the square at New California, after the close of the war.

On the 1st of September, 1862, the regiment left Camp Delaware, by way of Columbus, for Cincinnati, and, arriving in that city the same evening, crossed the Ohio River and quartered in the streets of Covington for the night. They remained there a week, sleeping at night in the streets, and were fed by the loyal citizens of that place.

On the 8th of October the regiment, in the brigade of General Burbridge, A. J. Smith commanding the Division of the Thirteenth Corps, marched to Falmouth, thence to Cynthiana, Paris, Lexington, and Nicholasville. At the latter place they remained in camp two or three weeks, then marched to Louisville, where they remained in the mud along the Ohio River for a few days; then embarked for Memphis, Tenn., on the 19th of November, where they were encamped for about a month. While there they were reviewed by General

Sherman and ordered to embark on the steamer Hiawatha and proceed down the river with the forces under his command, the objective point being Vicksburg, Miss.

The whole regiment and its outfit of wagons, teams, etc., together with the Seventeenth Ohio Battery with its guns, horses and mules, were packed on this small craft. Nearly every member of the battery was sick with the measles. The horses and mules were placed on deck, their heads tied on either side, forming between them a narrow aisle. Only partial rations of hard bread and roasted coffee could be had, the only resort being flour and green coffee, which required cooking and roasting. It may have been a necessity, but certainly it was a bitter fatality.

The only facility for cooking was a small stove on the after deck, to reach which it was necessary to run the gauntlet of two hundred pairs of treacherous heels and the filth of such a stable. First, the coffee and the meat were cooked and eaten with hard bread, but the supply of the latter was soon exhausted and the men were forced to mix flour with water and bake it on the same stove. With the best effort possible it was often 2 o'clock before all had their breakfast of the half-cooked material. As if this were not all that flesh and blood could endure, cold rain continually drenched all who were not under cover, and for want of room many were forced to remain on the hurricane deck, famished with hunger and tortured with sleeplessness.

All day and all night the little stove was used by men preparing the unhealthy rations which, while they staved off starvation, were not slow, in connection with other causes, in developing diseases that were equally fatal to those who were packed close in the ill-ventilated and overcrowded apartments. Surgeon Henderson, with his assistants, labored incessantly to check disease and relieve the sufferings of the men, but typhoid, measles and erysipelas were masters, everything seemingly rendering them aid. Death reaped a frightful harvest.

On its way the regiment disembarked at Milliken's Bend

on the 20th and made a forced march to Dallas Station, La., on the Vicksburg, S. & T. Railroad, a distance of twenty-eight miles over a narrow road cut through a dense cypress forest, over stretches of corduroy and thick intervening mud of the low marshes, burning depots and warehouses, destroying a large amount of railroad property, tearing up the track for miles, returning the following day in a pelting storm of cold rain, having marched fifty-six miles in less than forty hours.

The regiment was taken on down the river to the Yazoo (the River of Death), and up that river to Johnson's Landing; there disembarked and marched to Chickasaw Bluffs and participated in the first attack on Vicksburg, where the Union forces were defeated. Then proceeding to Arkansas Post, they took an active part in the assault upon the works, capturing 7,000 prisoners, losing ten killed and twenty-six wounded. After this engagement it at once accompanied the army under Grant in the flank movement to the rear of Vicksburg and took part in the siege until the surrender, July 4th, 1863. Then it marched on to Jackson, taking part in the siege until its evacuation on the 17th of July; thence back to Vicksburg, and from there by steamer to Carrollton, La. It was next engaged in what was called the Teche campaign, and participated in the battle of Grand Coteau on the 3rd of November. This was a desperate fight against overwhelming numbers, the regiment losing 110 men killed, wounded and missing.

In December the regiment was ordered to Texas, where it operated against Dick Taylor's forces until March, 1864, then returned to Brashear City, La., entered upon the Red River campaign under General Banks. On the 8th of April they were engaged in the battle of Sabine Cross Roads, losing fifty-six men killed, wounded and missing.

On the first of August the regiment, with the Thirteenth Corps, embarked for Dauphine Island, in the rear of Fort Gaines, and were the first troops to land in the rear of that fort and participated in the siege until the surrender on the

8th, with 1,000 prisoners. On the 1st of September the regiment returned to Louisiana, and in November proceeded to the mouth of White River, in Arkansas. The regiment was so reduced in numbers by continued losses that a consolidation became necessary, which was effected by special order on the 18th of November, making a battalion of five companies called the Ninety-sixth Battalion, Lieutenant Colonel A. H. Brown commanding.

Company B of Knox, E of Marion, and K of Union were consolidated, making Company C, commanded by Captain Evans. The battalion continued to operate in Arkansas until February, 1865, whence it removed to the rear of Fort Spanish, the key of Mobile, Ala., participating in the siege of that fort, which resulted in its capture on the 8th of April.

A few minutes after the surrender the regiment was marching to the assistance of General Steele, who had for some days been investing Fort Blakely, fifteen miles north of Spanish Fort. Upon the arrival of General Granger's corps on the field General Steele's troops stormed the fort, capturing 5,000 prisoners. This is said to be the last battle of the war. The battalion then proceeded to Stark's Landing on the 11th, and took passage on the morning of the 12th in company with a fleet of gunboats across the bay for the city of Mobile. A landing of the infantry was effected below the rebel stronghold and marched toward it, the gunboats sending shells of warning that we were upon them. The reason of no response soon appeared in the form of a white flag. After the surrender of Mobile the battalion joined an expedition to Nannahubbah Bluff, on the Tombigbee River, and also McIntosh Bluffs.

The last volley fired by the Ninety-sixth was on the 12th day of April, at Whistler Station, seven miles above Mobile, in a lively skirmish with Dick Taylor's retreating forces. The regiment returned to Mobile on the 9th of May, where it remained until mustered out, July 7th, 1865, excepting forty men whose term of service had not expired and who were transferred to the Seventy-seventh Battalion, Ohio Veteran

Volunteer Infantry, and served as a detachment in that battalion until March, 1866.

The Ninety-sixth, from the time of entering the field until the close of the war, was on continuously active and, most of the time, hard service. The regiment marched 1,683 miles, and was transported by boat 7,686 miles and by railroad 517 miles, making a total of 9,886 miles. The regiment participated in twelve battles, a score of minor fights, and the last shots fired by the regiment were on April 12th, 1865, three days after the surrender of Lee's army at Appomattox. As shown by the official records, the losses, killed, died of wounds and disease, were three hundred and thirty-nine.

110TH REGIMENT, OHIO VOLUNTEER INFANTRY. THREE YEARS' SERVICE.

The 110th was organized at Piqua, Ohio, in the late summer of 1862, and was mustered into the service October 3rd under Colonel J. Warren Kiefer. But one Jerome Township soldier served in this regiment, so far as can be ascertained.

Soon after the regiment was mustered into service it was ordered to Virginia, first going to Parkersburg and then to Clarksburg and on to New Creek, where it arrived November 26th, and was kept on drilling and fortifying until about the middle of December. In January, 1863, the regiment was ordered to Winchester and was assigned to the First Brigade, Second Division, Eighth Army Corps, where it was employed in scouting and reconnoitering during the winter months.

The regiment was under fire for the first time June 13th at Kernstown, meeting the advance of Lee's army, and after contesting the ground stubbornly on the 13th and 14th they were compelled to fall back before a large force of the enemy and retreated to Harper's Ferry. In July the regiment was ordered to Frederick City, Maryland, via Washington, and then to New York and back to the Potomac and Rappahannock in November, having frequent skirmishes during the fall months, capturing many prisoners, and remained in winter quarters at Brandy Station.

In the spring of 1864 the regiment was assigned to the Second Brigade, Third Division, Sixth Army Corps, and went into line for the Wilderness campaign. On the 5th of May they were heavily engaged, losing 19 killed, 88 wounded and 11 missing. In the assault at Coal Harbor, June 3rd, the loss in the regiment was five killed and thirty-four wounded. It participated in the battle of Monocacy and in this engagement the casualties were upward of seventy. The regiment was continuously on the move during July and August, skirmishing and guarding trains. In the battle of Winchester, October 19th, the regiment was on the front line and did heroic service in checking the advance of the rebels when the Eighth and Nineteenth Corps were driven back. During the late fall and winter the regiment was in winter quarters on the Weldon Railroad.

The first battle of the regiment in the spring campaign of 1865 was March 25th, attacking the outposts and capturing a large number of prisoners, and on the 2nd of April an attack was made on the enemy's works at Petersburg, routing the rebels and taking possession of the fortifications. The regiment having captured a larger number of flags than any regiment in the Corps, was selected as the guard of honor to escort all the flags captured by the Corps to General Meade's headquarters. The regiment, after Lee's surrender, marched via Richmond to Washington, and was in the Grand Review.

The regiment participated in upward of twenty battles, and the loss by death was 230. The total casualties were almost 800. The regiment was mustered out at Washington, D. C., June 25th, 1865. Colonel Kiefer was wounded three times and was promoted to Brigadier-General and Brevet Major-General.

113TH REGIMENT, OHIO VOLUNTEER INFANTRY.
THREE YEARS' SERVICE.

The 113th Regiment was organized at Camp Chase and Zanesville, Ohio, in the summer and fall of 1862. Seven companies rendezvoused at Camp Chase; then the regiment was ordered to Zanesville, where one company was added, and then to Camp Dennison, where a company was recruited, and the organization of nine companies was mustered in under Colonel James A. Wilcox. Two Jerome Township soldiers served in this regiment and William Sinsel died in the service.

Colonel Wilcox resigned April 29th, 1863, and Lieutenant Colonel John G. Mitchell was promoted to Colonel and commanded the brigade in some of the hardest battles in which the regiment participated. He was promoted to Brigadier-General January 12th, 1865.

December 27th, 1862, the regiment was ordered to Louisville, Ky., and encamped there and at Maldraughs Hill until February, 1863. The regiment was transported to Nashville from Louisville by river, and by reason of the lack of room and sanitary environments on the boats many of the men were taken sick, and on arrival at Nashville were in a serious condition. The regiment was ordered to Franklin and assigned to General Gilbert's Division, Army of the Cumberland; was on garrison duty at Franklin and Shelbyville during the spring and summer, worked on the fortifications, and was sent out on some scouting expeditions.

The regiment was assigned to the Reserve Corps commanded by General Gordon Granger, and moved with General Rosecran's army across the mountains to Chattanooga. In the last day's battle of Chickamauga, September 20th, 1863, the regiment, in General James Steadman's Division, arrived on the field at the most critical time, about 2 o'clock P. M., and reported to General George H. Thomas. They were ordered to charge Longstreet's Veteran soldiers, who were flushed with victory as they were steadily pushing the thin and depleted lines of Thomas' army to the rear with terrible slaughter. The regiment, with other regiments of the Division, made a fierce assault against the onrushing Confederate lines, checking and driving them from the ridge, but with a loss of almost fifty per cent in killed and wounded, numbering upward of one hundred and forty. They held the line until the army was ordered to fall back, late in the evening.

The regiment took an active part in all the campaigns around Chattanooga after the battle of Chickamauga, and marched to the relief of General Burnsides' army at Knoxville, after the battle of Lookout Mountain and Missionary Ridge. This was one of the hardest campaigns of their service, as the weather was bad and the men, being without sufficient clothing, suffered greatly. Returning to Chattanooga just before Christmas, the regiment went into winter quarters near McAfee's Church, a few miles south of Chattanooga. The regiment did some reconnoitering and scouting during the winter, but the duties were light, and the tenth company was organized, as up to this time there had been only nine.

The regiment moved with General Sherman's army on the Atlanta campaign May 5th, and was heavily engaged in many of the hard battles of that campaign. In the battle of Kenesaw Mountain, fought June 27th, in which the 113th was in the advance line charging up against impregnable breastworks through Chiver-de-frese, the loss in the regiment was very heavy, being upward of 150 in killed and wounded. After the fall of Atlanta the regiment marched with Sherman to the sea and the last battle in which they were engaged was Bentonville, N. C., March 19th, 1865. They then marched to Washington and took part in the Grand Review. The losses during the war in killed, died of wounds and disease were two hundred and sixty-nine. The regiment was mustered out at Louisville, Ky., July 6th, 1865.

121ST REGIMENT, OHIO VOLUNTEER INFANTRY.
THREE YEARS' SERVICE.

The 121st Regiment was organized at Delaware, Ohio, during the summer of 1862, under Colonel William P. Reid, Lieutenant Colonel William S. Irwin, and Major R. R. Henderson. Major Henderson had considerable military experience, as he served as a private in the Thirteenth Regiment, O. V. I., under the first call of the President for three months. He also served in the same regiment in the three years' service, was promoted to a Captaincy, and by reason of serious wounds in the battle of Shiloh was discharged from that regiment.

More Union County soldiers served in the 121st O. V. I. than in any other regiment. Marcenus C. Lawrence was mustered in as Captain of Company A, Aaron B. Robinson as Captain of Company I, and a number of soldiers from the county served in Company C. Captain Lawrence was promoted to Lieutenant Colonel, and Captain Robinson was promoted successively to Major, Lieutenant Colonel, and Colonel of the regiment. Fifteen Jerome Township soldiers served in this regiment, and Lieutenant Robert B. Fleming, Otway B. Cone, and Lewis J. Ketch were killed in battle and several others were wounded.

Company A went into camp with 102 men and Company I with 116. Recruits were assigned to the different companies during their service, making the total number of enlistments 300, this being the greatest number of men from this county serving in any one regiment. Of this number seventeen were killed, forty-two died of wounds and disease, eighty-two were wounded, and thirty-two were taken prisoners, making a total loss of one hundred and seventy-three.

The 121st went to Cincinnati, crossed the Ohio River and went into camp at Covington, Ky., on the 12th of September. At this place it was armed with a lot of condemned Austrian rifles, which were absolutely worthless. The regiment then moved to Louisville and was attached to General McCook's Division. Inexperienced and without an hour's drilling, the regiment marched with General Buell's forces against Bragg's rebel army, and on the 8th of October was led into the battle of Perryville, where it received its first baptism of blood. Many strong men were broken down in these first months of hard service and never afterward returned to their companies.

The regiment was detailed to bury the dead at Perryville; then continued in Kentucky performing guard duty until January, 1863. On the 31st of December, 1862, the regimental hospital was captured at Campbellsville, Ky., and S. B. Cone and James Cone were taken prisoners and paroled. On the 1st of February, 1863, the regiment moved into Tennessee and was employed in watching and protecting the right flank of General Rosecran's army, then stationed at Murfreesboro.

About this time Colonel H. B. Banning was transferred to the command of the regiment; the prisoners of Perryville had been exchanged and they, with many of the sick, returned to their companies.

The 121st moved from Stone River with General Rosecran's army, and on this march was engaged in a slight skirmish with the rebel General Forrest at Triune, on the 3rd of June. A few days later it occupied Shelbyville, Tenn., and after remaining there several weeks advanced to Fayetteville, where it continued until the 1st of September, when orders were received to join the Reserve Corps under General Gordon Granger and proceed to Chattanooga.

On the 20th of September, 1863, the regiment was engaged in that memorable charge of Steadman's Division at the battle of Chickamauga, in which they drove the enemy at the point of the bayonet from the field and held it against repeated attacks until the close of the battle. The 121st was the last regiment to leave the battlefield, and carried with them the flag of the Twenty-second Alabama Infantry, which was captured and borne away in triumph by one Solomon Fish, of Mill Creek Township, a member of Company C. It is concluded that this timely aid of the Reserve Corps saved General Thomas' army from defeat.

Captain Lawrence commanded the regiment on this occasion during the greater part of the battle, while yet ranking as a Captain, and Sergeant Otway Curry assumed command of Company A.

The loss of the regiment in this engagement was eleven officers and eighty-seven men. Of Company A, Amos Amrine was missing; Thomas Marshall, John J. Ramage, Solomon Hisey, O. S. Myers, Henry F. Jackson and Samuel Walters were wounded, and Solomon Hisey was also taken prisoner. Of Company I, Lieutenant Fleming, Harrison Carpenter and James Harden were killed, and Captain A. B. Robinson, A. R. Gage, George Deland, John S. Gill, John W. Bryan, James M. Lucas, Sheridan McBratney, Thomas Page, John G. Rupright, Edwin Sager and Richard White were wounded.

After the battle of Chickamauga the regiment shared in the battles of Lookout Mountain and Mission Ridge, and in the march to the relief of Knoxville, then remained quietly in camp at Rossville until entering upon the Atlanta campaign.

Captain Lawrence was promoted to Lieutenant Colonel in November, 1863, and was in command of the regiment during the winter of 1863 and 1864, Colonel Banning being home on recruiting service. On the 2nd of May, 1864, the 121st started on the Atlanta campaign. Companies A and I and two other companies were selected to make a dangerous charge upon Buzzards' Roost, which was successfully done with but little loss, then shared in the battle of Dalton a few days later, having passed through Snake Creek Gap, and from that point until the fall of Atlanta, September 1st, the regiment was continually under fire. It was in the engagement at Resaca and, as a part of General J. C. Davis' Division, was at the capture of Rome, Ga. At the battle of Kenesaw Mountain the regiment held the extreme right of the Union forces, and with fixed bayonet charged up nearly to the breastworks of the enemy in a vain effort to drive them from their strong position. A deadly cross-fire of shot, shell and grape killed and disabled 150 out of less than 400 of the 121st. With few exceptions all were killed or wounded in the open field in front of the enemy's works, in about five minutes.

Company A lost in this engagement John G. Perry, killed; O. B. Cone mortally wounded, and Henry F. Jackson, F. B. Hargrove, L. A. N. Craig, Henry Coats, W. H. Goff and Hiram Laughry wounded.

Company I lost, on the 20th, James Chapman, killed; on the 22nd A. Drake and John Vanderau were wounded, and on the 27th Edward Phillips, Alexander Scott, I. N. Dillon,

A. C. Rosecrans, John Kuhlman and Jeremiah Kirk were mortally wounded, and George Deland, J. Q. Converse, William H. Bonnett, A. W. Davis, Van Dix, Alexander Gandy, Wesley Hawn, George Holloway, Josiah Knight, C. P. Morse, David Rea, H. McVay, John A. Wood, James A. Snodgrass, Daniel Cooperider, J. P. Goodrich and John Reed were wounded, and Lewis Ketch was killed. The two companies lost twelve killed and died of wounds and thirty wounded.

From the 9th of July until the 17th the regiment was engaged on the banks of the Chatahoochie River; on the 18th and 20th it routed the enemy and occupied their position at Peach Tree Creek, Company A losing two men — S. B. Cone and John Jolliff — wounded in this engagement, and on the 22nd joined its brigade and took position on the right of the National line, three miles from Atlanta. In the movement upon Jonesboro it took the advance, acting as skirmishers for the Second Division, leading the Fourteenth Corps. Captain Henderson of Company K and John Cooperider of Company I were wounded in this battle, and John Ports of Company A was killed.

On the 2nd of September Atlanta surrendered, and on the 6th the regiment went into camp near that city. The 121st entered the Atlanta campaign with 428 non-commissioned officers and men and eighteen commissioned officers. Four officers were killed and eight wounded. Twenty-two men were killed, two hundred and five wounded, and one captured. On the 29th of September the regiment joined the expedition against Forrest's rebel cavalry, and having driven him across Tennessee into Alabama, returned and marched in pursuit of Hood's army.

On the 2nd of October Lieutenant Colonel Lawrence resigned, and on the 19th Colonel Banning left the regiment and the command devolved on A. B. Robinson, who had been promoted to Major and was mustered on the 17th of September. Major Robinson was afterward promoted to Colonel

GEORGE W. MITCHELL
96th O. V. I.

JACOB NONNEMAKER
96th O. V. I.

LIEUT. ROBERT F. FLEMING
121st O. V. I.

SAMUEL NONNEMAKER
136th O. V. I.

CAPTAIN JAMES D. BAIN
30th O. V. I.

ALONZO M. GARNER
1st O. V. C

DAVID BAIN
13th O. V. I.

SERGEANT ALANSON L. SESSLER
1st O. V. C.

and commanded the regiment from the fall of Atlanta until the close of the war with marked ability.

The 121st joined General Sherman at Rome, Ga., and marched with his army to the sea. After the fall of Savannah the regiment moved through the Carolinas, taking an active part in the engagement at Bentonville, losing six men killed and twenty wounded.

Company A lost John Sparks killed and J. L. Porter, T. Prosser, J. G. Irwin, and J. C. Warner wounded; and Company I lost C. B. Miller killed, Captain C. _ . Cavis mortally wounded, and P. Vanderau and James Dunn severely wounded.

The regiment joined the National forces in the march to Washington, was present at the Grand Review, and then proceeded to Columbus, Ohio, where it was mustered out on the 12th day of June, 1865.

The 121st was one of the fighting regiments, and the Jerome Township boys who served in the regiment had a most remarkable record for hard service. They participated in a number of the hardest battles fought by the Army of the Cumberland, and the losses in killed, died of wounds and disease were 349, including nine commissioned officers.

Many of the facts in this brief history of their services were furnished by Colonel A. B. Robinson and other members of the regiment.

The large number of casualties is the best evidence that can be given of the dangerous service rendered by these companies, and the members are justly proud of the record of the One Hundred and Twenty-first.

128TH REGIMENT, OHIO VOLUNTEER INFANTRY.
THREE YEARS' SERVICE.

The nucleus of the 128th O. V. I., known as the Hoffman Battalion, was composed of four companies, A, B, C, and D, recruited in 1861 and 1862. Two brothers, Samuel H. Carson and Andrew L. Carson, of Jerome Township, served in this regiment. This battalion was on duty at Johnson's

Island during the first part of its service, but was sent to Virginia on scouting and reconnoitering expeditions before the regiment was fully recruited and organized.

In the fall of 1863 six new companies were recruited and the regiment was organized and mustered in at Camp Taylor, Cleveland, Ohio, in January, 1864, including the Hoffman Battalion, under Colonel Charles W. Hill.

The regiment in the spring of 1864 was assigned to duty at Johnson's Island, near Sandusky, guarding rebel officers, as this island had been designated for the exclusive confinement of commissioned officers. A large number of officers were confined on the island, and the duty of guarding them carefully was arduous but very monotonous.

In 1862 the number of prisoners so confined was an average of about 850, as it varied during the different months by reason of an exchange of prisoners arranged by a cartel in July of that year. During the year 1863 the average number on the island was from 40 during the month of May to 2,623 in December.

In 1863, by reason of the organization of disloyal Orders in both Ohio and Indiana, and reported concentration of rebel troops in Canada for the purpose of releasing prisoners, the garrison at Johnson's Island was largely increased in November by a dismounted detachment of the 12th Ohio Cavalry, a Battery of the 24th Ohio Light Artillery, First Ohio Heavy Artillery, Pennsylvania Battery, and other detachments.

In the winter of 1864 a brigade of the Sixth Army Corps was also sent to Johnson's Island under General Shaler, with the 24th Battery stationed at Sandusky, all under command of General Terry.

In April, 1864, General Terry was relieved and Colonel Hill of the 128th Regiment was assigned to command of the garrison. In the fall of 1864 the Sixth Veteran Reserve Corps was duly assigned to duty on the island and there was a continuous transfer of troops to and from the front. Detachments of the 128th Regiment were detailed for duty and frequently sent to distant points guarding prisoners, thus reducing the force in the garrison, and their duties were very heavy at all times.

During the year 1864 the number of prisoners was largely increased, averaging from 2,500 in January to upward of 3,000 in December. As this prison was so near the Canadian border, and Canada was in sympathy with secession and the rebel army, there was great danger at all times that a release of the prisoners would be attempted by their emissaries in Canada, assisted by the Order of the Knights of the Golden Circle and Sons of Liberty, organized in the loyal States. The regiment was kept under the strictest discipline, at all times ready to repel an invasion or check any attempt of the prisoners to make their escape.

In addition to their duty of guarding prisoners, members of the regiment were required to perform a large part of the labor in erecting three forts, one at Cedar Point and two on the island, besides erecting magazine, so there was a great deal of physical labor necessary. The regiment was splendidly drilled, and had the opportunity offered they would have acquitted themselves with honor on the field, as strict discipline and drill had molded this organization into a fighting machine ready for any emergency.

Both officers and men would have hailed with delight an order to go to the front, but fortune was against them. The loss by death was sixty-four. The regiment was ordered from the island to Camp Chase July 10th, and was mustered out July 17th, 1865.

133RD REGIMENT, OHIO VOLUNTEER INFANTRY. ONE HUNDRED DAYS' SERVICE.

In the spring of 1864 the Army of the East, under General Grant in Virginia, and the Army of the Middle West, under General Sherman in Georgia, were organizing for a general forward movement all along the line. This was a most critical period in the progress of the war and it was determined to move all of the veteran organizations to the front and utilize the National Guard, organized in many of the Northern States, to garrison the forts and guard supplies, thus relieving the veterans from this service. Thirty thousand of the Ohio National Guard went into camp in one day in answer to the call of the President for "One hundred days' men."

The 133rd Regiment was organized under this call at Camp Chase, Ohio, by consolidation of two companies of the National Guard from Hancock County with the National Guard of Franklin County, numbering about 1,000 men in both organizations.

The regiment was mustered into the U. S. service May 6th, under Colonel Gustavus S. Innis, and was immediately ordered to Parkersburg, W. Va. Six soldiers of Jerome Township served in this regiment. In a few days it was ordered to New Creek and was there employed in guard duty and drill until about the 1st of June, when it was ordered to Washington and on to Bermuda Hundred, arriving June 12th, and was assigned to the First Brigade, First Division, Tenth Army Corps.

The Division was ordered out on an expedition June 16th to tear up and destroy the railroad between Petersburg and Richmond and cut off the enemy's communication between those two points.

The 133rd was engaged in a sharp fight as the regiment was ordered to support a battery that was shelling the rebel lines, and held the position for several hours while a detachment of the Division tore up several miles of railroad track. The troops then fell back slowly, keeping up a brisk fight all along the line and a few members of the regiment were wounded. This was their first experience on the firing line, and the men stood to their guns like veterans.

On the 17th of July the regiment was ordered to take steamer at Point of Rocks and move to Fort Powhatan, on the James River. Here the regiment was employed working on the fortifications for some time, and had frequent skirmishes with the enemy, in one of which two men were killed. The men were kept continuously at work on the fortifications when not employed on guard and picket duty. Many members of the regiment were stricken with malarial fever of a very malignant type, and about one-third of the command was on the sick list or in hospital during the month of July. Notwithstanding that fact, the men were kept on duty, although weakened by these continual fevers.

The losses by death during the Hundred Days' Service were forty-seven. The regiment was mustered out at Camp Chase, Ohio, August 20th, 1864.

129TH REGIMENT, OHIO VOLUNTEER INFANTRY.
SIX MONTHS' SERVICE.

The 129th Regiment, Ohio Volunteer Infantry, was organized at Camp Taylor, Cleveland, Ohio, in the summer of 1863. The regiment was mustered into service for six months August 10th, under Colonel Howard D. Johns. About twenty men were recruited in Union County and assigned as Company G, of which William H. Robinson was elected Second Lieutenant and Chester L. Robinson of Jerome Township was appointed a Sergeant. Four Jerome Township soldiers served in this regiment.

A large number of both officers and men had seen service in other regiments, and the 129th was composed of excellent material and was soon under good discipline and well drilled. Immediately after muster the regiment was ordered to Camp Nelson, Kentucky, and was brigaded with the 86th Ohio Volunteer Infantry, the 22nd Ohio Battery, Light Artillery, a detachment of Tennessee Mounted Infantry, and Colonel De Courcy was in command of the Brigade. The Brigade was attached to the Ninth Army Corps. August 20th they started on the march to Cumberland Gap by way of Crab Orchard, London and Barboursville.

The Brigade arrived at the Gap soon after the arrival of the army of General Burnsides from the opposite direction, and the rebel forces, strongly fortified, were completely invested. A few shells were fired from the forts, with some skirmishing on the picket lines as the Union froces advanced, but was a feeble resistance from the strongly fortified position.

As soon as the line of battle was formed and the 22nd Ohio Battery, under command of Captain Henry M. Neil, was in position, a demand was made on General Frazier, commanding the rebel forces, for the immediate surrender of his army. General Frazier accepted the terms at once and without firing a shot. About 2,500 prisoners were captured, with thirteen or fourteen pieces of artillery, several thousand stands of arms and a large amount of ammunition, commissary and quartermaster's supplies. A few companies of cavalry made their escape through the Union lines after the surrender. The Brigade was assigned to garrison duty at the Gap under command of Colonel Lemert of the 86th O. V. I. They were sent out frequently on reconnoitering expeditions and were so employed with guard and picket duty until about the 1st of December. Early in December the regiment received marching orders and arrived on the banks of Clinch River December 2nd. Here the regiment had a brisk fight with a detachment of Longstreet's corps near where the Knoxville road crosses the Clinch River.

After this fight the regiment was on duty scouting, patroling and watching the movements of the enemy along the river and had frequent skirmishes. Beginning with the "Cold New Year," January 1st, 1864, the weather was very cold and so continued during the winter. Having left their baggage at the Gap, the men were very thinly clad and suffered greatly, as their duties were very arduous and rations scarce.

About the last of December the regiment was ordered back to Tazwell, where they were in such close proximity to the enemy that they could not forage off the country for supplies without being in danger of an attack from a large force of rebel cavalry ever on the alert for foragers. This condition continued through all the month of January and many men of the Brigade died of exposure.

A number of the officers of the 129th had seen service in other regiments, where they had a thorough military training, and during these terrible days of suffering were untiring in their efforts for the comfort of the men. It was a campaign of terrible suffering, and it may well be doubted if any other Ohio regiment passed through such a siege of hardships as did the 129th Regiment in the same length of service.

During all of these days and weeks the men performed their duties like veterans, and without murmur or complaint, as attested by their officers. About the 1st of February the regiment was ordered back to the Gap and then marched to Camp Nelson, one hundred and thirty-five miles distant. From there the regiment moved by rail to Cleveland, Ohio, where it was mustered out March 4th, 1864.

The losses by death during the six months' service were twenty-five.

136TH REGIMENT, OHIO VOLUNTEER INFANTRY. ONE HUNDRED DAYS' SERVICE.

The 136th Regiment was organized under the call of the President for the "Hundred Days' Men," in May, 1864. It was composed of companies of the Ohio National Guard from Union County, Morrow County, Crawford County, and Marion County. Union County had three full companies in this regiment — Company D, Captain David S. Norvell; Company H, Captain Charles Fullington, and Company K, Captain Alpheus B. Parmeter, numbering in the three companies 274 men.

Twenty-eight men of Jerome Township served in this regiment, many of whom were married men and of the most substantial farmers, leaving their homes just when the corn and other crops were being planted, thus entaling heavy financial loss, as but few men were left at home to farm the land. A majority of the young men of the township were in the service and at the front, and this was a most critical time. A newspaper article published at the time gives a good idea of the situation, from which the following is a quotation:

"Fortunate was it for the country that the Governor of Ohio held in his hand this reserved thunderbolt of war. The crisis of the Rebellion was upon us. The rebel foe was insolent and sanguine. They were gathering their whole military power and preparing to hurl it upon the Union columns in one deadly and decisive conflict. The hearts of all brave men throbbed in unwonted anxiety as they looked upon the formidable array of rebel hosts. They saw that the impending conflict must speedily occur. They knew that failure to our arms would be an inexpressible disaster to the National cause; and all wanted the assurance of our success made doubly sure by giving additional strength to our armies in the field. To render that strength effective, it must be added at once. The exigency permitted of no delay. The reënforcements must come then, or their coming would be useless for the critical moment of the campaign. It was at this moment of public anxiety — a moment pregnant with the Nation's future — that Governor Brough sent forth the reserved power of thirty-five thousand brave and gallant National Guards."

This regiment was mustered into the service at Camp Chase May 13th, under Colonel W. S. Irwin, and was immediately ordered to Washington, where it arrived May 20th and was assigned to garrison duty at Fort Ellsworth, Fort Williams, and Fort North, south of the Potomac River, and was assigned to the Third Brigade, De Russey's Division.

Strict discipline and continuous drill were inaugurated by the commanding officer and the regiment was soon in fine condition for an active campaign. They not only drilled in infantry tactics, but details were made to man the heavy guns on the forts, and many of the men became efficient in artillery practice.

The regiment remained on garrison duty continuously in the defenses around Washington until the term of service expired, and won the praise of the commanding officer of the defenses by their soldiery bearing at all times. The regiment was mustered out August 30th, 1864, and the loss by death was twenty-five.

145TH REGIMENT, OHIO VOLUNTEER INFANTRY.
ONE HUNDRED DAYS' SERVICE.

This regiment was organized at Camp Chase, Ohio, May 12th, 1864, to serve one hundred days. It was composed of the Twenty-first Battalion, Ohio National Guard, from Delaware County, and the Thirteenth Battalion, Ohio National Guard, from Erie County. The regiment was immediately ordered to Washington City, and, on its arrival, was asigsned to General Augur as garrison for Forts Whipple, Woodbury, Albany and Tillinghast, comprising the southern defenses of Washington, on Arlington Heights.

The service of the regiment consisted principally of garrison and fatigue duty. On the 20th of August, the time of its enlistment having expired, the regiment was moved, by the Baltimore and Ohio Railroad, to Baltimore, and thence by the Northern Central, Pennsylvania Central, etc., to Camp Chase, where, on the 24th of August, it was mustered out on expiration of term of service.

But one Jerome Township soldier served in this regiment, and the loss by death was ten.

174TH REGIMENT, OHIO VOLUNTEER INFANTRY.
ONE-YEAR SERVICE.

Under the President's call of July, 1864, for troops to serve for one year, two full companies were recruited in Union County. Leaving Marysville for Camp Chase on the 31st of August, they were assigned as Companies B and C, of the One Hundred and Seventy-fourth Ohio Infantry.

The original commissioned officers of Company B were U. D. Cole, Captain; Peter Hill, First Lieutenant, and George Harriman, Second Lieutenant. During its term of service this company lost five killed in battle, six wounded and twelve died in hospitals.

Company C was mustered in under the following commissioned officers: William H. Robb, Captain; W. B. Brown, First Lieutenant, and Joseph Swartz, Second Lieutenant.

Captain Robb was discharged on account of wounds re-

ceived at Murfreesboro, and Lieutenant Brown was then promoted to Captain, and was in command of the company until
wounded at Kingston, March 10th, 1865, after which the command devolved upon Lieut. T. B. Myers.

Company C lost eight of its members on the fields and in
the hospitals, and fourteen wounded. Union County was represented among the field and staff officers of this regiment by
A. J. Sterling, who served as Lieutenant Colonel from the organization of the regiment until its muster out.

The One Hundred and Seventy-fourth Ohio was organized
September 21st, 1864, under Colonel John S. Jones, and, on
the 23rd, left Ohio for Nashville, Tenn., to report to Maj.
Gen. W. T. Sherman, then commanding the Military Division
of the Mississippi. On arrival at Nashville, orders were received to proceed to Murfreesboro, which was then threatened
by Forrest's rebel cavalry.

The regiment remained at Murfreesboro until October
27th, when it moved to Decatur, Ala., and assisted in defending
that garrison from an attack made by Hood's advance. After
a movement to the mouth of Elk Creek and back again, the
One Hundred and Seventy-fourth remained at Decatur, until
recalled to Murfreesboro to participate in the investment of
that stronghold. It took an active part in the battle at Overall's
Creek, losing two officers wounded, six men killed and thirty-
eight wounded.

After this engagement the regiment was ordered on dress
parade and was complimented in person by General Rousseau
for gallantry. In the battle of the Cedars it again distinguished itself by making a charge on the enemy's breastworks
and capturing two cannons, a stand of rebel colors belonging
to the First and Fourth Florida, and about two hundred prisoners. The regiment lost in this engagement one commissioned
officer killed and seven wounded; four men killed and twenty-
two wounded. It was complimented in general orders for its
conduct on this occasion.

After having participated in all the fighting around Murfreesboro, the One Hundred and Seventy-fourth joined the

Twenty-third Army Corps at Columbia, Tenn., and was assigned to the First Brigade, First Division of that corps. In January, 1865, it moved to Washington City, where it remained in camp until February 21st, then proceeded to North Carolina, and, joining the forces under General Cox, took a conspicuous part in the battle of Five Forks, at Kingston.

On the 10th of March it successfully resisted a fierce attack made by General Hoke. It lost two officers wounded, four men killed and twenty-three wounded.

This was the last battle in which the regiment was engaged. It joined Sherman's forces at Goldsboro, and served under General Schofield at Wanesboro, N. C., until mustered out at Charoltte, June 28th. Then returning to Columbus, Ohio, it was paid off, and discharged July 7th, 1865.

Colonel John S. Jones, who commanded the regiment, had served three years as a Captain in the Fourth Regiment, Ohio Volunteer Infantry, and had seen hard service at the front, participating, with his regiment, in twenty-one battles in the Army of the Potomac, including the battle of Gettysburg. Lieutenant Colonel James A. Sterling of Union County had served as a Captain in the 31st Regiment, Ohio Volunteer Infantry, Army of the Cumberland, having been discharged by reason of wounds received at the battle of Chickamauga.

Under these officers of long service, with many other veterans who had seen service at the front, the regiment became, in a short time, one of the best disciplined and best drilled regiments in the department to which it was assigned and was always depended on in any emergency. It may well be doubted if any other one-year regiment had a better record than the 174th, and the boys who served in it may well take a just pride in their services.

Fourteen Jerome Township soldiers served in this regiment. The losses by death were one hundred and seventeen.

187TH REGIMENT, OHIO VOLUNTEER INFANTRY.
ONE-YEAR SERVICE.

The 187th Regiment was one of the last full regiments recruited to serve one year under the call of President Lin-

coln in July, 1864. One company of this regiment was recruited in Union County by Captain William P. Welsh and
was the last company recruited in the county for Civil War
service. It was composed largely of farmers, strong of body
and lithe of limb, and there were great discrepancies in their
ages. Many of the members were mere boys of twelve or thirteen years of age when the war commenced. They had remained at home to do the farm work and care for the families
while the older brothers had enlisted, and many of them had
fallen on the battle line or died of disease.

The boys who had been left at home had now grown to
manhood and went forth to take the places of their fathers or
brothers who had fallen. Then there were men of more
mature years who had served in other organizations and were
true and tried veterans. This was very fortunate, as the young
boys, profiting by the experience and instructions of the veterans in the ranks, soon learned to care for their wants, both
in camp and on the march, and were ready for campaigning in
a few weeks, whereas if the regiment had been composed of
all raw recruits, it would have taken months. Fourteen Jerome
Township boys served in Company B of this regiment.

The regiment was mustered in at Camp Chase, Ohio, March
1st, 1864, under Colonel R. Z. Dawson and Lieut. Col. L. R.
Davis, both veterans of service in other organizations. On the
3rd of March the regiment received orders to report at Nashville and on to Dalton, Ga., where they went into camp, and
through the months of March and April were employed in
drilling and guard duty, and were brought to a high state of
efficiency in discipline by their veteran officers. At one time
the regiment was ordered out on a scout and made a hard night
march down through Sugar Valley, south of Chattanooga,
which was considered a hard introductory campaign, even by
the veterans. The regiment marched to Kingston, Ga., where
2,000 soldiers of the Confederate army of Lee and Johnson
surrendered and were paroled, after which they returned to
Dalton. When the railroads had been repaired the regiment
was ordered to Macon by rail.

During the summer and fall of 1865 the regiment was on garrison duty at Macon. As the Confederate soldiers were returning to their homes and the citizens were necessarily requesting many favors by reason of the fact that both the Union and Confederate armies, having passed through that section in the fall of 1864, had stripped the country very largely of both forage and provisions, the duties of the regiment were complicated and arduous.

The war having ended, the discipline among the troops outside the garrison was very lax and caused a great deal of trouble to the Provost Guard, as they had to make many arrests. During the service of the regiment as Provost Guards they were very highly commended for discipline and soldierly bearing at all times as one of the best regiments in the service of that department.

The losses in the regiment by death were fifty-four. The regiment was mustered out at Macon, Ga., January 20th, 1866, and was discharged and paid off at Camp Chase, Ohio, January 23rd.

191ST REGIMENT, OHIO VOLUNTEER INFANTRY.
ONE-YEAR SERVICE.

The 191st Regiment was organized at Camp Chase, Ohio, and mustered into the service March 10th, 1865, under Colonel Robert B. Kimberly, who had served as Lieutenant Colonel of the 41st O. V. I.; Lieut. Col. Edward M. Driscoll, who had served as a Captain in the Third Ohio Infantry, and Maj. Nathaniel J. Manning, who had served as a Captain in the 25th O. V. I. It was very fortunate that the regiment was organized under these veteran officers, and it was soon equipped and ready for the field.

On the day of organization, the regiment was ordered to Winchester, Va., and reported to General Hancock, who was in command of the First Army Corps, but was intercepted by an order to stop at Harper's Ferry, and was assigned to a brigade composed of the 192nd O. V. I., 193rd O. V. I. and 196th O. V. I., thus forming an Ohio brigade.

Colonel Kimberly having been promoted to Brigadier General, was assigned to command the brigade. Soon after the organization of the corps, the designation was made Second Brigade, Second Division, Army of the Shenandoah. Strict discipline was inaugurated by Colonel Kimberly in the regiments composing the brigade, and a great deal of time was devoted to drill and practice marching. The brigade was reviewed by General Hancock during the month of May, and was very highly complimented for their soldierly appearance while marching in review.

The regiment served on garrison duty in the Shenandoah Valley during the summer, and during a part of its service was stationed at Winchester. The regiment was kept on duty continuously until the latter part of August, and was the last regiment retained in the Shenandoah.

The losses by death were twenty-nine. Two Jerome Township soldiers served in this regiment, Lieut. Henry Hensel and David B. Lattimer. The regiment was mustered out at Camp Chase, Ohio, September 3rd, 1865.

197TH REGIMENT, OHIO VOLUNTEER INFANTRY.
ONE-YEAR SERVICE.

The 197th Regiment was organized at Camp Chase, Ohio, under the last call of the President for volunteers during the Civil War. It was mustered into service, one thousand strong, April 12th, 1865, for one year, under Colonel Benton Halstead, and was the last regiment to leave the state. A majority of the officers and many of the rank and file had seen service in other regiments and were fully equipped and ready for service in the field as soon as mustered in. The regiment left Camp Chase for Washington April 25th, and on arrival was assigned to the Ninth Army Corps and went into camp near Alexandria, Va. It was assigned with the 215th Pennsylvania, 155th Indiana, as the Provisional Brigade.

Soon after this organization was completed the brigade was ordered by rail to Dover, Delaware, and was in camp for one month, employed in guard duty and drill. During the month of June the headquarters of the regiment were at Havre-de-Grace, Maryland, and detachments were sent out to guard the railroads and bridges toward Baltimore. While stationed here the designation of the regiment was changed to the Separate Brigade, Eighth Army Corps.

During the month of July the regiment was stationed at Fort Worthington, near Baltimore, and performed garrison duty continuously until ordered to Ohio to be mustered out. But one Jerome Township soldier served in this regiment, Emanuel Lape.

The regiment was composed of a splendid body of men, well drilled and disciplined, who were anxious for service in the field, but the war closed just as the regiment was mustered into service and before it reached the front. The loss by death was eighteen. The regiment was mustered out at Tod Barracks, Columbus, Ohio, August 6th, 1865.

7TH INDEPENDENT COMPANY, OHIO SHARP-
SHOOTERS, OR GEN. SHERMAN'S BODYGUARD.
THREE YEARS' SERVICE.

Ten companies of Sharpshooters were organized in Ohio and an effort was made to organize a regiment to be known as "Birge's Western Sharpshooters," but the organization was never completed. As the companies were recruited and sent to the front, they were attached to some regiment that did not have a full quota of men to commission the regimental officers.

The Seventh Company of Independent Sharpshooters was organized at Cleveland, Ohio, and mustered into the three years' service on the 27th of January, 1863.

Twenty-five men were recruited in Union County for this company, and Lieut. William M. McCrory, from Jerome Township, was promoted to a Captaincy. The soldiers from Union County who served in this company were farmer boys who had been accustomed to hunting with a rifle, and were fine shots. They preferred this service with the expectation of being permitted to serve on the skirmish line and defenses as sharpshooters. Watson C. Squires was mustered in as Captain of the company; William M. McCrory, First Lieutenant, and James Cox, Second Lieutenant.

This company first served under Generals Rosecrans and Thomas, and participated in the battles of Chickamauga, Lookout Mountain and Mission Ridge. At the commencement of the Atlanta campaign it was ordered to Gen. Sherman's headquarters, and remained on duty near the person of the Commanding General until the close of the war.

The company was commanded by Captain Squire until he was detailed as Judge Advocate, after the battle of Chickamauga; then by Captain McCrory, except during the march to the sea, when, in the absence of Captain McCrory, Lieutenant Cox assumed command.

I saw Captain McCrory on the Atlanta campaign when he had command of the company. He informed me that the duties at General Sherman's headquarters were very pleasant and agreeable, yet he was anxious to be relieved and get out on the skirmish line, but General Sherman would not consent and the company was retained as his escort during the march to the sea and until the close of the war.

Captain William McCrory was a fine shot himself and felt perfectly at home with a rifle in hand watching for a shot on the picket or skirmish line. After the march to the sea and through the Carolinas the company was in the grand review at Washington. It was ordered to Camp Chase, Ohio, and mustered out July 28th, 1865.

Three Union County soldiers of this company died in the service, and a number were taken prisoner at Kingston, Ga., November 8th, 1864. Sergeant William B. Haines was a prisoner of war, was in Andersonville for some months, and can relate some harrowing incidents of the sufferings of Union soldiers in that prison.

The company took an honorable part in fifteen battles and skirmishes. The loss by death was eighteen. On its departure for Ohio for muster-out General Sherman issued the following:

"The General Commanding tenders to officers and men of

JOSEPH KAHLER
18th U. S. I.

CLARK L. BARLOW
95th O. V. I.

HENRY KAHLER
86th O. V. I.

DAVID F. McKITRICK
174th O. V. I.

SAMUEL H. CARSON
128th O. V. I.

DELMORE SNODGRASS
40th O. V. I.

CORPORAL CHARLES S. COMSTOCK
46th O. V. I.

CORPORAL JOHN T. McCULLOUGH
136th O. V. I.

the Seventh Independent Company of the Ohio Sharpshooters his personal thanks for their long and valuable services near his person in the eventful campaign beginning at Chattanooga, Tenn., and ending with the war. He commends them as a fine body of intelligent young volunteers, to whom he attributes his personal safety in the battles, marches and bivouacs in Georgia and the Carolinas. He wishes them long life and a proud consciousness of having done their duty with a cheerfulness, precision and intelligence worthy the great cause in which they were engaged, and he bespeaks for them a kind and generous welcome back to their old home in Ohio."

TENTH OHIO BATTERY, LIGHT ARTILLERY.
THREE YEARS' SERVICE.

This battery was organized at Xenia, Ohio, and was mustered into the service at Camp Dennison on the 3rd day of March, 1862, under Captain Hamilton B. White. It was armed and equipped soon after muster in, and was ordered to St. Louis, and from there to go up the Tennessee River by boat to Pittsburg Landing, where it arrived April 13th, one week after the battle of Pittsburg Landing, fought April 6th and 7th.

The 13th Ohio Battery, which had participated in the battle of Pittsburg Landing, was unfortunate in taking a position where the horses were shot down, and the battery was captured by the enemy. The members of the battery were transferred to other batteries and the Thirteenth was disbanded. Among the number so transferred was Charles M. Adams of Jerome Township, who was transferred to the Tenth Battery.

I saw him on the battlefield the next day after the battle, and he was very much depressed. As tears came to his eyes he informed me that he was a gunner in the 13th Battery and was mourning the loss of the gun and the unfortunate condition of his command. He served in the 10th Ohio Battery until January 16th, 1863, was discharged on disability, but

11

again reënlisted in Company C, 174th O. V. I., and served to the end of the war.

The 10th Ohio Battery participated in the siege of Corinth, Miss., in April and May, 1862, and after the evacuation of Corinth was on garrison duty at Corinth until September, and during September was at Iuka. The battery participated in the battle of Corinth October 4th, and did yeoman service in repelling the attacks of the rebel infantry by firing grape and canister at short range.

In November the battery moved to Grand Junction. During the winter of 1863 it was at Milliken's Bend a part of the time; in May was sent to Grand Gulf, and from this point went on a number of expeditions and had considerable skirmishing with cavalry of the enemy. In June the battery was on duty at Vicksburg, Big Black, and Jackson.

During the winter the battery was at Vicksburg and vicinity and was remounted and equipped at Cairo in May, 1864. The battery was then ordered to join General Sherman's army in Georgia, arrived at Ackworth May 16th, and was continuously on the firing line during the Atlanta campaign. After the fall of Atlanta the battery was ordered to Nashville with General Thomas' army, remaining at Nashville through the winter and in March the Tenth and Fourth Ohio Batteries were consolidated.

In April it was ordered to East Tennessee and was on duty at London until ordered to Camp Dennison, Ohio, and mustered out July 17th, 1865. The losses by death were eighteen.

THE SQUIRREL HUNTERS, OR MINUTE MEN.

In September, 1862, the Confederate Army under General Kirby Smith, marching up through the State of Kentucky, threatened to invade Ohio.

Governor Tod issued a proclamation calling upon the citizens of Ohio to rally to the defense of Cincinnati. He said: "Our Southern border is threatened with invasion. I therefore recommend that all loyal men form themselves into military companies to beat back the enemy at all points he may attempt to invade the State."

In response to this call two companies went from Union County, aggregating about one hundred men in all, many of them old and gray-haired, prominent among whom was the Rev. B. D. Evans, a very intelligent old Welshman and Presbyterian minister of Jerome Township. They went with their shotguns, rifles, powder horns and shot pouches. "They responded gloriously to the call for the defense of Cincinnati, and you should acknowledge publicly this gallant conduct," said Governor Tod in a dispatch to the Secretary of War. These men were denominated "Squirrel Hunters" and were, by act of the Legislature, given honorable discharges.

Sixteen men of Jerome Township responded to this call and went to Cincinnati. Some of them crossed over the Ohio River into Kentucky and assisted in building the breastworks around Covington. While their service was not arduous, yet they responded to the call cheerfully and patriotically, and no doubt this prompt response had a great moral effect and was a revelation to the rebels that the North had a great reserve army ready at all times to respond to the call "to arms," as did the "Minute Men" of the War of the Revolution.

About 14,000 assembled at Cincinnati under this call of Governor Tod, and a few years ago the Legislature of Ohio made an appropriation to pay each survivor $13.00 in full for his services, this being the regular pay per month of volunteers at that time. They were all given discharges, of which the following is a copy:

Our Southern Border was menaced by the enemies of our Union. David Tod, Governor of Ohio, called on the Minute Men of the State and the "Squirrel Hunters" came by thousands to the rescue. You (..........................) were one of them and this is your HONORABLE DISCHARGE.

September, 1862.   CHAS. W. HILL,

DAVID TOD, *Governor.*   *Adj. Gen. of Ohio.*

18TH REGIMENT, UNITER STATES INFANTRY.
THREE YEARS' SERVICE.

The 18th Regiment, United States Infantry, was organized and largely recruited at Camp Thomas, near Columbus, Ohio, in the summer and fall of 1861. It was the intention to organize a regiment of twenty-four companies in three battalions of eight companies each, but the third battalion was not fully recruited and the regiment was organized in two battalions of ten companies each.

Henry B. Carrington, who was Adjutant General of Ohio, was appointed the first Colonel, but never served with the regiment in the field, although he remained in the service on detached duty and was promoted to Brigadier-General. About forty men were recruited in Union County for this regiment, and of this number fifteen died on the field. Twelve enlisted from Jerome Township, and of that number six died in the army.

In the winter of 1861-62 the regiment was on duty in Kentucky and was ordered to Nashville in the early spring of 1862. From Nashville they marched with General Buell's army to Pittsburg Landing in General George H. Thomas' Division, but did not arrive in time to participate in the battle of April 6th and 7th.

The regiment was actively engaged in that terrible campaign of rain and mud from Pittsburg Landing to Corinth during the months of April and May. After the evacuation of Corinth they moved with General Buell's army east toward Chattanooga, and on to Nashville during the summer. Up to this date the regiment had not been engaged in any hard battles, but had some sharp skirmishes during the siege of Corinth.

A brigade of Regular Army regiments was organized at Nashville, Tenn., in December, 1862, composed of battalions from the 15th, 16th, 18th and 19th U. S. Infantry and the 5th U. S. Battery. Lieutenant Colonel Oliver S. Shepherd of the 18th Infantry was assigned to command the brigade. The brigade was designated as the Fourth Brigade, First Division,

14th Army Corps, Army of the Cumberland. This was one of the best organized fighting machines in the "Grand Old Army of the Cumberland," and a brief statistical history of its campaigns, terrific fighting and great losses on the battle lines is all that can be given in the limited space that can be taken in this Township History.

On the 31st of December, 1862, the 18th Regiment, with the brigade, was engaged in the battle of Stone River. The regiment was under fire continuously during the day and was ordered to different weakened lines on the field and suffered its heaviest loss in the cedars, as they were in such close contact with the enemy the Union lines were being driven back when the 18th Regiment arrived as support. General Rousseau, commanding the Division, says in his report:

"On that body of brave men the shock fell heaviest, and the loss was most severe. Over one-third of the command fell killed or wounded, but it stood up to the work and bravely breasted the storm. * * * Without them we could not have held our position in the center." The 18th Regiment went into this battle with 571 men and the loss in killed and wounded was 278.

The campaign closing with a victory for the Union arms, the brigade, having buried its dead on the battlefield, where there is now a monument erected to their memory, marched on the fifth day of January, 1863, from its last position on the field to Murfreesboro and encamped between the Shelbyville and Salem Turnpikes, near the town.

The regiment moved with the army from Murfreesboro on the Tullahoma and Chickamauga campaign, June 24th, and took a prominent part in all of that campaign up to the battle of Chickamauga. Just before this battle the brigade was placed under command of General John H. King. The regiment participated in the battle of Chickamauga on both the 19th and 20th of September, 1863. The fighting was terrific and some of the battalions were almost annihilated.

Here the battery of the brigade was captured, but was soon retaken by a charge of the Ninth Ohio Infantry. The loss in the regiment in the two days' fighting was 291. In the battle of Missionary Ridge the regiment captured a battery with a loss of twenty-nine. During the fall and winter months of 1864 the regiment was in camp near Chattanooga, but was sent out on a number of reconnoitering expeditions. When the Atlanta campaign commenced, in May, 1864, the 18th Regiment had been recruited up to 650 men from 270 after the battle of Chickamauga.

On the Atlanta campaign from May 5th to September 1st, 1864, the regiment participated in almost every battle for 100 days, and in the last battle of the campaign, at Jonesboro, the loss was forty-eight. The total loss on the Atlanta campaign was two hundred and twenty-six. After the fall of Atlanta the regiment was sent back to Lookout Mountain, where it remained on duty until August, 1865, and the battalions were sent to different parts of the country. Colonel Oliver L. Shepherd commanded the regiment during the greater part of the Civil War with most distinguished ability.

The battalions were under command of line officers in many of the campaigns. Major Frederick Townsend was in command of a battalion during many of the hard battles and until he was promoted successively to Colonel and Brigadier-General. Many other officers whose names might be mentioned commanded battalions, but they cannot all be named. The percentage of killed and wounded among the officers was very heavy, and among others Lieutenant James Mitchell of Union County died near Chattanooga, Tenn., a short time before the battle of Chickamauga.

The regiment served continuously in the Army of the Cumberland and participated in every great battle of that army and in scores of skirmishes. The best evidence of their hard service is a statement of the losses:

Total losses by death	470
Killed and wounded	606
Missing in action	135
Total casualties	741

The reports of the officers of the command, from brigade to company commanders, which have been examined, speak in the highest terms of the bravery and devotion of both officers and men in the many hard battles in which the regiment participated, in many cases mentioning the names of private soldiers for heroic deeds on the battlefield. To the boys who served in this regiment from Jerome Township is due the gratitude of all patriotic citizens for their devotion to the cause of the Union.

27TH REGIMENT, U. S. COLORED INFANTRY.
THREE YEARS' SERVICE.

This regiment was organized at Camp Delaware, Ohio, from January 16th to August 6th, 1864, to serve three years. Shortly after being mustered into the service of the United States the regiment was ordered to Camp Casey, Washington, D. C., where it was stationed awhile, doing garrison duty. Thence the regiment went to City Point and Petersburg, Va., it being at the latter place that it distinguished itself for unsurpassed gallantry and good conduct upon the battlefield. The bravery of this regiment was also displayed at Chapin's Farm and at Weldon Railroad.

The regiment was sent down into North Carolina, where it was engaged a part of the time in doing garrison duty, and the other part of the time in taking part in the operations, including the skirmishes in and around Fort Fisher, Wilmington, Goldsboro and Raleigh. It did heroic service, won the confidence and approval of its superior officers, and after as honorable service as any of the regiments, it was mustered out of the U. S. service September 21st, 1865, at Smithville, N. C. The Roll of Honor of this regiment will show eighteen killed in action and one hundred and forty-nine died in hospital of disease or wounds received in battle.

Joseph Butcher of Jerome Township served in this regiment with nine other soldiers who enlisted in Union County.

Wherever colored troops were engaged in battle during the Civil War they acquitted themselves in a manner which fully justified the Government in enlisting their services. The first colored regiment organized during the war was recruited in New Orleans, was mustered into the service September 27th, 1862, and was known as the First Louisiana Native Guard. The first colored regiment organized in Northern States was the 54th Massachusetts, recruited in the spring of 1863.

The total number of colored troops enlisted during the Civil War was 178,975, and the losses by death were 36,847.

47TH REGIMENT, U. S. C. T.

The 47th Regiment, United States Colored Troops, served in the Southwest and participated in the battles of Milliken's Bend, the campaign against Mobile, Alabama, the siege and storming of Fort Blakely, and other minor engagements. The total losses in the regiment by death were four hundred and thirty-two.

Dunallen M. Woodburn of Jerome Township served in this regiment from the summer of 1864 until January 5th, 1866, as Drum Major. He first enlisted in the 58th Regiment, O. V. I., January 16th, 1862, and was transferred to the 47th Regiment, U. S. C. T., having a total service of three years and eleven months.

UNITED STATES NAVY.

Major Llewellyn B. Curry, Paymaster.
Daniel R. Cone.

So far as can be ascertained by careful inquiry, the above named are the only two young men who enlisted from Jerome Township in the U. S. Navy during the Civil War. They served under Admiral Farragut in the Mississippi Squadron on the same gunboats, and participated in some of the hardest naval battles on the Cumberland, Tennessee, and Mississippi Rivers. They were first assigned to the gunboat "St. Louis," and during their service the name was changed to the "Baron de Kalb," which was sunk on the Yazoo River by a torpedo.

They participated in the battle of Fort Henry on the Tennessee River; Fort Donelson on the Cumberland River; Island No. 10, Columbus, Ky; Fort Wright; the destruction of the rebel fleet off Memphis, and an expedition up White River, Ark. They were afterward on duty at Memphis.

The Baron de Kalb was in continuous service patroling the river and shelling forts until she was sunk. Admiral Farragut was one of the most distinguished naval officers of the war, and these boys were very fortunate in having had the opportunity to serve under him and participate in these decisive naval battles.

Fort Donelson surrendered February 16, 1862, and my regiment passed up the Cumberland River on boats about the 1st of March and saw the wreck and havoc of the fort, and timber along the river banks mowed down by the shells from the gunboats, which gave us the after-glimpse of that terrible battle.

Daniel R. Cone wrote a letter to his family at home, in which he gave a most thrilling description of the battle of Fort Danelson, equal to that given of the storming of the castle in "Ivanhoe." A part of this letter was written during the engagement, giving the time and the location on the gunboat where the balls from the guns in the fort were striking the vessel with such terrific force that it was expected the hulls of the boats would be pierced and the boats sunk at any moment.

They enlisted January 14th, 1862, and were discharged September 30th, 1862, and during that period were in a sufficient number of engagements to have satisfied even Paul Jones.

SPANISH-AMERICAN WAR.

In the Spanish-American War, 1898, soldiers of Jerome Township served in three different regiments. Three served in the Fourth Regiment, Ohio Volunteer Infantry, and were engaged in a battle with the Spaniards at Guayama, Porto Rico, August 5, 1898. Three served in the First Ohio Cavalry, but did not leave the United States. Three served in the

Seventeenth Regiment, United States Infantry, and participated in the battle of El Caney, Cuba, July 1, 1898. The history of the services of each of the above named regiments appears in this volume.

SPANISH-AMERICAN WAR—1898.
4TH REGIMENT, OHIO VOLUNTEER INFANTRY.

After the sinking of the battleship "Maine" at Havana, Cuba, and declaration of war with Spain, the Ohio National Guard responded to the first call for troops and were the nucleus to which the volunteers rallied, and with their well-drilled and disciplined officers, within thirty days a great army was organized and ready to take the field.

The United States was at peace with the world and had a standing army of 25,000 men. In three months after war was declared an army of a quarter of a million men was organized, equipped, and a campaign was conducted on both land and water, separated by thousands of miles, and the enemy was defeated without a single reverse—all in a period of but one hundred days. As a writer has stated, "It was an achievement unparalleled in the history of warfare, which will be referred to by military critics of the future as the military marvel of the age."

Many members of the National Guard Volunteers were sons of veterans of both the blue and the gray; they were of the same blood and had the vim and pluck of their fathers who fought the battles of the war which cost nearly 1,000,000 lives. These soldiers marched shoulder to shoulder and touched elbows on the line of battle, under the same flag.

The Fourteenth Regiment, Ohio National Guard, with headquarters at Columbus, Ohio, was the first regiment to go into quarters at Camp Bushnell, near Columbus. On the 9th day of May, 1898, the regiment was mustered into the United States service, and the designation was changed to the Fourth Regiment, Ohio Volunteer Infantry. The field officers were Colonel Alonzo B. Coit, Lieutenant Colonel Barton Adams, and Majors of the three battalions were John C. Speaks, John L. Sellers and Charles V. Baker.

The Fourteenth Regiment was organized during the summer of 1877, had been in the state service continuously, and had been called into active service in the state during strikes and riots, fifteen times. Company D was mustered into the state service at Marysville July 18th, 1877, and the writer was the first Captain of the Company. There had been many changes in the company officers as well as in the rank and file. During the more than twenty years' service, several hundred men had been in the ranks and the *esprit du corps* was always of a high standard.

Company D of Union County was mustered into the United States service for the Spanish War under Captain Charles F. Sellers, one hundred and five strong. Captain Sellers was a charter member of the company, as was Major John L. Sellers, when the company was organized in 1877. Three Jerome Township soldiers served in this company during the Spanish War. They have the proud distinction of serving in the only Ohio regiment which was under fire during the war, and this baptism of fire was at Guayama, Porto Rico, August 5, 1898.

May 15th the regiment was ordered to Camp George H. Thomas, Chickamauga Park, Ga., and on arrival was assigned to the Second Brigade, Second Division, First Army Corps. The regiment was in camp at Chickamauga Park, drilling and equipping, until orders were received to proceed to Newport News by rail, July 22nd.

Arriving at Newport News the regiment boarded the steamer St. Paul, commanded by Captain Sigsbee, and on August 1st arrived off Guanico, Porto Rico. General Miles boarded the St. Paul at this point and ordered the regiment armed with the Krag-Jorgensen rifles, of which a supply was aboard the ship. The regiment arrived at Arroyo August 2nd, and was immediately landed. Under orders from General Haines the regiment made a demonstration toward Guayama with a section of artillery and the Third Illinois in support.

With Major Speaks conducting the advance, the regiment

moved forward. The advance soon struck the enemy, the skirmishers were hotly engaged and the enemy fell back. The flankers advanced cautiously and balls from the Mausers whistled thick and fast, but too high to do much damage, as the Spaniards were firing from an elevation, and were overshooting.

The regiment, after the first skirmish, moved forward rapidly and the firing was general all along the line. The city was soon reached by the advance, and finding that the enemy had retreated, the American flag was hoisted over the city buildings. The Spaniards kept up a desultory fire as they fell back until the dynamite guns of the Fourth Regiment were brought into action, which soon silenced their Mausers.

Reconnoitering parties were sent out frequently for some days. A number of skirmishes were had with the enemy, and the dynamite guns were brought into action a number of times. In one of these skirmishes six men were wounded, including William Walcutt of Company D, wounded in the foot.

In their baptism of fire at Guayama, the officers and men acquitted themselves like veterans of long service and were highly complimented by the commanding officer.

After the signing of the peace protocol, August 13th, the regimental headquarters were retained at Guayama until the 5th day of October. A number of the companies were sent out to various parts of the island on detached duty, while others were retained as Provost Guards at headquarters. Company D was sent to Humocoa under Captain Sellers and he proved himself a diplomat in the reorganization of civil affairs, as he was the governor in fact during the time he occupied the town with his command.

There was a great deal of sickness in all of the commands, the prevailing diseases being some form of tropical fever, and the surgeons and hospital corps were kept busy.

The regiment sailed from San Juan on the U. S. steamship Chester, October 29th, arriving at Jersey City November 3rd. By telegraphic orders from President McKinley the regiment was ordered to Washington, where it was reviewed by the President and arrived in Columbus November 6th. Sixty days' furlough was given and the regiment again assembled at Columbus and was discharged January 20th, 1899.

The citizens of Union County were particularly interested in the service of Company D of the Fourth Regiment, as there was scarcely a family in Marysville or vicinity that did not have some member of the family in the company during the many years' service in the National Guard. Two Lieutenant Colonels of the regiment, W. L. Curry and Wm. M. Liggett, were from Jerome Township. Colonel Liggett had been seriously wounded in the Cincinnati riots in 1884. Therefore, not only the families of the members of the Company in the service during the war were solicituous to hear from the front as the war progressed, but all patriotic citizens were interested.

While the company was not permitted to participate in any severe battles, yet it had many hard marches in that tropical climate, and I confess that I was very much delighted when the news was received that the regiment had been "under fire" and heard the whistling of the Mauser balls from the guns of the Spaniards.

Had the war continued and the opportunity been given for further service and severe fighting, the Fourth Regiment would not have been "found wanting," no matter what the service may have been. The members of the regiment and their friends can always point with pride to their good work, both in the National Guard and the Spanish-American War.

THE FIRST OHIO CAVALRY — SPANISH-AMERICAN WAR.

Eight companies of cavalry were recruited and organized in Ohio for the Spanish-American War. The two battalions of four companies each were mustered into the service at Camp Bushnell, near Columbus, Ohio, May 9th, 1898. On the 14th day of May the regiment was ordered to Camp Thomas, Chickamauga Park, Ga. By the 1st of June the companies were fully recruited, equipped and mounted. The command was to be armed with Krag-Jorgensen carbines and their mounts and equipments were of the best that could be furnished by the government. They were assigned to the Second Brigade, Cavalry Division, General Joseph Wheeler commanding.

The regiment proceeded to Lakeland, Florida, by rail, leaving Camp Thomas July 13th, and was entrained at Ringold, Ga. Before transportation could be secured for either Cuba or Porto Rico, the peace protocol was signed and the services of the regiment were not required. They went into camp at Lakeland and were employed in camp duty and drill until August 20th, when they were ordered to Huntsville, Alabama.

The regiment was encamped at Huntsville until September 13th; then proceeded to Columbus, Ohio, for muster out. The troops were given thirty days' furlough. Troops A, B, and C were mustered out at Cleveland, Ohio, October 22nd, Troop H was mustered out at Cincinnati, and the other four troops were mustered out at Columbus, Ohio, on expiration of their furloughs.

The regiment was composed of good material, was well officered, and had become quite efficient in drill for the short period of their service. It was unfortunate that they were not fully armed when General Wheeler's command embarked for Cuba, as they would have had opportunity for active service under a cavalry leader who had seen long and hard service during the Civil War.

Troop G of this regiment was largely recruited in Union County, and three members of the troop were Jerome Township soldiers. It was no fault of officers or men of the command that they did not have opportunity for active service, as every effort was made to secure arms and full equipment before the cavalry command embarked for Cuba, but the fates were against them, much to their disappointment.

THE 17TH REGIMENT, UNITED STATES INFANTRY.
SPANISH-AMERICAN WAR, 1898.

When war was declared against Spain, the Seventeenth Regiment was stationed at the U. S. Barracks, Columbus,

Ohio, where they had been on duty for several years. They were a splendid body of men and many of the officers had seen long service, a number of them having served in the Civil War. Among the names recalled are Major Sharp, Captain O'Brien, Captain Roberts and Captain Rogers. Colonel Poland and Lieutenant Colonel Haskell had long service, and it may well be doubted if there was a better officered or better equipped regiment in the service of the 25,000 men composing the United States Army at that time.

Having been personally acquainted with many of these officers, some of whom were members of the military order of the Loyal Legion and others of the Society of the Sons of the American Revolution, now that the majority have been mustered out by the Great Commander, the cherished memories of those pleasant meetings come trooping thick and fast. Not only were they brave soldiers, but gentlemen of intelligence and high character.

Under orders the regiment left the Columbus (Ohio) Barracks in April, 1898, under command of Colonel Poland, for Tampa, Florida, and was encamped at Tampa, employed in usual garrison duty, drilling and equipping for an active campaign in the field. Colonel Poland died of disease at Tampa and Lieutenant Colonel Joseph T. Haskell succeeded to the command of the regiment. June 2nd, under orders, the regiment embarked on transports and landed at Bagarie, Cuba. General Shafter, commanding the United States Army, numbering 15,000 men, was preparing for an aggressive campaign against the Spaniards, who were strongly fortified at El Caney.

The regiment had their first skirmish with the Spanish army in the advance on El Caney, June 30th. The battle of El Caney was fought July 1st, 1898, in which the regiment participated, together with the United States Army of 15,000 soldiers under General Shafter, and was particularly distinguished for the bravery of the officers and men. The losses in the regiment is the best evidence of the prominence of the regiment in that battle, there being forty-four killed and wounded and seven missing.

Of this number Lieutenant Miche and Lieutenant Dickenson were killed, and Lieutenant Colonel Haskell, commanding the regiment, was mortally wounded. The total losses in General Shafter's army were twenty-two officers and two hundred and eight men killed; eighty-one officers and twelve hundred and three men wounded; and twenty-seven missing, a total of fifteen hundred and forty-one.

Sergeant George Kelley, who was seriously wounded in the battle, made a miraculous recovery. A Mauser ball passed entirely through his body, and he gives a most graphic description of that battle. He is now in business near the U. S. Barracks, Columbus, Ohio, and his place of business is a favorite stopping place for his old comrades and all soldiers.

The regiment returned to the U. S. Barracks at Columbus in the fall of 1898, and had a parade through the streets. Colonel Haskell, although suffering from his wound and very weak, rode at the head of his regiment in a carriage, looking every inch the brave soldier that he was. The same evening he died from the result of his wounds and was mourned by the officers and men of his regiment as the "brave mourn for the brave."

After recruiting, one battalion of the regiment was ordered to the Philippine Islands for duty in February, 1899, and was soon followed by the other battalions. The regiment saw a great deal of hard service in the insurrection and the losses by death were quite heavy.

The regiment is now stationed at Fort Oglethorp, Chickamauga Park, Georgia, under command of Colonel Van Orton.

Three Jerome Township soldiers served in the 17th Regiment during the Spanish-American War, as shown by the roster.

BIOGRAPHICAL SKETCH OF COLONEL GEORGE RUEHLEN, UNITED STATES ARMY.

Born in Wurtemberg, Germany, September 21st, 1847. Came to the United States in the early winter of 1852 and settled in Jerome Township, Union County, Ohio. Attended the common schools of Jerome Township, and from Septem-

JOHN B. ROBINSON
32nd O. V. I.

SAMUEL B. ROBINSON
40th O. V. I.

DELMORE ROBINSON
66th O. V. I.

SERGEANT CHESTER L. ROBINSON
129th O. V. I.

HEBER WOODBURN
187th O. V. I.

SERGEANT ANDREW J. SMITH
96th O. V. I.

DAVID H. WOODBURN
96th O. V. I.

DUNALLEN M. WOODBURN
Drum Major, 47th U. S. C. T.

ber, 1863, to June, 1866, the Central High School of Columbus, Ohio, from which he was graduated in June, 1866.

He then entered the law office of Mr. James W. Robinson in Marysville, Ohio, as a student, in the summer of 1867. Entered the United States Military Academy at West Point, New York, under an appointment received through Hon. John Beatty, M. C., in June, 1868, and was graduated at that institution number 16 in a class of 56 members, June, 14th, 1872.

He was appointed Second Lieutenant in the 17th U. S. Infantry and joined his company, which was then stationed at the Cheyenne River Indian Agency, on the Missouri River in South Dakota. Served at that post on the Indian frontier among the Sioux and Minnecoujoix Indians until the spring of 1877, when he was detached from his command and sent with an expedition to the junction of the Big Horn and Little Big Horn Rivers in Montana, where he served as quartermaster in charge of the construction of the military post, Fort Custer, remaining on that duty until June, 1878, when he was transferred to the Black Hill country in South Dakota and as quartermaster had charge of the construction of the military post, Fort Meade, near Deadwood, South Dakota, until the spring of 1879, when he again joined his company at Fort Sisseton, Minnesota, and remained with it until June, 1881, when he was appointed Professor of Military Science and Tactics at the Ohio State University at Columbus, Ohio, at which place he served until July, 1884.

Returned to duty with his company, then stationed at Fort Totten, North Dakota, in September, 1884, and went with the company to Fort D. A. Russell, near Cheyenne, Wyoming. Appointed Adjutant of the 17th Infantry in September, 1889, and transferred to the Quartermaster's Department as Captain and Assistant Quartermaster, in August, 1890. As Quartermaster he took part in the Pine Ridge Indian uprising and campaign from December, 1890, to February, 1891. Was transferred in the spring of 1891 to El Paso, Texas, to take charge of construction of the new post, Fort Bliss. Transferred to Detroit, Mich., for construction work at Fort Wayne,

12

thence to Fort Riley, Kansas, and from there, in the winter of 1897-98, to Southeastern Alaska, as Quartermaster of the Alaska Relief Expedition.

At the outbreak of the Spanish war, in the spring of 1898, Captain Ruehlen was at Dyea, Alaska, and in May, 1898, was sent to San Francisco, Cal., where he was assigned to duty in connection with the preparation of transports carrying troops and supplies to the Philippine Islands. Was transferred to Honolulu, Hawaii, in August, 1898, as Depot Quartermaster and in charge of the transport service there, where he remained until September, 1900, when he was sent to Seattle, Washington, for duty as Depot Quartermaster there.

On duty in the office of the Quartermaster General in Washington, D. C., in charge of the Department of Construction and Repair, from March, 1902, to May, 1908. Depot Quartermaster at Jeffersonville, Ind., May, 1908, to May, 1909. In the Quartermaster General's office, Washington, D. C., from May, 1909, to June, 1911.

Retired from active service, having reached the limit of age established by law, in September, 1911.

His successive promotions in the Regular Army were: Second Lieutenant, 17th Infantry, June 14th, 1872; First Lieutenant, 17th Infantry, September, 1876; Captain-Assistant Quartermaster, August, 1890; Major and Quartermaster, January, 1900; Lieutenant Colonel, August, 1903; Colonel and Assistant Quartermaster General, February, 1908.

MEXICAN WAR — 1846.

On the 4th day of July, 1845, Texas became a State of the Union. The Mexican Minister at Washington had, previous to this time, ceased diplomatic relations with the United States, and soon after General Zachary Taylor was ordered to enter Texas with his arms to protect the border, and by reason of the annexation of Texas it became evident that war was inevitable.

When the call was made for volunteers in 1846 and 1847 to invade Mexico and settle the question of the annexation of

Texas, the young men of Ohio responded gallantly to the call. The State furnished four full regiments of infantry, several companies of cavalry, and quite a large number for the artillery service—in all, upward of sixty companies, and now but one muster roll can be found on file in the Adjutant General's office at Columbus.

Thirty-four Union County soldiers served in the Mexican War, two of whom were from Jerome Township—William Clevinger and Alexander Oliver—who served in Company E, Fourth Regiment, Ohio Volunteer Infantry. Captain James Cutler, who enlisted in Jerome Township during the War of the Rebellion, served in the Second Regiment, United States Infantry, in the Mexican War, and the service of William Lamme, buried at New California, is not known.

The regiment in which Captain Cutler served participated in many of the hard battles and was a part of the army which first entered Mexico City.

As the majority of the Union County soldiers served in the Fourth Ohio Regiment, an extract from a history of their services is copied, as follows:

"On May 29th, 1847, a company recruited at Columbus moved to Cincinnati, which was the place appointed for the regimental rendezvous, and was assigned as Company E of the Fourth Ohio Regiment, commanded by Colonel C. H. Brough, Lieutenant Colonel Warner, Major Young, and Adjutant Kessler.

"On the 1st of July boats were ready in the river opposite the camp and the regiment took passage for New Orleans. Company E, under the command of Captain M. C. Lilley, was placed on the steamer Alhambra.

"New Orleans was reached on the 7th, and after remaining at this place until the 11th, the troops went on board the steamer Telegraph, arriving in sight of Brazos, Santiago, on the morning of the 16th. On the 18th Matamoras was reached and the regiment went into camp certain of being in the enemy's country. The camp was situated nearly opposite Fort Brown, on the Texas side, and adjacent to it was a fine parade ground, of which good use was made every day. In the latter part of August orders were received to proceed to Vera Cruz and march to General Scott's line of operations. Accordingly on the 4th of September the regiment took steamboats and descended the Rio Grande to the mouth. Here it remained until the 11th, when shipping being ready at Brazos, it marched over to that place, embarked on the sailing ship Tahmroo on the 12th, and on the evening of the 15th hove in sight of the sand hills near Vera Cruz. The following morning the Tahmroo ran in to the bay and cast anchor near the great castle of San Juan de Ullua.

Having landed the torops, they marched to a place about four miles north of the city and encamped on the beach. On the 19th a brigade was formed of the following troops: Fourth Ohio Regiment, Fourth Indiana Regiment, Captain Simmons' Battalion of Detached Regulars, and the Louisiana Dragoons, all under the command of General Joseph Lane of Indiana. Tents were struck and the long march commenced.

"About noon on the following day, as the troops entered a kind of woodland, the advance guard fell in with a party of guerillas, gave them chase, and killed and captured several. In this chase Lieutenant Coleman of Columbus died from the effects of heat and fatigue. On the 21st the troops again moved forward, but after marching several miles, stopped at Paso de Ovejas, where they remained until the 25th, then proceeded to Plan del Rio, and on the morning of the 27th moved forward, ascending the hills between the river and the heights of Cerro Gordo. This place, though picturesque in appearance, is remarkable only from the fact that here Santa Anna and his army met with a signal defeat.

"On the 1st of October the brigade started on the march toward the hills of Montezumas; on the 7th arrived at a place near the Aguas Calientes, or Hot Springs, and on the 8th proceeded on the way with the understanding that Santa Anna was at Huamantla and would probably intercept them at Pass el Pinal. Early on the morning of the 9th General Lane drew off all the troops except the Fourth Ohio, Captain Simmons' battalion, and two pieces of artillery, which were left behind to guard the train, and proceeded toward Huamantla; when within two or three miles of the place he ordered Captain Walker, with his mounted force, to gallop on, and if the Mexicans were in considerable force, not to attack them but to wait for the arrival of the infantry and artillery.

"On arriving near the town, the Captain found that the main body of the enemy had started for the pass, while perhaps five hundred remained in the plaza. Upon these he made a furious charge, killing several of them and dispersing the rest, while he and his troops took possession of their artillery and ammunition. But before the arrival of the infantry the Captain was surprised by a charge from some 2,500 lancers. In this fearful fray the Captain was mortally wounded and fell from his horse while encouraging his men to still withstand the fearful odds against them until the other troops should arrive. Soon they came to their relief, and before many minutes the place was cleared of the enemy. Among the prisoners taken on this occasion was Colonel La Vega, brother to the General of the same name; also Major Iturbide, son of the former Emperor of Mexico.

"On the 11th the troops entered the pass and after the principal part of the train had proceeded some distance a wagon in the rear broke down and seven companies of the Fourth Ohio were left to protect it until another wagon could be brought back and the baggage shifted into it. While thus detained a party of lancers, about 1,500 in number, appeared on the right and to the rear. The companies immediately concealed themselves behind some brushes and awaited the attack. After considerable firing and maneuvering on the part of the enemy, the wagon that had been sent for came rattling and thundering through the mountain pass, which they probably mistook for the approach of artillery, and with no little haste these valorous Mexicans took their exit to the opposite side of the plain.

"Continuing the march, the troops arrived at Amazuque, and, after resting a few hours, pressed forward, intending to enter Puebla and relieve Colonel Childs and his gallant band before night. On nearing the city the clash of arms was distinctly heard, and also the Colonel firing a salute on his eighteen-pounder. The troops passed through the principal parts of the city, only occasionally being fired at by the foe concealed on the tops of the houses. This firing was kept up for some minutes, when, being returned with compound interest, the bells rang for a truce and the Mexicans abandoned the city.

"The joy of Colonel Childs and his men seemed to have no bounds; and no wonder, for they had been hemmed up in the northern part of the city for nearly à month, and a good part of that time they had been scant of provisions and water. Day after day they had lived upon flour, water and coffee, and these not in abundance. The enemy, finding that Colonel Childs would not surrender the place, had attempted to starve him out. So destitute of meat were the Colonel's men that it has been told they even ate cats! Their ammunition was so nearly spent that they had to wrap six-pound balls to fire from the twelve-pound guns.

"On the 19th of October details from the Fourth Ohio and other regiments started on an expedition against a party of Mexicans under General Rea, the noted guerilla chief. When about ten miles from Puebla the enemy was met with and a close conflict ensued. Retreating some distance, they again made a stand and fought desperately with the dragoons, but on receiving a shot or two from the artillery they again fled and ran into Atalixco. The loss of life in this engagement was considerable. The report of the Mexicans was 219 killed and 300 wounded; the Americans, two killed and one wounded. The forces were about 1,500 Americans and about the same number of Mexicans.

"A detachment of some 300 men was sent to a little town called Huacalcingo, for the purpose of capturing two pieces of cannon belonging to the enemy. The guns were hid on the arrival of the troops, but by a diligent search they were found and spiked, and the Americans reassembled at Puebla, elated with their success and the probable cessation of hostilities. The stay in Puebla was somewhat long — from the 12th of October, 1847, to the 2nd of June, 1848 — during which time the prospects of peace and war were alternating with a regularity perplexing and vexatious to the American forces.

"On the 2nd of June orders were received to take up the line of march for Vera Cruz, and the 3rd found the troops hastening homeward."

WAR OF 1812.

From 1811 to 1814 was an exciting war period in the history of this country. Union County was then on the frontier and near to the seat of war of the Northwest.

The territory which now comprises Union County was but sparsely settled. The settlements were along the Southern border on Big Darby Creek and Sugar Run, and comprised the families of the Robinsons, Mitchells, Currys, Ewings, Sagers, Kents, Snodgrasses, Shovers and a few others.

From the close proximity of these settlements to the seat of hostilities it would be expected that there would be ample material for an extended chapter on the services of the citizens of this county during the war of 1812. But the early history of this territory is very meager from which to obtain any data of the stirring events of that period. There are but few rolls now on file at the Adjutant General's office, and from these can be gleaned but little history, save the names of the members of the companies.

Almost every citizen within the limits of the county who was a military subject at that time was in the service at some time during the war.

The first military company organized in the county was recruited during the year 1813, by Captain James A. Curry. He was appointed enrolling officer of the district, including all the settlements along Darby Creek and Sugar Run, and organized a company of which he was elected Captain, Samuel Mitchell First Lieutenant, and Adam Shover Second Lieutenant. Strange as it may seem, but very little can be learned of the other members of this company, although they were recruited from the old families of Robinsons, Mitchells, Ewings, Kents, Sagers and others.

After a diligent search among the records and inquiring among the oldest of the descendants now living, the following named citizens are known positively to have been members of this company:

James A. Curry, Captain; Samuel Mitchell, First Lieutenant; Adam Shover, Second Lieutenant; James Buck, Calvin Carey, Ewing Donaldson, David Mitchell, Andrew Noteman, Clark Provins, Christian Sager, George Sager, Abe Sager and William Taylor.

They were attached to a regiment the number of which cannot be ascertained. They first rendezvoused at Delaware, where orders were received to join General Harrison's army in the Northwest. They marched by way of Upper Sandusky and the Falls of St. Mary's to Fort Meigs, then returned by Wapakoneta and Piqua. The majority of them were called out the second time to build and garrison blockhouses on the frontier. The names of several citizens of this county appear on the rolls of Captain McClellan's company, among which are those of four brothers, James, William, Samuel and Robert Snodgrass.

Captain James A. Curry first enlisted in June, 1812, at Urbana, in a company of light horse from Highland County, and was attached to Colonel Carr's regiment, composed mainly of Kentucky troops, and served in this campaign under General Tupper on the Maumee and River Raisin. He was detailed as a scout during that summer, and being an experienced woodsman, was kept constantly in service. I have heard him say he never performed a day's camp duty during this campaign. He was a fine horseman, was splendidly mounted on his own horse "Jack." He and the scouts serving under him were constantly on the move examining the streams for Indian signs and watching the movements of the enemy.

A company was organized at Plain City during the summer of 1812 or 1813, of which Jonathan Alder was elected Captain and Frederick Loyd First Lieutenant. They were directed to march north toward the lakes, about twenty miles beyond the settlements of Darby, and erect a blockhouse for the protection of the settlements. They marched to the banks of Mill Creek, and after working three or four days a blockhouse was completed. Mr. Alder says: "There were seventy in all, and one, Daniel Watkins, was made Colonel and Commander-in-Chief."

Mr. Alder, who had been a captive among the Indians for fifteen years and well knew their mode of warfare, condemned this as a very unwise move in the Governor to order so many men from the settlements, for he claimed the tactics of the Indians would be to "attack the women and children in the settlements and avoid the forts."

They remained at the bolckhouse only a few weeks. There being a false alarm, it was not possible to keep men from returning to the settlements. This blockhouse was situated on the west bank of Mill Creek, about three miles northwest from Marysville.

Thomas Killgore, who died at the residence of his son, Simeon Killgore, in Mill Creek Township, a few years ago, was a member of the company that erected this fort and was the last one left of the company. A short time before his death he gave a detailed account of this campaign and the building of the blockhouse, which was transmitted by Judge Cole to the Pioneer Association of Union County. So far as can be learned, this is the only fort ever erected within the borders of this county, and this is probably known to but few of our citizens. Of the company that erected this blockhouse it has not been possible to learn the names of any except those already mentioned.

A number of the young men in the settlements enlisted in companies outside of the county and saw hard service during the war. Simon Shover, who lived on Darby near the old Sager mill, in Jerome Township, enlisted in and was Orderly Sergeant of Captain Langham's company, of Chillicothe, Ohio. He was a brave and gallant soldier, and had many hair-breadth escapes. At one time he was taken prisoner by the Indians and saved his life by imitating a rooster crowing, by jumping up on logs or stumps, and flapping his arms and hands. This seemed to please the Indians very much, as they laughed immoderately at his antics. Simon always claimed that this saved his life. He was taken prisoner at Winchester's defeat, and often expressed his indignation at the treatment of General Winchester, who was abused and insulted by the Indians, without any check from the British. Simon Shover was one of fifty picked men, who made a sortie from Fort Erie, and spiked the guns of the British during the night; and was, perhaps, the most distinguished soldier that went from the county. He was of a good family, and honorable and brave to a fault. He learned many of the traits of the Indians, and was accustomed to entertain large crowds of citizens at all kinds of gatherings, such as "log-rollings," "huskin'-bees," "house and barn raisings" and "musters," with many interesting incidents of his adventures, both thrilling and ludicrous. Wherever "crowds were wont to assemble," Simon could always be counted as one of the number, and furnished much amusement by giving the "Indian war whoop."

His voice was as clear and shrill as a trumpet, and he could give a genuine war whoop that would have caused old Tecumseh to have marshaled his warriors for the field. Many anecdotes might be related of his efforts to amuse the crowd during court term and on "training day." He was anxious to live a hundred years, and on meeting or parting with old friends he was wont to exclaim: "Hurrah for a hundred years!"

The territory now comprising the county of Union was but thinly populated in 1812, yet many of her citizens left their homes in response to the call to arms with the full knowledge that their women and children were at the mercy of the Indians prowling along the northwestern border, and not a few of them rendered good service to the government in her hour of need. Ever may our citizens hold in grateful remembrance the services of the patriotic veterans of Union County in the War of 1812.

The names of twenty-three soldiers who served in the War of 1812 are given in the attached roster. Of this number, Christian Adams, Elijah Hoyt, F. Hemenway and Titus Dort and Simon Rickard did not enlist from Jerome Township, but were old residents and bruied in the different cemeteries of the township. Major Edward Barlow lived on the border of the township and was a well-known prominent citizen, member of the old red-brick Presbyterian Church congregation. He was an officer and participated in the battle of New Orleans under General Andrew Jackson.

A number of other residents along Darby Creek in Darby and Union Townships, served during the war, among whom may be named James and Samuel Mitchell, George, Robert and James Snodgrass, James, Thomas, John and Samuel Robinson.

In 1812-13 Colonel James Curry, a soldier of the Revolutionary War, was called to Delaware to assist in organizing a regiment of soldiers in which his oldest son, James A. Curry, was a Captain, leaving his wife with several small children, the oldest of which was but eleven years of age, in the cabin on the banks of Sugar Run, with no neighbor nearer than John Kent and family, one mile distant through the dense forest. One day, during Colonel Curry's absence, the horses were attacked by the wolves, and stampeded with such a noise as to make Mrs. Curry believe the Indians were going to attack their home. Young Stephenson, then a boy of but eleven years, but with the coolness of an old backwoodsman, took down the two rifles, and, loading one, placed his younger brother, Otway, as a sentinel at the fence, in rear of the cabin, and while he attempted to load the other, the charge became fastened in the barrel. The two boys stood on guard for some time, ready to meet the invasion of the redskins. When night came on they, with their mother, went to John Kent's house and spent the night. The next morning, on their return with some of the neighbors, they found that the wolves had attacked the horses, badly injuring one of them, but that no Indians, or traces of them, were to be found. One of the old flint-lock rifles used on this occasion is still in possession of W. L. Curry, son of Stephenson Curry.

Sugar Run Falls, on the land of Colonel Curry, now owned by his great-grandson, Thomas H. Curry, was in the early days a beautiful and attractive place. The stream wound its way through a little valley, shaded by burr oaks and black walnut timber, and, surrounded as it was by good hunting and fishing grounds, it was a favorite place for the Indians in the early years of the present century. The old Indian trace, leading from the Wyandot nation south, ran past the Falls, and the Indians continued to travel this route after there was quite a settlement along Sugar Run.

The last Indians who visited this vicinity came about the year 1816-17. In the early spring, four Indians came from the north, and encamped at the falls for a few days. They visited Colonel Curry's house, and, as usual, were supplied from his table, as he was well known to the Indians passing along this route, and he was one in whom they had great confidence. When they left the falls they separated, two following the old trail and two traveling in a southwesterly direction. In a few weeks two of them again reached the falls, and had with them an Indian pony. They remained a day or two, and their two companions not arriving (it is supposed this was to be their place of meeting), they then stripped the bark from a burr oak tree, and taking yellow keel, which was in great abundance along the stream, traced on the trunk of the tree in rude characters an Indian leading a pony, while another Indian was in the rear with a gun on his shoulder and the ramrod in his hand, as if in the act of driving the pony, traveling northward. This done, they covered their camp fire and took the old Indian trail north. A few evenings after their departure, their two comrades arrived from the south, and learning by the drawings on the tree that their companions had preceded them, they remained over night and the next morning took the trace and moved rapidly north. And thus the last Indians ever seen on the southern border of Union County took their departure from their once happy hunting grounds.

WAR OF THE REVOLUTION—1776.

At the close of the war of the Revolution, the soldiers were given lands in payment for their services. The territory comprising Union County is all "Virginia Military Lands," being a part of that between the Scioto and the Miami Rivers, all of which was set apart for the Revolutionary soldiers by the United States Government.

Many of these old patriots took up these lands and in this way quite a number found homes in Union County. From this grand old Revolutionary stock sprang Union County's brave and patriotic sons who fought in the War of 1812, the Mexican War and the War of the Rebellion.

Of these old heroes of '76, several are buried in the cemeteries of this county. But little can be learned, even traditionally, of their services, although many of their descendants reside in the county. Some of them are known to have fought at Yorktown, Monmouth, White Plains, Germantown and other historic battlefields of the war of the Revolution.

Colonel James Curry and Henry Shover both served in Virginia regiments during the war of the Revolution. Mr. Shover enlisted in Louden County and emigrated to the territory in which Jerome County is situated, before the breaking out of the War of 1812, and two of his sons, Adam and Simon, served in that war. No information can be secured of the service of Henry Shover in the War of the Revolution. Colonel Curry resided near Staunton, Augusta County, Virginia, and as shown by the records in the War Department, he served as an officer in the Fourth and Eighth Virginia Infantry, Continental Line.

He was a private in the Staunton, Virginia, Company, under General Lewis, in Dunmore's war with the Indians on the Ohio River was severely wounded at Point Pleasant, Va., October 10th, 1774, in battle with Indians under Cornstalk. He was a private in the 4th Virginia Infantry, Continental Line, at beginning of the Revolution; Second Lieutenant, Eighth Virginia, December, 1776; First Lieutenant, June 24th, 1777; transferred to Fourth Virginia September 14th, 1778; Captain,

September 23rd, 1779; was in battles of Brandywine, Germantown, etc.; at Valley Forge, 1777-78; taken prisoner with Lincoln's army at Charleston, May 12th, 1780; exchanged June,
1781; on staff of General Nathaniel Gist; severely wounded
at siege of Yorktown; acted as second in two duels between
officers while in service; with Washington at triumphal entry
into New York, November 25th, 1783; served nearly eight
years; subsequent to war, was Brigade Inspector of Virginia
militia, Clerk of Court of Augusta County, Virginia, Colonel of
Ohio militia, County Judge, and member of Ohio Legislature.

The battle of Point Pleasant, Virginia, is called "A First
Battle of the Revolution" by Chambers' Encyclopedia, from
which the following account of the battle is copied. As it was
fought before war was declared and at least one citizen of the
township was a participant, it will be of interest to all citizens
of the township.

"An important battle, fought October 10th, 1774, between
Colonial troops of Virginia, under General Andrew Lewis, and
the Shawnees, Delawares and other Indians composing the
Northern Confederacy, led by Cornstalk as king and sachem
of the Shawnee tribe, on the east bank of the Ohio River, and
just above the great Kanawha. The village of Point Pleasant
has since grown up on the spot where this battle was fought,
which was and is to this day spoken of as the first battle of
the Revolution. The 'Boston Tea Party' had already been
held in the spring of the same year, and the 'Boston Port Bill'
was received in May—the signal of actual conflict between the
colonies and the Mother Country. Lord Dumore, Governor
of Virginia, had been busy in the interests of England by way
of stirring up a hostile feeling between the hardy white settlers
and the various tribes of Indians, the object of which had become apparent. At last a crisis was reached. The legislature
took action, under which General Andrew Lewis gathered together 1,200 men at Lewis Springs, now Lewisburg, W. Va.,
and from thence proceeded to Point Pleasant, acting as was
understood, in concert with the Colonial governors, who in
person led about 1,000 men through the wilderness, striking

the Ohio at Wheeling, from which point he was to meet General Lewis. All this time, unbeknown to General Lewis, the agents of Lord Dunmore had been busy concentrating the Indians in the neighborhood of Point Pleasant, and subsequent events show that he never intended to join his forces with the troops under Lewis. Our space will not admit of our giving the various facts substantiating this statement made so emphatic in the history of the 'Border Wars' by Withers and others.

"In this bloody battle, about one-fifth of the entire army of General Lewis were either killed or wounded, and of the Indians, the number must have been even greater. It was the most severely contested battle of the kind of which we have any account, and was fought on both sides from behind trees in a dense forest of primeval growth, on one of the richest bottoms of the Ohio. It was wholly unexpected, the object being on the part of General Lewis, in fulfillment of the purposes on the part of the legislature, to proceed with an overpowering force in conjunction with Governor Dunmore, from Point Pleasant to the Indian settlement on the Scioto, beyond the Ohio. In vain did the brave Lewis look for troops from Wheeling. During the night of the 9th and 10th, a body of Indians was reported by a scouting party as having encamped near the site of an old Shawnee village, about six miles above.

"At the same time advices were received that Lord Dunmore would cross the country directly to the Scioto. Before sunrise on the morning of the 10th, a hunting party returned and brought the startling report of 'four acres of Indians,' about a mile above the camp of General Lewis. The party had been fired upon. At once, on receipt of this news, the main body of the troops, under Colonel Charles Lewis and Colonel Fleming, were mustered into line. The battle soon began, and raged with varied fortune through nearly the entire day. The brave Colonel Lewis fell mortally wounded. Colonel Fleming was soon after disabled, when Colonel Field, who had come up with a re-enforcement, took command. This officer had learned a lesson from the unfortunate Braddock;

but he, too, soon fell. At times the battle raged like a tempest. The roar of the musketry was continuous. The clarion voice of Cornstalk was, nevertheless, everywhere heard bidding his warriors, 'Be strong!' Be strong!' Seeing a warrior shrink, he sunk his tomahawk into his skull. The most unyielding and desperate courage was on both sides displayed until late in the afternoon, when three companies that had been retained in camp, perhaps on account of the Indians in large numbers on the opposite shore of the Ohio, under Captains John Stewart, Isaac Shelby and George Matthews—distinguished names—reached the rear of Cornstalk by a well-planned movement, and decided the fortunes of the day.

"A treaty was entered into at Camp Charlotte, in Ohio, at which Lord Dunmore was present, who seemed to have a perfect understanding with the Indians; though the colonists were indebted mainly to Cornstalk for the treaty of peace which Dunmore seemed determined to postpone, as we might show. It was in view of the surprising valor displayed by the troops under General Lewis in this decisive battle that Washington, in the darkest days of the Revolution, was led to exclaim: 'Leave me but a banner to plant upon the mountains of Augusta, and I will rally around me the men who will lift our bleeding country from the dust and set her free."

OUR BOYS OF OTHER STATES.

A number of Jerome Township boys left the parental home and the old farm soon after the close of the Civil War, in 1865, and took up the duties of citizenship in other States. Robert A. Liggett went to Detroit, Mich., and was for many years a prominent official in the Michigan Mutual Life Insurance Company. William M. Liggett, after serving two terms as Treasurer of Union County, moved with his family to Minnesota, where he was very prominent. First serving as Commissioner of Railroads, for eighteen years he was Dean of the Agricultural Experiment Station in connection with the University of Minnesota.

David G. Robinson, after graduation at college, was also

DAVID CURRY
121st O. V. I.

CORPORAL IMMER ROBINSON
174th O. V. I.

ADDISON CURRY
86th O. V. I.

FORESTER BEARD
88th O. V. I.

CAPTAIN OTWAY CURRY
121st O. V. I.

CORPORAL JAMES CURRY
187th O. V. I.

CAPTAIN WILLIAM L. CURRY
1st O. V. C.

ANDREW GILL
86th O. V. I.

graduated as a theological student of the Presbyterian Church and was an ordained minister of that church. William Mc-Crory went to Minneapolis, Minn., where he was a prominent business man. He projected and built the first interurban railroad line from Minneapolis to Lake Minetonka. James D. Bain was graduated as a physician, went to Great Bend, Kansas, where he practiced a number of years and was elected a member of the Legislature in that State.

All of the above named are deceased.

Of those who survive, Henry A. Brinkerhoff, who first served as a Lieutenant in the 30th O. V. I., was promoted to Lieutenant Colonel in the U. S. Army before the close of the Civil War. He remained in the Army and was retired a few years ago with the rank of Colonel, and resides in Oak Park, Illinois.

James Curry was graduated from the University of Wooster, Ohio, in 1872. He then went immediately to San Francisco, California, where, after two years' study, he was graduated from the Presbyterian Theological Seminary in that city. He was immediately ordained as pastor of the Presbyterian Church of San Pablo and Berkeley, and has been in the ministry continuously for 40 years in the vicinity of San Francisco. He is a Doctor of Divinity, and in service is the oldest Presbyterian minister on the coast. He has written a history of Presbyterianism on the Pacific Coast, of which a large edition was published, and he has for a number of years been the Secretary of the Board of the Theological Seminary of San Francisco. He is now pastor of the Presbyterian Church at Newark, California.

James Cone, Stephenson B. Cone, Daniel R. Cone, with their families, emigrated to Oregon many years ago. They live in the vicinity of McMinnville, excepting Stephenson and family, who live in Portland, and they have all prospered in a business way.

Alexander D. Gowans resides at Centerview, Mo., and is now Mayor of that city. Thompson O. Cole is a successful business man of Great Bend, Kansas. James L. McCampbell

13

resides at Orange, California. David Curry, for many years a fruit grower in California, has recently changed his residence to Seattle, Washington. William B. Brinkerhoff, piano manufacturer, Brazil, Indiana. Immer Robinson, produce merchant, Champaign, Ill.

Robert McCrory served two years as Clerk of the Courts of Union County and afterward practiced law quite successfully a number of years, is now a resident of Spokane, ,Wash. James F. Chapman, Pomona, Cal.; Heber Woodburn, Minneapolis, Minn.; Jacob Ruehlen, Hiawatha, Kan.; George Butler, Rush Center, Kan.; Festus Edwards, Chase, Mich.; Samuel Nonnemaker, Topeka, Kan.; Dunallen M. Woodburn, Hessington, Kan., druggist; A. M. Garner, railroad engineer for forty years, Mattoon, Ill.; Edgar G. Magill, a prominent physician of Peoria, Ill.

They were all schoolboys of Jerome Township, and it is a pleasure to note that some of them have been prominent in public life and all are respected citizens of other States. There may be others whose names are not recalled, but every effort has been made to ascertain the present address of all who reside in other States.

OUR HEROINES.

Soon after the first war meeting was held in the Seceder Church, April 24th, 1861, the company was organized and commenced drilling under Dr. James Cutler, afterward a Captain in the First Ohio Cavalry, the mothers, wives and sisters said: "We can and will help." Busy hands were plying the needles, and in a few days uniforms consisting of red flannel blouses and black caps were ready to don. Flags were not so plentiful in those early days of the war, and the sisters and sweethearts were not content to purchase an ordinary bunting flag, but one stitched by their own hands should be carried by the boys as they marched to the wild music of the war-drums. A messenger was dispatched to Columbus, silk was purchased, and a beautiful flag was manufactured by these patriotic girls.

Then came the call for 500,000 three-year volunteers, and

as a number of companies were organized in the county, they were all called to assemble at Milford Center July 4th for regiment drill. A wagon was equipped with a great platform decorated with bunting and was drawn by four white horses driven by Moderwell Robinson. In this wagon were seated thirty-one girls, dressed in white with red, white and blue sashes, representing all the States in the Union. The wagon was driven to the square in New California, and with appropriate ceremonies and great enthusiasm the flag was presented to the company. Preceded by this wagon with the bevy of girls singing patriotic songs a procession was formed, some in wagons, buggies or carriages, and many on horseback, proceeded to Milford, where the regimental drill was held, viewed by thousands of patriotic citizens.

The flag was not taken to the field during the war, but the enthusiasm of that flag presentation by the loyal young ladies of this community — our own sisters and sweethearts — was an inspiration that followed the soldiers to the front and cheered them on battle lines.

During our Civil War the loyal women of our country did not have the inspiration of the war-drums — no hope of fame for heroic deeds amid the clash of arms — no hope of reward but that of a nation saved. But her courage was equal to that of the soldier who carried the sword or the musket — when she sent father, husband, brother or sweetheart with prayers and blessings.

The names of many of these girls are recalled and herewith published as our heroines — many of whom have passed to the other shore:

LIZZIE GOWANS	ABI SHAFFER
JEANNETTE GOWANS	MAGGIE NUNEMAKER
AMANDA MCCAMPBELL	MARTHA JANE FLECK
LOVINA LIGGETT	SUSIE RUEHLEN
MARY MCCAMPBELL	SARAH MARY LIGGETT
SUSANNAH ROBINSON	ELVIRA ROBINSON
LOU ROBINSON	BELLE BUCK
OLLIE CURRY	LIZZIE LAUGHEAD

MARY CURRY

PHEBE CURRY

MARTHA J. ROBINSON

GEORGIANA ROBINSON

JENNIE TAYLOR

SALLIE BAIN

ESTELLE MCCAMPBELL

NAN BEARD

SARAH GILL

FLORENCE WOODBURN

LOVISA KETCH

EMMA ROBINSON

SARAH WOODBURN

ELIZA HILL

FIDELIA ROBINSON

BELINDA KETCH

NAN BAIN

HESTER MITCHELL

LOU CONE

HANNAH BEARD

MARY ANN DODGE

SALLIE RUEHLEN

I recall vividly a scene on the battlefield of Shiloh which can never be effaced from my memory. The next day after the battle, fought April 6th and 7th, 1862, along the banks of the Tennessee River, I saw upon that terrible field of carnage a woman of my own kin. Her maiden name was Nancy Snodgrass, and when a girl she resided in Jerome Township. Her father, William Snodgrass, a cousin of my mother, one of the early pioneers of Union County, Ohio, had emigrated to Iowa in the early fifties when the daughter was a girl in her teens.

Just at the beginning of the war she was married to a young man by the name of Vastine, who enlisted in an Iowa regiment. He was stricken with fever, and she came from her prairie home in Iowa to nurse him in the hospital at Fort Donelson. When he was restored to health he was detailed as a nurse and his young wife remained as a nurse in the hospital.

She was on the field during the two days' battle, fought amid the forests and along the ravines, without breastworks or protection of any kind, where the loss in the two armies was upward of 24,000. The only woman on the field for many days after the battle, there she moved about among the dead and wounded, an angel of mercy, ministering to the wants of the suffering soldiers of both the blue and the gray; the bravehearted, sympathetic country girl, as true as the soldier who fell upon the field with sword or musket in hand. Any picture I could draw would give but the faintest idea of the reality.

The rain had been pouring in torrents, the little streams and ravines flowing toward the Tennessee were at high flood, while ambulances with sick and wounded, supply and ammunition wagons, were plunging through the mud and miring everywhere, as they wound their slow way back and forth from the field to the landing, where the hospital boats were floating in the river waiting to receive their loads of mangled bodies. Then there were the details burying the dead in shallow graves, or long narrow trenches, with not even a blanket to cover their faces or bodies. There had been a victory, and cheers went up from the camps of the living, and night was coming on. It was a weird scene, as plain to me as if but a few months ago. Yet more than half a century has passed since that bloody war tragedy on the battlefield of Shiloh.

The groans of the suffering and dying carried in on the litters or in the ambulances; the broken neigh of some warhorse in ravine or tangled brush, shot through body or limb, vainly trying to struggle to his feet, and with a look of despair almost human as he raises his head in the throes of death; a few camp-fires glimmering here and there, with a white tent which had not been disturbed by shot or shell in the terrible struggle just ended. A dim light of candle or lantern in some headquarters of the commander gleams through the mist. The splash of a horse's hoofs in the mud is heard as a weary staff officer or courier dashes off on the gallop to some distant part of the line with orders for the movements and pursuit of the defeated foe at early dawn on the morrow. Many a soldier, with the dead piled thick around him, in his agonizing pains was thinking of the loved ones at home in the far-off Northland as he gazed at the starless sky — of mother, sister, or wife — when the flutter of a woman's garments was seen and he spoke softly, "A sister of mercy." Yes, a sister of mercy caring for the wounded that dark night. It was Nancy Vastine, the brave country girl, the only woman on that awful field of carnage, April 7th, 1862. A drop of cordial, a cool bandage, a cup of hot broth, are trifles for a man-of-arms to long for, but the getting of them from a woman thrills the faltering heart with warrior blood, and many a life was saved on the field because a woman was around.

ROSTER.

ABBREVIATIONS.

Adjt.	Adjutant	inf.	infantry
art.	artillery	Lieut.	Lieutenant
Bat.	Battalion	Maj.	Major
Col.	Colonel	Regt.	Regiment
Capt.	Captain	re-e.	re-enlisted
Corp.	Corporal	res.	resigned
com.	commissioned	Sergt.	Sergeant
cav.	cavalry	trans.	transferred
disc.	discharged	vet.	veteran
e.	enlisted	wd.	wounded
Gen.	General	*	died in army

Roster of Soldiers who enlisted from Jerome Township, Union County, Ohio, during the War of the Rebellion.

COMPANY K, 1ST O. V. C.

Capt. James Cutler, e. Sept. 1, 1861; disc. April 20, 1863.
Capt. William L. Curry, e. Sept. 1, 1861; disc. Dec. 30, 1864.
Sergt. Patterson Bradley, e. Sept. 23, 1861; disc. Aug. 7, 1862.
Sergt. A. L. Sesler, e. Oct. 26, 1861; disc. Sept. 13, 1865.
Corp. William B. Herriott, e. Feb. 26, 1864; disc. Sept. 14, 1865.
Clark, Sanford P., e. Dec. 5, 1861; disc. Feb. 11, 1863.
*Ewing, James S., e. Feb., 1864; March 19, 1864, died.
*Goff, Presley E., e. Oct. 15, 1861; July 10, 1864, died Andersonville Prison.
Garner, Alonzo M., e. Feb. 26, 1864; disc. Sept. 13, 1865.
*Lucas, Benjamih F., e. Oct. 15, 1861; July 23, 1862, killed.
Ruehlen, Samuel H., e. Nov. 28, 1861; disc. Dec. 4, 1864.
Ruehlen, William, e. Sept. 28, 1861; disc. Oct. 6, 1864.

COMPANY C, 12TH O. V. C.

*Corp. William S. Channell, e. Sept. 7, 1863; Aug. 10, 1864, died.

COMPANY D, 12TH O. V. C.

Adams, Nelson C., e. Sept. 1, 1864; disc. June 15, 1865.
Cary, Isaac, e. Sept. 5, 1864; disc. June 15, 1865.
Hawn, Philip, e. Sept. 3, 1863; disc. Nov. 14, 1865.
*Heath, Daniel, e. Sept. 12, 1863; March 30, 1864, drowned.

COMPANY F, 13TH O. V. I. (Three Months).

Bain, James D., e. April 25, 1861; disc. Aug. 25, 1861.
Wood, Harvey S., e. April 25, 1861; disc. Aug. 25, 1861.
Collumber, Joseph, e. April 25, 1861.

COMPANY F, 13TH O. V. I. (Three Years).

Bain, David, e. June 5, 1861.
*Taylor, David O., e. June 5, 1861; May 27, 1864, killed.

COMPANY G, 17TH O. V. I. (Three Months).

Lieut. Daniel Taylor, e. April 22, 1861; disc. Aug. 15, 1861.
Black, James, e. April 22, 1861; disc. Aug. 15, 1861.

Beach, Joseph, e. April 22, 1861; disc. Aug. 15, 1861.
Durboraugh, Washington, e. April 22, 1861; disc. Aug. 15, 1861.
Bancroft, William, e. April 22, 1861; disc. Aug. 15, 1861.
*Fleming, Robert F., e. April 22, 1861; disc. Aug. 15, 1861.
Hill, Andrew, e. April 22, 1861; disc. Aug. 15, 1861.
Hobert, Leander, e. April 22, 1861; disc. Aug. 15, 1861.
Hobert, Lorenzo, e. April 22, 1861; disc. Aug. 15, 1861.
Kent, David, e. April 22, 1861; disc. Aug. 15, 1861.
Kile, William N., e. April 22, 1861; disc. Aug. 15, 1861.
Kilbury, James M., e. April 22, 1861; disc. Aug. 15, 1861.
Langstaff, James G., e. April 22, 1861; disc. Aug. 15, 1861.
Langstaff, Justin O., e. April 22, 1861; disc. Aug. 15, 1861.
Lucas, Benjamin F., e. April 22, 1861; disc. Aug. 15, 1861.
McClung, John, e. April 22, 1861; disc. Aug. 15, 1861.
McCune, David, e. April 22, 1861; disc. Aug. 15, 1861.
McDowell, John P., e. April 22, 1861; disc. Aug. 15, 1861.
Norris, George, e. April 22, 1861; disc. Aug. 15, 1861.
Patch, Esley, e. April 22, 1861; disc. Aug. 15, 1861.
Perry, John F., e. April 22, 1861; disc. Aug. 15, 1861.
Perry, Luther, e. April 22, 1861; disc. Aug. 15, 1861.
Ruehlen, Samuel, e. April 22, 1861; disc. Aug. 15, 1861.
Ruehlen, William, e. April 22, 1861; disc. Aug. 15, 1861.
Stevens, Marion, e. April 22; 1861; disc. Aug. 15, 1861.
Surface, Reuben W., e. April 22, 1861; disc. Aug. 15, 1861.
Taylor, William, e. April 22, 1861; disc. Aug. 15, 1861.
Wells, Lewis W., e. April 22, 1861; disc. Aug. 15, 1861.
Williams, John P., e. April 22, 1861; disc. Aug. 15, 1861.

COMPANY E, 30TH O. V. I.

The only full company recruited in the Township. One hundred and two (102) men served in this company and thirty-two (32) were killed or died of wounds and disease.

Maj. Elijah Warner, e. Aug. 19, 1861; disc. Nov. 9, 1864.
Capt. James D. Bain, e. Aug. 28, 1861; disc. Aug. 13, 1865.
Asst. Surgeon Philander F. Beverly, e. Aug 5, 1862; disc. April 6, 1863.
First Lieut. Henry R. Brinkerhoff, e. Aug. 19, 1861; promoted to Lieut. Col., 2nd Miss. U. S. C. T.
Second Lieut. Henry Hensel, e. Aug. 9, 1861; disc. May 15, 1862.
Sergt. Horace Beach, e. Aug. 19, 1861; disc. Aug. 31, 1864.
Sergt. Bazil Burton, e. Feb. 1, 1864; disc. Aug. 13, 1865.
Sergt. James Collier, e. Aug. 19, 1861; disc. Aug. 13, 1865.
*Sergt. John Engle, e. Aug. 19, 1861; Aug. 10, 1864, died.
Sergt. Hiram Roney, e. Aug. 19, 1861; disc. July 6, 1865.
Corp. Amos Beach, e. Aug. 19, 1861; disc. Aug. 13, 1865.
*Corp. James Brobeck, e. Aug. 19, 1862; Aug. 10, 1864, killed.
*Corp. Caleb Green, e. Aug. 19, 1861; Dec. 16, 1863, died.
*Corp. Benjamin Gamble, e. Aug. 19, 1861; Sept. 1, 1863, died.
Corp. Alexander Harkness, e. Aug. 19, 1861; disc. Aug. 31, 1864.
Corp, James G. Langstaff, e. Aug. 19, 1861; disc. Aug. 31, 1864.
Corp. Robert McCrory, e. Aug. 19, 1861; disc. Sept. 3, 1863.
Corp. John A. Porter, e. Aug. 19, 1861; disc. Aug. 13, 1865.
Corp. Addison Wells, e. Aug. 19, 1861; disc. Aug. 13, 1865.
Ashbaugh, David R., e. Aug. 13, 1862; disc. June 18, 1865.
Ashbaugh, Milton O., e. Aug. 19, 1861; disc. Aug. 31, 1864.

Beach, Joseph, e. Dec. 25, 1861; disc. June 25, 1865.
Beaver, William, e. Aug. 19, 1861; disc. April 13, 1863.
Bercaw, Jeremiah, e. Aug. 19, 1861; disc. Feb. 24, 1863.
Borland, William, e. Sept. 5, 1861; disc. Jan. 29, 1863.
Brinkerhoff, William B, e. Aug. 19, 1861; disc. Feb. 24, 1863.
Brown, William G., e. Aug. 19, 1861; disc. Aug. 31, 1864.
Bogan, Joseph, e. Aug. 19, 1861; disc. Aug. 31, 1864.
Buckley, Joseph, e. Aug. 19, 1861; disc. Aug. 13, 1865.
Buckley, Samuel, e. Aug. 19, 1861; disc. Aug. 13, 1865.
Cabo, John, e. Aug. 19, 1861; disc. Aug. 31, 1864.
Collier, William, e. Sept. 5, 1861; disc. Oct. 4, 1864.
Cowen, James, e. March 10, 1862; disc. Aug. 17, 1863.
Dennis, William H., e. Aug. 29, 1861; disc. Aug. 13, 1865.
*Donaldson, David M., e. Aug. 13, 1862; Feb. 8, 1863, died.
*Ellis, Daniel W., e. Aug. 19, 1861; March 6, 1862, died.
Fleck, Thaddeus S., e. Aug. 19, 1861; disc. Dec. 2, 1862.
Forquer, Peter, e. March 26, 1862; disc. March 29, 1865.
Freshwater, George, e. Aug. 19, 1861; disc. Aug. 13, 1865.
*Fultz, John, e. Aug. 13, 1862; August 15, 1863, died.
Graham, Hezekiah, e. Aug. 19, 1861; disc. Aug. 13, 1865.
*Grubb, Benjamin C., e. Aug. 13, 1862; May 9, 1863, died.
Grubb, William, e. Aug. 19, 1861; disc. Dec. 29, 1864.
Hahn, William F., e. Aug. 19, 1861; disc. Feb. 1, 1864.
Hahn, William H., e. Aug. 24, 1861; disc. Aug. 13, 1864.
*Hamilton, John E., e. Aug. 19, 1861; May 6, 1862, died.
Hill, Andrew, e. Aug. 19, 1861; disc. Aug. 13, 1865.
Hobbs, Sylvester, e. Aug. 22, 1862.
Hoffiner, Lewis, e. Aug. 19, 1861; disc. Feb. 1, 1862.
Huffvine, Moses, e. Aug. 19, 1861; disc. Nov. 14, 1862.
Huffvine, William H., e. Aug. 19, 1861; disc. Nov. 24, 1864.
*Houts, Joseph, e. Aug. 19, 1861; Oct. 18, 1861, died.
*Hudson, Joseph, e. Aug. 19, 1861; Sept. 14, 1862, killed.
*Jackson, William H., e. Aug. 13, 1862; Aug. 16, 1863, died.
*Johnson, Samuel, e. Aug. 19, 1861; April 29, 1862, died.
*Langstaff, Juston O., e. Sept. 5, 1861; Nov. 25, 1863, killed.
Lacourse, Alonzo, e. Aug. 19, 1861; disc. June 25, 1865.
Lacourse, William C., e. Aug. 24, 1861; disc. Aug. 31, 1864.
*Laymaster, David D.; Aug. 24, 1864, killed.
Mahaffy, Alexander, e. Aug. 19, 1861.
*Marsh, David, e. July 13, 1862; July 17, 1863, died.
Martin, Theodore, e. Aug. 19, 1861; disc. Aug. 13, 1865.
Merryman, James M., e. Aug. 19, 1861; disc. Aug. 13, 1865.
Moore, Albert, e. March 7, 1862; disc. March 6, 1863.
Moore, Frank M., e. Aug. 19, 1861; disc. Aug. 13, 1865.
Moore, Sylvester, e. Aug. 19, 1861; disc. Sept. 31, 1863.
*Morrow, Henry, e. Aug. 13, 1862; Aug. 13, 1863, died.
*Mullen, Ezekiel, e. Aug. 19, 1861; April 11, 1862, died.
McCumber, Walter, e. Aug. 19, 1861; disc. July 6, 1862.
McCumber, William, e. Aug. 19, 1861; disc. Dec. 10, 1862.
*McCumber, Zeno, e. Aug. 19, 1861; June 1, 1863, died.
*McIntire, James, e. Aug. 24, 1861; May 11, 1864, died.
*McIntyre, Joseph, e. Aug. 19, 1861; Sept. 23, 1863, died.
*McKim, David, e. Aug. 19, 1861; April 9, 1864, died.
Noble, Lewis C., e. Aug. 28, 1861; disc. Aug. 13, 1865.
Norris, Robert, e. Aug. 13, 1862; disc. May 31, 1865.

*Patterson, John, e. Aug. 19, 1861; April 16, 1862, died.
*Patterson, Robert, e. Aug. 13, 1862; July 28, 1864, killed.
*Perkins, Atlas, e. Aug. 19, 1861; Oct. 3, 1861, died.
Perry, Daniel, e. Aug. 13, 1862; disc. May 31, 1865.
Perry, Luther, e. Aug. 19, 1861; disc. Feb. 28, 1865.
Preston, Thomas H., e. Aug. 13, 1862; disc. May 31, 1865.
Roney, Jesse, e. Aug. 19, 1861; disc. Aug. 13, 1865.
Ruehlen, Solomon, e. Aug. 19, 1861; disc. Nov. 4, 1863.
Schofield, James, e. Aug. 19, 1861; disc. Aug. 31, 1864
*Scott, David S., e. Aug. 19, 1861; Feb. 26, 1862, died.
Shaw, Thomas, e. Aug. 13, 1862.
*Skinner, Lyman B., e. Aug. 19, 1861; July 22, 1864, killed.
*Smith, David, e. Aug. 13, 1862; Aug. 18, 1863, died.
Smith, Orville D., e. Aug. 19, 1861; disc. April 17, 1865.
*Stevens, James, e. Aug. 19, 1861; Jan. 9, 1862, died.
Stephens, Saulsbery, e. Aug. 19, 1861; disc. Aug. 13, 1865.
Taylor, Adam, e. Aug. 19, 1861.
Thomas, Byron, e. Aug. 19, 1861; disc. Aug. 13, 1865.
*Urton, Thompson P., e. Aug. 19, 1861; June 27, 1864, died.
Wagner, James, e. May 10, 1864; disc. Aug. 13, 1865.
Wells, William, e. Aug. 29, 1861; disc. Sept. 1, 1863.
Wolfe, John M., e. Aug. 13, 1862.
*Wollam, Andrew J., e. Aug. 19, 1861; June 27, 1864, killed.
*Wood, Aaron, e. Aug. 19, 1862; May 23, 1863, died.

COMPANY B, 32ND O. V. I.

Converse, Henry M., e. Aug. 9, 1861; disc. Nov. 11, 1861.
McDowell, John P., e. Aug. 9, 1861; disc. July 20, 1865.
*McDowell, Robert N., e. Aug. 9, 1861; Oct. 4, 1862, died.
Robinson, John B., e. Aug. 9, 1861; disc. July 20, 1865.

COMPANY G, 34TH O. V. I.

Highland, Seth G., e. Feb. 26, 1864; disc. July 27, 1865.

COMPANY D, 40TH O. V. I.

Conklin, David, e. Sept. 23, 1861; disc. Oct. 7, 1864.
Hawn, Philip, e. Sept. 8, 1861; disc. May 1, 1863.
Myers, Henry, e. Sept. 1, 1862; disc. June 21, 1865.
*McDowell, Jesse V., e. Sept. 17, 1861; Feb. 24, 1862, died.
Snodgress, Delmore, e. Aug. 30, 1861; disc. Oct. 7, 1864.
Robinson, Samuel B., e. Aug. 30, 1861; disc. Oct. 7, 1864.
Bancroft, William, e. Sept. 21, 1862; transferred to Co. I, 51st
 O. V. I.

COMPANY B, 46TH O. V. I.

Herriott, William B., e. Sept. 9, 1861; disc. July 22, 1863.
Pence, David M., e. Oct. 14, 1861; disc. Aug. 11, 1862.
Williams, John P., e. Oct. 2, 1861; disc. July 22, 1865.

COMPANY E, 46TH O. V. I.

Corp. Charles S. Comstock, e. Sept. 27, 1861; disc. July 14, 1862.

COMPANY H, 46TH O. V. I.

Sergt. Ammon P. Converse, e. Dec. 14, 1861; disc. July 22, 1865.
*Sergt. James E. Gowans, e. Oct. 16, 1861; Nov. 25, 1863, killed.

COMPANY G, 46TH O. V. I.

Buckley, Edward R., e. Nov. 17, 1861; disc. July 26, 1866.

*Hudson, William, e. Nov. 15, 1861; Dec. 25, 1862, died.
*Uray, Thomas, e. Nov. 21, 1861; March 25, 1862, died.

COMPANY K, 54TH O. V. I.

Sergt. David Cook, e. Nov. 16, 1861; disc. Sept. 22, 1862.
Sergt. Marion Stevens, e. Nov. 30, 1861; disc. Aug. 15, 1865.
*Sergt. James Clark, e. Nov. 26, 1861; Feb. 18, 1864, died.
Beaver, George, e. Dec. 11, 1861; disc. Dec. 21, 1864.
Hobert, Lorenzo, e. Feb. 8, 1862; disc. June 19, 1862.
*Kent, David, e. Nov. 23, 1861; July 4, 1862, died.
Lape, Jeremiah, e. Nov. 12, 1861; disc. July 21, 1862.
Lape, Zachariah, e. Nov. 11, 1861; disc. July 21, 1862.
Martin, Charles, e. Nov. 9, 1861; disc. Sept. 29, 1862.
McClung, William, e. Nov. 11, 1861; disc. Aug. 20, 1862.
Surface, Reuben W., e. Nov. 23, 1861; disc. Dec. 21, 1864.
Nessle, George, e. Nov. 12, 1861; disc. Aug. 15, 1865.
Norris, Jacob, e. Feb. 26, 1864; disc. June 15, 1865.
Norris, George K., e. Nov. 23, 1861; disc. Aug. 15, 1865.

COMPANY C, 58TH O. V. I.

Drum Maj. Dunallen Marion Woodburn, e. Jan. 16, 1862; transferred to the 47th Regiment, U. S. C. T.

COMPANY H, 63RD O. V. I.

*Sergt. Eli Casey, e. Dec. 12, 1861; Oct. 4, 1862, killed.

COMPANY F, 66TH O. V. I.

*Corp. Delmore Robinson, e. Nov. 13, 1861; July 10, 1862, died.
Collumber, Jesse, e. Jan. 27, 1864; disc. June 28, 1865.
McKitrick, James H., e. Nov. 1861; disc. June 28, 1865.
Smith, Jacob H., e. Nov. 28, 1861; disc. March 27, 1863.
Smith, John T., e. Nov. 28, 1861; disc. June 28, 1865.
*Stithem, Leonard, e. Nov. 30, 1861; Jan. 20, 1862, died.

COMPANY H, 66TH O. V. I.

*Shineman, David, e. Oct. 14, 1861.

COMPANY F, 82ND O. V. I.

Oliver, Alexander H., e. Oct. 4, 1864; disc. May 26, 1865.

COMPANY E, 85TH O. V. I.

*Smeck, Henry, e. June 6, 1862; Sept. 23, 1862, died.

COMPANY E, 86TH O. V. I. (Three Months).

Beach, William, e. June 3, 1862; disc. Sept. 25, 1862.
Beaver, John, e. June 3, 1862; disc. Sept. 25, 1862.
Beaver, Nathaniel, e. June 3, 1862; disc. Sept. 25, 1862.
Chapman, James, e. June 3, 1862; disc. Sept. 25, 1862.
Huffvine, Lewis, e. June 3, 1862; disc. Sept. 25, 1862.
Post, Frank W., e. June 3, 1862; disc. Sept. 25, 1862.
Robinson, Chester L., e. June 3, 1862; disc. Sept. 25, 1862.
Robinson, David G., e. June 3, 1862; disc. Sept. 25, 1862.

COMPANY B, 86TH O. V. I. (Six Months).

Corp. R. L. Woodburn, e. June 26, 1863; disc. Feb. 10, 1864.
Collier, Arthur, e. July 13, 1863; disc. Feb. 10, 1864.
*Curry, Addison, e. June 26, 1863; Oct. 2, 1863, died.
Gill, Andrew, e. July 28, 1863; disc. Feb. 10, 1864.

Hohn, Daniel, e. July 28, 1863; disc. Feb. 10, 1864.
Hopkins, LaFayette B., e. June 25, 1863; disc. Feb. 10, 1864.
Kahler, Henry, e. July 12, 1863; disc. Feb. 10, 1864.
*Ketch, Lewis, e. June 20, 1863; Feb. 10, 1864, killed.
Moffitt, John, e. June 20, 1863; disc. Feb. 10, 1864.
McCampbell, William, e. June 23, 1863; disc. Feb. 10, 1864.
McNeal, William, e. June 20, 1863; disc. Feb. 10, 1864.
Robinson, Imer, e. June 26, 1863; disc. Feb. 10, 1864.
Wise, Eli, e. June 22, 1863; disc. Feb. 10, 1864.
*Wise, William, e. June 29, 1863; Jan. 4, 1864, died.
Woodburn, Heber, e. July 28, 1863; disc. Feb. 10, 1864.

COMPANY D, 88TH O. V. I.

Corp. Isaac Mummy, e. Oct. 1, 1862; disc. Aug. 12, 1864.
Bethard, James H., e. Oct. 1, 1862; disc. July 3, 1865.
Fleck, William H. H., e. May 14, 1863; disc. July 3, 1865.
*Fulk, William, e. Oct. 1, 1862; April 12, 1863, died.
Jackson, James, e. Oct. 1, 1862; disc. March 4, 1865.
*McIntyre, George F., e. Oct. 1, 1862; Jan. 22, 1864, died.
Mummy, Jacob, e. Oct. 1, 1862; disc. July 3, 1865.
Norris, Jacob, e. Oct. 1, 1862; disc. Oct. 2, 1863.
Wise, David B., e. March 7, 1863; disc. July 3, 1865.

COMPANY H, 88TH O. V. I.

Beard, Forrester L., e. July 22, 1863; disc. July 3, 1865.

COMPANY H, 94TH O. V. I.

Capt. Andrew Gowans, e. Aug. 7, 1862; disc. June 5, 1865.

COMPANY A, 95TH, O. V. I.

Sergt. Daniel W. Ellis, e. Aug. 13, 1862; disc. Aug. 14, 1865.

COMPANY D, 95TH O. V. I.

O'Harra, William, e. Aug. 8, 1862; disc. Jan. 6, 1863.

COMPANY K, 95TH O. V. I.

Allen, Benjamin F., e. Aug. 11, 1862; disc. June 20, 1865.
Allen, Calvin J., e. Aug. 11, 1862; disc. Feb. 2, 1863.
*Beard, S. B., e. Aug. 11, 1862; June 17, 1864, died.
Bethard, James F., e. Aug. 11, 1862; disc. Aug. 14, 1865.
Chief Musician Clark L. Barlow, e. Aug. 11, 1862; disc. June 20, 1864.
Bethard, William, e. Aug. 11, 1862; disc. March 17, 1863.
Myers, Jacob, e. Aug. 11, 1862; disc. June 9, 1865.
McClung, John, e. Dec. 6, 1862.
Williams, John P., e. Aug. 11, 1862; disc. April 11, 1863.

COMPANY K, 96TH O. V. I.

*Sergt. Wm. D. Laughead, e. Aug. 6, 1862; Nov. 28, 1862, died.
Sergt. Andrew J. Smith, e. Aug. 6, 1862; disc. Nov. 18, 1864.
Sergt. Robert A. Liggett, e. Aug. 6, 1862; disc. July 7, 1865.
Corp. George Butler, e. Aug. 6, 1862; disc. July 7, 1865.
Corp. David Edwards, e. Aug. 6, 1862; disc. Feb. 20, 1863.
Cole, Thompson O., e. Feb. 29, 1864; disc. March 8, 1866.
*Green, William J., e. Feb. 23, 1864; July 23, 1864, died.
Gowans, A. D., e. Aug. 6, 1862; disc. July 7, 1865.
Kent, William, e. Aug. 6, 1862; disc. Dec. 24, 1862.

Liggett, William M., e. Feb. 29, 1864; disc. March 8, 1866.
*Liggett, Alfred P., e. Feb. 11, 1864; Sept. 15, 1864, died.
*Mitchell, George W., e. Aug. 4, 1862; Feb. 11, 1863, died.
Morford, John W., e. Aug. 4, 1862; disc. July 7, 1865.
McGill, Edgar, e. Feb. 13, 1864; disc. March 8, 1866.
McCampbell, James L., e. Aug. 4, 1862; disc. June 4, 1863.
McIntire, David, e. Aug. 4, 1862; disc. July 7, 1865.
McIntire, George, e. Aug. 22, 1864; disc. July 7, 1865.
*Nonnemaker, Jacob, e. Aug. 4, 1862; Jan. 20, 1863, died.
*Perry, Jesse N., e. Aug. 4, 1862; Jan. 9, 1863, died.
*Ruehlen, George W., e. Aug. 6, 1862; Oct. 4, 1864, died.
Woodburn, David H., e. Feb. 29, 1864; disc. March 8, 1866.

COMPANY F, 96TH O. V. I.

Williams, William H., e. Aug. 7, 1862; disc. July 7, 1865.

COMPANY K, 110TH O. V. I.

Heath, George W., e. May 3, 1864; disc. June 25, 1865.

COMPANY H, 113TH O. V. I.

Hudson, David, e. Aug. 14, 1862; disc. July 6, 1865.
*Sinsel, William, e. Aug. 12, 1862; Feb. 9, 1863, died.

COMPANY A, 121ST O. V. I.

Capt. Otway Curry, e. Aug. 15, 1862; disc. June 8, 1865.
Corp. Stephenson B. Cone, e. Aug. 15, 1862; disc. March 20, 1865.
Cone, James C., e. Aug. 15, 1862; disc. July 6, 1865.
*Cone, Otway B., e. Aug. 15, 1862; July 21, 1864, died of wounds received June 27, 1864.
Curry, David, e. Aug. 15, 1862; disc. July 12, 1865.
McClung, John, e. Aug. 8, 1862.
Warner, Joshua C., e. Aug. 9, 1862; disc. June 24, 1865.

COMPANY H, 121ST O. V. I.

Baker, Bernard, e. Aug. 17, 1862; disc. July 14, 1865.

COMPANY I, 121ST O. V. I.

*Lieut. Robert F. Fleming, e. Aug. 16, 1862; Sept. 20, 1863, killed.
Corp. John N. Bryan, e. Aug. 3, 1862; disc. June 8, 1865.
Corp. J. M. Fookes, e. Aug. 18, 1862; disc. June 8, 1865.
*Ketch, Lewis J., e. Feb. 22, 1864; Aug. 6, 1864, killed.
Lamme, Bowin J., e. Aug. 16, 1862; disc. March 30, 1863.
Patch, Esley, e. Aug. 16, 1862; disc. June 8, 1865.
Patch, Harmon, e. Aug. 19, 1862; disc. July 15, 1865.

COMPANY C, 128TH O. V. I.

Carson, Andrew L., e. Aug. 14, 1862; disc. June 5, 1865.
Carson, Samuel H., e. May 1, 1862; disc. June 5, 1865.

COMPANY G, 129TH O. V. I.

Sergt. Chester L. Robinson, e. July 21, 1863; disc. March 8, 1864.
Clark, James, e. July 24, 1863; disc. March 8, 1864.
Edwards, Festus, e. July 22, 1863; disc. March 8, 1864.
Huffvine, Lewis, e. July 20, 1863; disc. March 8, 1864.

COMPANY E, 133RD O. V. I.

Sergt. Edward S. Churchman, e. May 2, 1864; disc. Aug. 20, 1864.
Corp. Lucas B. Goff, e. May 2, 1864; disc. Aug. 20, 1864.
Pence, David M., e. May 2, 1864; disc. Aug. 20, 1864.

COMPANY K, 133RD O. V. I.

Evans, Benjamin W., e. May 2, 1864; disc. Aug. 20, 1864.
Goff, Tillman, e. May 2, 1864; disc. Aug. 20, 1864.
South, Samuel, e. May 2, 1864; disc. Aug. 20, 1864.

COMPANY H, 136TH O. V. I.

Ryan, Nathaniel, e. May 2, 1864; disc. Aug. 31, 1864.

COMPANY K, 136TH O. V. I.

Lieut. Bowen J. Lamme, e. May 2, 1864; disc. Aug. 31, 1864.
Sergt. William Green, e. May 2, 1864; disc. Aug. 31, 1864.
Sergt. James Guy, e. May 2, 1864; disc. Aug. 31, 1864.
Corp. Isaac D. Mapes, e. May 2, 1864; disc. Aug. 31, 1864.
Corp. David McCune, e. May 2, 1864; disc. Aug. 31, 1864.
Corp. John Q. Adams, e. May 2, 1864; disc. Aug. 31, 1864.
Corp. John McCullough, e. May 2, 1864; disc. Aug. 31, 1864.
Chapman, James F., e. May 2, 1864; disc. Aug. 31, 1864.
Dall, Francis, e. May 2, 1864; disc. Aug. 31, 1864.
Kahler, Henry, e. May 2, 1864; disc. Aug. 31, 1864.
Kent, Marion, e. May 2, 1864; disc. Aug. 31, 1864.
Kent, William, e. May 2, 1864; disc. Aug. 31, 1864.
McCullough, Zenis O., e. May 2, 1864; disc. Aug. 31, 1864.
McCune, Zachariah, e. May 2, 1864; disc. Aug. 31, 1864.
Mapes, Jacob, e. May 2, 1864; disc. Aug. 31, 1864.
Martin, George, e. May 2, 1864; disc. Aug. 31, 1864.
Martin, William, e. May 2, 1864; disc. Aug. 31, 1864.
Nonnemaker, Samuel S., e. May 2, 1864; disc. Aug. 31, 1864.
Preston, M. A., e. May 2, 1864; disc. Sept. 1, 1865.
Palen, William, e. May 2, 1864; disc. July 20, 1864.
Ruehlen, Jacob, e. May 2, 1864; disc. Aug. 31, 1864.
Scott, John M., e. May 2, 1864; disc. Aug. 31, 1864.
Tarpening, Ira, e. May 2, 1864; disc. Aug. 31, 1864.
Warner, Isaac H., e. May 2, 1864; disc. Aug. 31, 1864.
Wilcox, William, e. May 2, 1864; disc. Aug. 31, 1864.
Windall, Jacob, e. May 2, 1864; disc. Aug. 31, 1864.
Windall, Joseph, e. May 2, 1864; disc. Aug. 31, 1864.

COMPANY K, 145TH O. V. I.

Bowersmith, Jacob, e. May 10, 1864; disc. Aug. 23, 1864.

COMPANY B, 174TH O. V. I.

Corp. Robert E. Benson, e. Aug. 29, 1864; disc. June 28, 1865.
Benson, John, e. Aug. 29, 1864; disc. June 28, 1865.
Beach, Amos, e. Aug. 16, 1864; disc. June 28, 1865.
Edwards, George C., e. Aug. 20, 1864; disc. June 28, 1865.
Oliver, James, e. Aug. 29, 1864; disc. June 28, 1865.
Oliver, William M., e. Aug. 29, 1864; disc. May 30, 1865.
Swank, Thomas L., e. Sept. 1, 1864; disc. June 28, 1865.

COMPANY C, 174TH O. V. I.

Corp. Charles M. Adams, e. Aug. 30, 1864; disc. June 28, 1865.

McKitrick, David F., e. Sept. 3, 1864; disc. May 22, 1865.
Myers, Henry A., e. Aug. 30, 1864; disc. June 28, 1865.
Perry, Albert T., e. Aug. 19, 1864; disc. June 28, 1865.
Perry, Chas. W., e. Aug. 22, 1864; disc. June 28, 1865.
Perry, Ezra, e. Sept. 3, 1864; disc. June 29, 1865.
Wells, Marvel W., e. Sept. 17, 1864; disc. June 28, 1865.

COMPANY B, 186TH O. V. I.

Roney, Chas. M., e. Feb. 21, 1865; disc. Sept. 18, 1865.

COMPANY B, 187TH O. V. I.

Corp. James Curry, e. Feb. 6, 1865; disc. Jan. 20, 1866.
Corp. James G. Langstaff, e. Feb. 13, 1865; disc. Jan. 20, 1866.
Beathard, Charles W., e. Feb. 6, 1865; disc. Jan. 20, 1866.
Brake, Lewis A., e. Feb. 15; 1865; disc. Jan. 20, 1866.
Collier, Arthur, e. Jan. 31, 1865; disc. Jan. 20, 1866.
Dickson, Adelbert, e. Jan. 13, 1865; disc. Aug. 14, 1865.
Edwards, Festus, e. Feb. 14, 1865; disc. Jan. 20, 1866.
Hawn, Philip M., e. Feb. 15, 1865; disc. Jan. 20, 1866.
McCampbell, Addison, e. Feb. 14, 1865; disc. Jan. 20, 1866.
Post, Frank W., e. Jan. 15, 1865; disc. Jan. 20, 1866.
Romine, Henry C., e. Jan. 7, 1865; disc. Jan. 20, 1866.
Romine, Jacob M., e. Feb. 3, 1865; disc. Jan. 20, 1866.
Woodburn, Heber, e. Feb. 14, 1865; disc. Jan. 20, 1866.

COMPANY C, 191ST O. V. I.

Lieut. Henry Hensel, e. March 2, 1865; disc. Aug. 27, 1865.
Lattimer, David B., e. Feb. 25, 1865; disc. Aug. 27, 1865.

COMPANY B, 197TH O. V. I.

Lape, Emanuel, e. March 23, 1865; disc. July 31, 1865.

COMPANY 1, 27TH U. S. C. T. I.

Butcher, Joseph, e. Aug. 29, 1864; disc. Sept. 4, 1865.

EIGHTEENTH U. S. I.

*Beal, George, died.
*Converse, H. G., e. March 12, 1862, died.
Converse, Jasper, e. Aug. 27, 1861; disc. Aug. 27, 1864.
*Ditmus, Gotfried, died.
Kahler, Joseph, e. Aug. 6, 1861; disc. March 7, 1867.
McClung, James, e. March 4, 1862; disc. 1865.
Patch, Lemuel.
*Rider, Henry, died.
*Stierhoff, George, Dec. 31, 1862, killed.
Swank, George W.
*Williams, David, died.
*Latham, Alexander, died Nashville, Tenn., April 2, 1863.

FOURTY-SEVENTH REGIMENT, U. S. C. T.

Dunallen M. Woodburn, drum major, transferred from the Fifty-eighth Regiment, Ohio Volunteer Infantry; disc. Jan. 5, 1866.

SEVENTH OHIO INDEPENDENT SHARPSHOOTERS.

Capt. William McCrory, e. Oct. 8, 1862; disc. July 28, 1865.
Dickson, Samuel, e. Oct. 11, 1862; disc. Sept. 8, 1863.

TENTH OHIO BATTERY LIGHT ARTILLERY.

Adams, Charles M., e. Dec. 23, 1861; disc. Jan. 16, 1863.

U. S. NAVY.

Daniel R. Cone served on "Baron De Kalb" and other gunboats of Mississippi Squadron.

Llewellyn B. Curry served as Major and Paymaster on "Baron De Kalk" and other gunboats of Mississippi Squadron.

SIGNAL CORPS.

George W. Lattimer.

COMPANY D, 9TH MINNESOTA INFANTRY.

Kent, Philo.

INDIANA INFANTRY.

*Hill, James, regiment unknown, died in service Feb. 1, 1864.

JAMES HILL.

James Hill died Feb. 1, 1864. He was an English boy who had been in the United States but a few years. He died in the service, and his remains are buried in the cemetery at New California. Every effort to ascertain his service has failed, but he served in an Indiana Regiment. The service of this young boy, who gave his life in defense of his adopted country, must be marked "unknown."

SQUIRREL HUNTERS, SEPTEMBER, 1862.

Capt. James S. Ewing	Huff, L. G.
Beard, David D.	Kimerly, Frederick
Beard, Forester	Kilbury, James
Curry, Addison	McCune, Zachariah
Dort, J. B.	Taylor, John
Evans, Rev. B. D.	Wilcox, William
Ewing, Salatheil	Windle, Joseph
Fleck, W. H.	Wise, Samuel

JEROME TOWNSHIP.

The following named soldiers who enlisted in the Township were Commissioned Officers:

Majors.

Maj. Llewellyn B. Curry   Maj. Elijah Warner

Captains.

Capt. James Cutler   Capt. James D. Bain
Capt. Otway Curry   Capt. William McCrory
Capt. W. L. Curry

Surgeon.

Asst. Surg. P. F. Beverly.

Lieutenants.

First Lieut. H. R. Brinkerhoff, promoted to Lieutenant Colonel, U. S. A.

Second Lieut. Henry Hensel   Lieut. Robert F. Fleming
Lieut. Daniel Taylor   Lieut. B. J. Lamme

SPANISH WAR.

Jerome Township.

Colonel George Ruehlen, Quartermaster, U. S. Army.
James Beaver, Company D, Fourth O. V. I.
Wassen Beaver, Company D, Fourth O. V. I.
Wm. Wise, Company D, Fourth O. V. I.
John Parmenter, Company G, First O. V. C.
Thomas Parmenter, Company G, First O. V. C.
Irwin Patch, Company G, First O. V. C.
Chester M. Fletcher, Company I, Seventeenth U. S. I.
Harry Hill, Company I, Seventeenth U. S. I.
Wm. Peaks, Company I, Seventeenth U. S. I.

WAR OF REVOLUTION—1776.

Col. James Curry served in the Fourth and Eighth Virginia Infantry, Continental Line, eight years.
Henry Shover served in Virginia Regiment.

WAR OF 1812.

Capt. James A. Curry
Alder, Jonathan
Buck, James
Kent, Daniel
Kent, John
Shover, Simon
Shover, Adam
Noteman, Andrew
Taylor, William
Ricard, Simon
Adams, Christian
McClung, Joseph

Provin, Clark
Dort, Titus ·
Donelson, James E.
Ewing, Scott
Ewing, Donelson
Hemenway, F.
Hoyt, Elijah
Kent, James
Kent, William
Sager, Abraham
Barlow, Major Edmund

MEXICAN WAR—1846.

Cutler, James, Second U. S. I.
Clevenger, William W., Company E, Fourth O. V. I., e. May 12, 1847; disc. July 18, 1848.
Lamme, William, service not known.
Oliver, Alexander G., Company E, Fourth O. V. I., e. May 12, 1847; disc. July 18, 1848.

NAMES OF SOLDIERS BURIED IN THE CEMETERIES OF JEROME TOWNSHIP.

NEW CALIFORNIA CEMETERY.

Civil War.

Robert N. McDowell
William Little
Jesse V. McDowell
Daniel Straw
George F. McIntire
James McClung
Andrew J. Murray
David Bain
Charles S. Comstock

Joseph Porter
James E. Gowans
Leonard A. Stithem
James Hill
Henry Smeck
Frederick J. Hinderer
William Wise
Otway B. Cone

War of 1812.

Joseph McClung
Capt. James A. Curry

William Taylor
Elijah Hoyt

Mexican War.

William Clevenger

William Lamme

JEROME CEMETERY.

Civil War.

Joseph Beach
Henry Hensel
John Patterson
Robert Norris
Hobbs Jackson

Charles Beach
Calab Green
Robert Patterson
D. R. Ashbaugh

War of 1812.

Titus Dort

Christian Adams

EWING CEMETERY.

Civil War.

James E. Ewing

Samuel B. Beard

War of 1812.

James E. Donaldson

Scott Ewing

MITCHELL CEMETERY.

Simon Rickard

CURRY CEMETERY.

War of 1812.

James Buck

War of the Revolution.

Colonel James Curry, buried July 6, 1834; remains removed to Oakdale Cemetery, Marysville, Ohio.

OUR HEROIC DEAD.

Names of Jerome Township Soldiers Who Died in the Army.

COMPANY K, 1ST O. V. C.

James Ewing, died at Columbus, Ohio, March 19, 1864.
Presley E. Goff, died in Andersonville Prison of wounds.
Benjamin F. Lucas, killed at Courtland, Ala., July 23, 1862.

COMPANY D, 12TH O. V. C.

Daniel Heath, drowned in the Ohio River, March 30, 1864.

COMPANY C, 12TH O. V. C.

William S. Channell, died in hospital at Lexington, Ky., August 10, 1864.

COMPANY F, 13TH O. V. I.

David O. Taylor, killed at New Hope Church, Ga., May 27, 1864.
Joseph Collumber, died in hospital at Louisville, Ky., 1864.

COMPANY E, 30TH O. V. I.

John B. Engle, killed at Atlanta, Ga., August 10, 1864.
Andrew J. Wollam, killed near Atlanta, Ga., August 10, 1864.
Benjamin Gamble, died September 1, 1863, in hospital at St. Louis, Mo.
James Brobeck, killed in action near Atlanta, Ga., August 10, 1864.
David M. Donaldson, died in hospital at St. Louis, Mo., February 8, 1863.
Daniel W. Ellis, died in hospital at Camp Union, Va., May 6, 1862.
John Fultz, died near Vicksburg, Miss., July 24, 1863.
Benjamin Grubb, died at Young's Point, La., May 9, 1863.
Caleb Green, died December 16, 1863, at Columbus, O.
Joseph Hudson, killed in action near South Mountain, Md., September 14, 1862.
John E. Hamilton, died in hospital at Camp Union, Va., May 6, 1862.
Joseph Houtz, died in hospital, Camp Ewing, Va., October 18, 1861.
Joseph McIntyre, died while at home on furlough, September 23, 1863.
James McIntyre, died in hospital at Columbus, O., May 11, 1864.
David McKim, died while en route home on veteran furlough, April 9, 1864.
Zeno McCumber, died at Van Buren Hospital, La., June 1, 1863.
Ezekiel Mullen, died in hospital at Camp Union, Va., April 11, 1862.
Henry Morrow, died on United States hospital steamer McDougal, August 13, 1863.
David Marsh, died in hospital at Jackson, Miss, July 17, 1863.
Robert Patterson, killed at Atlanta, Ga., August 24, 1864.
John Patterson, died at Cincinnati, O., April 16, 1862.

Atlas Perkins, died at Gauley's Bridge Hospital, Va., October 3, 1861.

Lyman B. Skinner, killed at Atlanta, Ga., July 22, 1864.

David Smith, died in regiment hospital, Camp Sherman, Miss., August 18, 1863.

David S. Scott, died in hospital at Camp Union, Va., February 26, 1862.

Thompson Urton, killed at Kenesaw Mountain, Ga., June 27, 1864.

Aaron Wood, died in hospital at Young's Point, La., May 23, 1863.

James Stephens, died in regiment hospital at Camp Union, Va., January 9, 1862.

Samuel Johnson, died in hospital at Camp Union, Va., April 29, 1862.

William H. Jackson, died in hospital at St. Louis, Mo., August 16, 1863.

Juston O. Langstaff, killed at Mission Ridge, Tenn., November 25, 1863.

David D. Laymaster, killed at Atlanta, Ga., August 24, 1864.

COMPANY B, 32ND O. V. I.

Robert N. McDowell, died in prison at Winchester, Va., October 4, 1862.

COMPANY D, 40TH O. V. I.

Jesse B. McDowell, drowned in Big Sandy River at Piketon, Ky., February, 1862.

COMPANY H, 46TH O. V. I.

James E. Gowans, killed November 25, 1863, at Mission Ridge, Tenn.

COMPANY K, 46TH O. V. I.

William Hudson, died June, 1862, at Memphis, Tenn.

COMPANY K, 54TH O. V. I.

James Clark, died at home.

David Cook, died at home.

David Kent, died July 6, 1864, at Nickojack Creek, Ga.

COMPANY H, 63RD O. V. I.

Eli J. Casey, killed at Corinth, Miss, October 4, 1862.

COMPANY F, 66TH O. V. I.

Delmore Robinson, died July 10, 1862, in hospital, Alexandria, Va.

COMPANY F, 66TH O. V. I.

Leonard Stithem, died at Urbana, O., January 20, 1862.

COMPANY H, 66TH O. V. I.

David Shinneman, died Cumberland, Md.

COMPANY E, 85TH O. V. I.

Henry Smeck, died at home.

COMPANY B, 86TH O. V. I. (Six Months).

James A. Curry, died at Crab Orchard, Ky., October 2, 1863.

William Wise, died at Cumberland Gap, Tenn., January 4, 1864.

COMPANY D, 88TH O. V. I.

William Fulk, died at Camp Chase, Columbus, O., April 2, 1863.
George F. McIntire, died in hospital, January 22, 1864.

COMPANY K, 95TH O. V. I.

S. B. Beard, died June 17, 1864, in hospital at Memphis, Tenn.

COMPANY K, 96TH O. V. I.

Jesse N. Perry, died on board the Hiawatha, January 9, 1863.
William D. Laughead, died in hospital at Nicholasville, Ky., November 28, 1862.
George W. Mitchell, died at St. Louis, February 11, 1863.
Jacob Nonnemaker, died on board hospital steamer near Vicksburg, January 20, 1863.
George W. Reuhlen, died at Baton Rouge, La., October 4, 1864.
Alfred P. Liggett, died at home while in the service, September 15, 1864.
William J. Green, drowned in Mississippi River, at New Orleans, July 23, 1864.

18TH U. S. INFANTRY.

George Stierhoff, killed at Stone River, Tenn., December 31, 1862.
Gotfried Ditmus, died in service.
H. G. Converse, died March 12, 1862.
George Beal, died at Nashville, Tenn., 1862.
David Williams, died in the service.
Henry Rider, killed at Ringgold, Ga., 1863.
Alexander Latham, died at Nashville, April 2, 1863.

COMPANY A, 121ST O. V. I.

Otway B. Cone, died July 21, 1864, in hospital at Chattanooga, Tenn., of wounds June 27.

COMPANY I, 121ST O. V. I.

Robert F. Fleming, killed at Chickamauga, Ga., September 20, 1863.
Lewis J. Ketch, killed at Atlanta, Ga., August 6, 1864.
James Hill served in an Indiana regiment and died in the army.

CIVIL WAR.

SPANISH WAR.

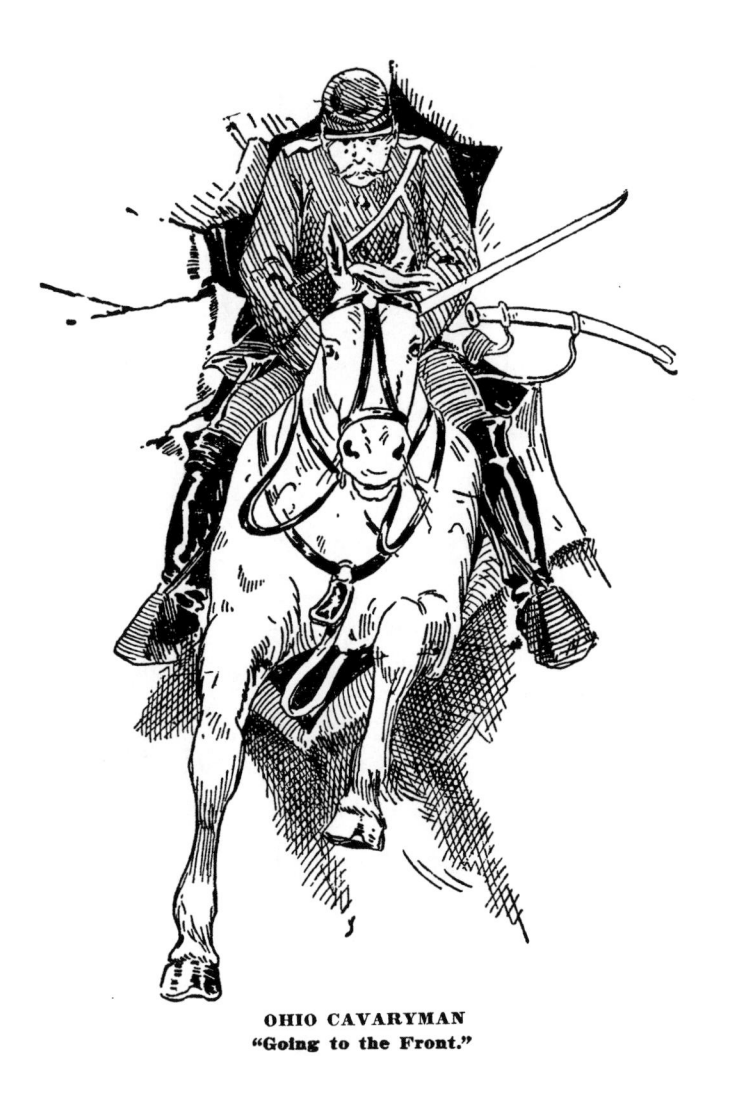

OHIO CAVARYMAN
"Going to the Front."

RAID OF THE UNION CAVALRY, COMMANDED BY GENERAL JUDSON KILPATRICK, AROUND THE CONFEDERATE ARMY IN ATLANTA, AUGUST, 1864.

By W. L. Curry,

Captain, First Ohio Volunteer Cavalry.

In military parlance, cavalry is called the "eyes of the army," and the life of a cavalryman in time of war is one of constant activity, hard and dangerous service. During the winter season, when the main army is snugly ensconced in winter quarters, cavalry is the most active and has the hardest service to perform, as it is kept constantly patroling and scouting. All these movements of the cavalry arm of the service require vigilance, secrecy, energy, promptness and dash; and whether the command is composed of a platoon or division, the commander must not halt or hesitate in an emergency, but must act immediately and supply by strategy what he lacks in numbers.

During the last two years of the War of the Rebellion, cavalry officers were composed largely of young men, who were at the beginning of the war privates or non-commissioned officers. The older officers could but with rare exceptions endure the hard duty of picket guard, routs, raids, and scouts of fifty and sixty miles a day, which were of usual occurrence. Many of the most dangerous expeditions were under command of officers of the line, penetrating the lines of the enemy with a company or squadron, capturing outposts and couriers with dispatches that were of vital importance. Scores of instances of bravery and heroism in the rank and file could be related that would do honor to a Kilpatrick or a Custer, and instances

1

of individual adventure and heroic deeds in the cavalry service could be multiplied by the hundred.

As an instance of the importance of a cavalry expedition ordered by General Sherman on the Atlanta campaign, and how little the loss of life was considered, the order to General Kenner Garrard, bearing date of July 20, 1864, read in part as follows: "I do wish to inspire all cavalry with my conviction that caution and prudence should be but a small element in their character." "It is a matter of vital importance and must be attempted with great vigor." "The importance of it will justify the loss of a quarter of your command." Garrard's division numbered four thousand men, and the order meant that one thousand men should be sacrificed in this one raid, rather than it should fail.

A cavalry raid is defined in a military sense "to be an incursion or irruption of mounted troops into the theater of war, occupied by or under the control of the enemy."

One of the main duties of cavalry in time of war is to make raids in the rear of the enemy's army. These raids, when successful, always add to the efficiency and raise the morale of the cavalry arm of the service and give forces engaged confidence for any expedition, however hazardous it might seem.

In fact, the cavalryman is always in his element when on reconnoissance or raid, teeming with dash and adventure. Cavalry raids have been in vogue more or less from the earliest times of which we have any history of the cavalry service, yet in no prior war was it practiced to the extent that it was during the War of the Rebellion.

There is no kind of service that so develops the skill of the officer and the endurance and intelligence of the soldier as the cavalry raid. From the time he cuts loose from the main army until the object of the raid is accomplished, the commander must depend on his own resources, as he has nothing to draw from, and his command is being constantly weakened by contact with the enemy. His men are being killed and wounded; his horses are exhausted, or killed by hard marching or by the bullets of the enemy; his ammunition is being rapidly consumed; his rations eaten up, and there is a continuous destruction of his forces.

The object of the raid is to destroy the enemy's communication by burning bridges, filling up tunnels and railroad cuts with rocks and timber; cutting telegraph wires; burning ties; heating and destroying rails; burning and destroying army supplies; capturing railroad and bridge guards, and creating general consternation and havoc in rear of the enemy's lines. Raiding expeditions must carry all their ammunition from the start, as they have no resources from which to draw should their ammunition become exhausted. Therefore they usually avoid all large bodies of the enemy, excepting those in their immediate front, who are endeavoring to repel the expedition from striking some point on a railroad or depot of supplies.

They capture all prisoners that come in their line of march, but the prisoners are usually paroled, as the command moves so rapidly, often marching fifty and sixty miles a day, that prisoners can not be guarded if they are mounted, and if on foot could not march the distance required; besides, all the good mounts captured are needed for the dismounted troopers of the command, as many horses become exhausted, while others are killed or wounded by the enemy.

When prisoners are captured on such raids, they are taken to the commanding officer and questioned very persistently as to their commands, strength, name of commanding officer, and any other information that may be of interest or benefit to the commander.

No rule can be adopted for the time and place of raids, but the commander must be governed by the developments of the campaign. If he sees an opportunity that he may think desirable to draw the enemy's cavalry away from the front, before making an attack in force, if he has the cavalry to spare from his own army, a raid may be made in the enemy's rear; or if he fears the enemy will receive reinforcements, he may attempt to cut his communications. All these matters must be governed by circumstances, and the commander considers carefully all the surroundings, and whether or not the sacrifice will justify sending out the expedition.

One of the most daring and successful raids made by the cavalry of the Army of the Cumberland during the Civil War was the raid made by two divisions of cavalry, commanded by General Judson Kilpatrick, in August, 1864, and as an officer of the First Ohio Volunteer Cavalry, I participated with my regiment in that expedition.

General Sherman's magnificent army moved out from Chattanooga May 5, 1864, and the Confederate army, commanded by General Joseph E. Johnston, had been driven back steadily through the mountain passes and across the rivers of Northern Georgia during that great battle summer of 1864 — the "one hundred days under fire from Chattanooga to Atlanta." The battle of bloody Kenesaw Mountain had been fought, the Chattahoochee River had been crossed, and by the middle of August the Union army was closing in around the "Gate City."

During the month of July two cavalry expeditions had been sent out, one under General Stoneman from the left flank, and the other under General Ed. McCook from the right flank. Neither of these expeditions had been as successful as General Sherman had hoped for, as McCook's division had been repulsed by an overwhelming force of the enemy, and Stoneman, with about one thousand of his command, had been captured. Sherman, therefore, decided to make another effort to break the enemy's communication before beginning his grand flank movement to the right. General Kilpatrick, who had been severely wounded early in the campaign at the battle of Resaca, had just returned to the front, and was chafing to again be in the saddle for a raid full of dash and danger, was selected to command the two divisions of cavalry detailed for this hazardous undertaking.

The expedition was composed of five brigades of cavalry and two batteries of artillery. The Third Cavalry Division, commanded by Brigadier-General Kilpatrick, was, on August 17th, encamped on the Chattahoochee River at Sandtown, on the right and rear of the army. The three brigades were present; Lieutenant-Colonel Robert Klein commanding the First Brigade, composed of the Third Indiana; Major Alfred Gaddis, and the Fifth Iowa, Major J. Morris Young. Lieutenant-Colonel Fielder A. Jones, commanding the Second Brigade, composed of the Eighth Indiana, Major Thomas Herring commanding; Second Kentucky, Major Owen Starr commanding, and Tenth Ohio, Lieutenant-Colonel Thomas W. Sanderson commanding. Colonel Eli H. Murray, commanding the Third Brigade, composed of the Ninety-second Illinois Mounted Infantry, Colonel Smith D. Atkins commanding; the Third Kentucky, Lieutenant-Colonel Robert H. King commanding; Fifth Kentucky, Colonel Oliver L. Baldwin commanding; the Tenth Wisconsin Battery, Captain Yates V. Beebe commanding.

The First and Second Brigades and a battery of artillery of General Kenner Garrard's division were ordered to report to General Kilpatrick at Sandtown, to engage in the movement against the Macon Railroad. The First Brigade, commanded by Colonel Robert H. G. Minty, consisted of the Fourth Michigan Cavalry, commanded by Major Frank W. Mix; Seventh Pennsylvania, Major William H. Jennings; Fourth United States, Captain James B. McIntyre. The Second Brigade, commanded by Colonel Eli Long, consisted of the First Ohio, Colonel Beroth B. Eggleston; Third Ohio, Colonel Charles B. Seidel; Fourth Ohio, Lieutenant-Colonel Oliver P. Robie, and the Chicago (Illinois) Board of Trade Battery, Lieutenant George Robinson commanding.

The whole command, numbering about 4,800 men, was composed of veterans of long service, well drilled, splendidly officered, and was ready and anxious for any expedition which had promise of adventure and fighting.

The brigades of Minty and Long were on the extreme left of the Union army at Buck Head, and marched all night on the 17th of August in the rear of the army and joined the Third Division at Sandtown, on the right of the Union army, on the morning of the 18th of August at sunrise, and General Kilpatrick assumed command and turned over the command of his division to Colonel Eli H. Murray, who in turn turned over the command of his brigade to Colonel Robert L. King.

We lay in bivouac all day, and on the same evening at sundown we were in the saddle, and the order from General Kilpatrick was read, stating that we "had been selected as the last hope of the Commanding General to break the enemy's communication, and we must go forth with the determination to do or die."

General Sherman, in a communication to General Thomas, bearing date of August 17th, said: "I beg you will convey the following orders to govern Kilpatrick in his movement on the Macon road. It is not a raid, but a deliberate attack for the purpose of so disabling that road that the enemy will be unable to supply his army at Atlanta. He will have his own division of cavalry and two brigades from General Garrard's division. With these he will move to-morrow night, aiming to cross the West Point road between Red Oak and Fairburn. If he has time, he should remove a small section of the road without using fire, simply to lessen the chances of an infantry force being sent to intercept his return. He should move then in force to the nearest point on the Macon road, about Jonesborough, and should destroy as much of that road as he possibly can do, working steadily until forced to take to his arms and horses for battle.

"He should avoid battle with infantry or artillery, but may safely fight any cavalry he encounters, and all the army should so engage the attention of the enemy that he can not detach infantry as against General Kilpatrick. Instruct the General to advise at the earliest possible moment of his success.

"I wish to notify General Garrard to have one of his brigades ready to make a demonstration, without risking battle, on our left, and have this effective part of two brigades, under Long, if possible, ready to move this night by moonlight by Pace's Ferry and Sandtown bridges, to operate with Kilpatrick. on our right."

Strong demonstrations were made along the front of the Union army as soon as the command drew out from Sandtown, by infantry and artillery, making feints by the display of troops as if to assault on both the 19th and 20th. General Garrard with his remaining cavalry force made a demonstration to the left toward Stone Mountain, and drew a force of Hood's army in that direction. General Jefferson C. Davis, with his division of the Fourteenth Corps, moved out from the right and drove the enemy across the West Point Railroad and destroyed a portion of the track.

In spite of all these aggressive movements of Sherman's army, Hood detached a division of his army to attack Kilpatrick's cavalry, which was seen from the signal station, as shown by the following dispatch:

HOWARD'S HEADQUARTERS, August 20, 1864 — 5 p. m.

General Schofield: The following just received from signal officer: "A train of fifteen freight cars just left Atlanta, loaded with troops inside and outside; tops of cars were crowded."

O. O. HOWARD,
Major-General.

This force proved to be Clebourne's division, which fought Kilpatrick at Lovejoy.

Every officer and soldier in the command realized that the proposed expedition was very perilous, and the chances were

213

that many of us would be either killed or wounded, or, what seemed worse, land in a rebel prison. After the order was read, the command was given for "the pack train to fall out and all troopers whose horses were lame or exhausted should go to the rear." In a few minutes, and just as the sun was dropping behind the mountain, the command was given, "Right, forward, fours right!" and we were off on what proved to be one of the hardest cavalry raids during our four years' service. Soon after dusk we struck the enemy's pickets, which proved to be the advance of Ross' and Ferguson's brigades of cavalry, and a brisk skirmish was kept up all night, and during a greater part of the time we were dismounted, as the enemy would throw up barricades at every good position at bridges or along the edge of a wood, and they gave us so much trouble that instead of reaching the West Point Railroad at midnight, as we intended, we did not strike it until just at daybreak of the 19th. King's brigade of the Third Division had the advance during the night, but before daylight and before we struck the West Point Railroad near Fairburn, King's brigade swung to the left, and Jones' brigade of the Third Division had the advance when we reached the railroad. When the railroad was reached Long's brigade dismounted and commenced tearing up and destroying the railroad track near and southwest of Fairburn.

Cavalry, when they become accustomed to this kind of work, would tear up a track very rapidly. When the order is given to dismount, number one, two and three dismount, and number four always holds horses, remains mounted, and leads the other three horses. Number three hands his reins to number four; number two ties his reins to the bit of number three, and number one to rein of number two. The men then form along one side of the track in close order, and at command grasp the rails and ties and turn the track over, and sometimes a half mile of tracks is turned before a joint is broken. The men move along rapidly, and many rods of the track will be standing up on edge. If there is time, the rails are then torn loose from the ties by picks and axes, carried for that purpose; the ties are piled up and the rails on top of them, and then the ties are fired; thus the rails are heated in the middle and bent out of shape by being twisted around trees or telegraph poles, are left there to cool, and no doubt some of them are there yet to mark the trail of the cavalry raiders. The brigade destroyed about a mile of track, when we were attacked by the cavalry and artillery of the enemy in both the rear and left flank. The brigade was ordered to mount, and galloped forward to join the First Brigade, under Minty, which had crossed the track and had the advance.

Long's brigade formed a line of battle facing toward the left, and as we began to advance a battery galloped into position on a little knoll to the right of our line. Just at this moment General Kilpatrick, who had been giving orders to the commander of the battery, came dashing along in front of our line, mounted on an Arabian horse, looking the ideal cavalryman. He directed Colonel Long to move his brigade forward at a gallop, and we dashed across a field in front, over ditches and fences, and into the woods, routing the enemy and taking a number of prisoners.

Still farther to the left the First Brigade, under Minty, had a sharp fight with cavalry, mounted infantry and a battery of artillery, which had been carefully masked, and the fighting was terrific for a short time. The Eleventh Wisconsin Battery was brought into action, shelled the woods to the left, and very soon the enemy retreated in confusion toward Atlanta, and were driven back a mile or two from the left of our column.

During all of this time General Kilpatrick's headquarters' band, mounted on white horses near the railroad track, where the work of destruction was being prosecuted vigorously, was enlivening the scene with patriotic airs, which was rather an unusual innovation during a fight.

As the real objective point was the Atlanta and Macon Railroad, as soon as the left of the column was cleared of the enemy harassing the flank, that part of the command which had been participating in the fight joined the main column and moved forward toward Jonesborough, Long's brigade having the advance, while Minty's brigade was in close support in column, and the Third Division was protecting the rear and flanks.

We struck the enemy in a short time and attacked them at once, pushing them back slowly but steadily. The country was thickly wooded, and a very bad place for cavalry to operate. The enemy would throw up barricades at every favorable position, such as woods, streams or ravines, firing on the advance from ambuscades. The progress of the column was much retarded, and the enemy made every effort to keep our column back from the railroad until reinforcements could be moved down from Atlanta. About noon the advance halted, and dismounted in a thick piece of woods to let the horses rest, and to eat a hard-tack, raw-pork sandwich. The men were all sitting or lying down, when all at once the rebels fired a volley and charged the advance guard, driving them back on the reserves before we could mount.

Colonel Long ordered the brigade forward, dismounted and on the double-quick, and the bang of the carbines was soon ringing out and the rebel horsemen were suddenly checked and sent scurrying back through woods and fields. The brigade then advanced, dismounted, with a strong skirmish line in front and flankers to protect the column, as the rebel cavalry kept a continuous fire from the woods to the right and left. The rebel force was pushed back steadily until we reached Flint River, and on the east side of this stream they had thrown up works, dug rifle-pits, and had a strong position.

216

As soon as our advance appeared a rebel battery opened up and the Chicago Board of Trade Battery was put in position, and after a lively artillery duel the rebel battery was silenced. The First and Second Brigades of the Second Division dismounted, advanced some distance in the woods on the west side of the stream, where we halted, and both of our batteries, with eight guns, were put in position on a hill in our rear, and at a signal they opened up by volleys for several rounds, and as soon as the batteries ceased firing the two brigades rushed forward with a yell, and the rebel line left their works and rifle-pits and fell back rapidly toward Jonesborough.

When the bridge was reached the planks had been torn up, and there was nothing left but the stringers, on which the First and Third Ohio and Fourth Michigan crossed. As we crossed, Kilpatrick himself came up, and was ordering the men to jump into the stream after the planks to repair the bridge. The dismounted men moved forward, and reached Jonesborough about sundown. The bridge across the stream was soon repaired, and the artillery, mounted men and led horses were closed up by the time we reached the town.

We had some skirmishing in the outskirts of the town, and to the south on the opposite side of the town a strong force of rebel cavalry was drawn up in line of battle in plain view, and the officers could be seen dashing to and fro forming the lines. Our lines were straightened up, and, moving forward, the rear guard of the enemy dismounted, opened up fire on our skirmishers from houses and buildings, and a brisk fire was kept up from a brick church. A section of the Chicago Board of Trade Battery came dashing down the street up to the skirmish line, unlimbered, and sent a few shells into the church, making the bricks and mortar fly, and the church was evacuated in short order.

The sound of the guns and scream of the shells was sweet music to the ears of the skirmishers, and they moved forward

217

with a shout, and the bang! bang! of their sharp-ringing carbines swelled the chorus as the mayor and a few citizens appeared in the main street with a white flag to surrender the town and claim protection for the citizens.

The line advanced rapidly through the town, the rebels fell back along the railroad, and we soon had undisputed possession. The shells from the artillery had fired the cotton bales, used as barricades around the railroad building, and soon both cotton and buildings were blazing, and the water tank at the station had been shivered by a shell. Our men took possession of the telegraph office, and it was reported that an old operator in our command caught a dispatch stating that reinforcements were on the way from Atlanta, which was very important news to Kilpatrick. Jonesborough is about twenty-five miles south from Atlanta, and a considerable amount of clothing and commissary stores were found, with whisky and other necessary munitions of war. All of these supplies that we did not need for immediate use were burned and destroyed.

As Hood's whole army was now between us and Sherman's army, it was not particularly desirable for less than five thousand cavalrymen to remain in this position very long, and the destruction of the railroad, which ran through the main street of the town, was commenced at once. Tearing up the track and destroying the rails and ties was done principally by the Third Division, as they had not been engaged in the fight when we entered the town. The Second Brigade formed a line of battle south of the town and across the railroad; the First Brigade was formed facing Atlanta, and skirmishing was kept up all night. It was a wild night and a most graphic scene. The sky was lighted up with burning timbers, buildings and cotton bales; the continuous bang of carbines, the galloping of staff officers and orderlies up and down the streets carrying orders or dispatches, the terrified citizens peering out of their windows, the constant marching of troops changing position,

Kilpatrick's headquarters' band discoursing national airs, with the shouts of men — all made up a weird scene never to be forgotten by the troopers who were on that raid.

By midnight about two miles of the road had been effectually destroyed, and in attempting to move farther south along the road a strong force of infantry was found posted behind barricades, with timber cut in front. This position could not have been taken without a hard fight and heavy loss, and Kilpatrick then determined to withdraw from Jonesborough, make a detour to the east and strike the road again farther south. The movement was commenced about 2 o'clock on the morning of the 20th by Murray's division and Minty's brigade of the Second Division marching on the McDonough road to the east, and the Second Brigade, under Colonel Long, remaining in the barricades to hold the infantry in check The Second Brigade withdrew just as the first streaks of dawn began to appear in the east, and they were followed up closely by the enemy, both cavalry and infantry, the First Ohio holding the rear. After we had marched about five miles, the advance regiments halted to feed their horses, and the enemy made an impetuous attack on the rear guard, and one battalion was dismounted, throwing up barricades hurriedly of logs and rails, and prepared to give the enemy a warm reception.

The enemy attacked the barricades, and as their line was much longer, the battalion was outflanked on both sides, and the balls were soon whizzing from the flanks, and, as the Johnnies would say, they took us "end ways." Although heavily outnumbered, this battalion of the First Ohio held its position until reinforcements were ordered by Colonel Long, and the rebels were soon driven back in confusion toward Jonesborough. General Kilpatrick, in speaking of the fight, complimented Colonel Long for the manner in which he maneuvered his command. As General Phil Kearney once said to a brigade commander who reported to him during one of the great battles in Virginia, and asked as to the position his brigade should take, "Fighting Phil" replied, "Just go in anywhere; there is lovely fighting all along the line." This seemed to be about the situation at this time.

As soon as the enemy was repulsed, Long's brigade was ordered to the front on a gallop of three or four miles toward Lovejoy Station, where we found that Minty's brigade, on striking the railroad, had been attacked by a heavy force of cavalry and Reynolds' division of infantry. The infantry line was concealed in a railroad cut, and the Seventh Pennsylvania and the Fourth U. S. Cavalry dismounted, drove the enemy's line in, and were within twenty or thirty rods of the railroad, when the infantry line raised up, delivered a very destructive volley, and, rushing from the cut, drove the line of Minty's brigade back in considerable confusion. Just at this moment Long's brigade arrived on the field with the Chicago Board of Trade Battery. The brigade was dismounted, formed a line of battle, and by this time some of the dismounted men of Minty's brigade came rushing back through our line, and it was not safe to fire, as it would endanger the lives of some of our own men. Although the balls from the rebel infantry were whizzing on all sides, the officers of Long's brigade made every effort to keep their men from firing until the rebel line was almost upon us, but when our troops did open up, the rebel line was repulsed and driven back with heavy slaughter. The Chicago Board of Trade Battery was up on the front line, and did excellent execution, and the rebel infantry fell back into the railroad cut. During this fight the lines were so close together that the officers of the First and Second Brigades used their revolvers with good execution.

Our ammunition was exhausted, and a detail was sent back to the ammunition train and got a supply in boxes, and the boxes were broken open with stones, and the cartridges were distributed in a few moments, much to the delight of the troopers.

The Second Division held this line for an hour, and during this time staff officers were busily engaged in forming the led horses in columns of fours facing the rear. One of the guns of the Chicago Board of Trade Battery was disabled in a cornfield just to the left of the First Ohio, and it was hauled to the rear by some of the troopers of the Second Division. When the Second Division had driven the rebel line back, and the firing had about ceased, Colonel Long and Minty were ordered to withdraw their brigades and fall back to the led horses, a few hundred yards in the rear.

Now we began to realize that we were surrounded, and the chances began to look desperate, as our ammunition had already been pretty well exhausted, and we must cut our way through the lines. The distance between the two lines of the enemy could not have been more than three-fourths of a mile. When the Second Division was fighting along the railroad and near the station, King's brigade was in support of the rear and right and had some hot work. Jones' brigade was protecting the rear, and was hard pressed by the divisions of Ross, Ferguson, and Martin, and kept up a continuous fight for two hours all along the lines. The rattling volleys from the front and rear echoed back and forth alternately, mingled with the shouts and cheers from both the Union and rebel lines.

At this critical time the situation was as follows: In our rear were two brigades of Clebourne's division of infantry, the cavalry brigades of Ross and Ferguson, and about a thousand State troops which had been sent from below Lovejoy Station, and on the right were the remaining brigades of Clebourne's division. Martin's and Jackson's brigades of cavalry were on the left, while Reynolds' division of infantry, with a brigade

221

of infantry and a six-gun battery sent up from Macon, were along the railroad at Lovejoy Station, with twelve pieces of artillery sent down from Atlanta. A total of five brigades of infantry, eighteen pieces of artillery, six brigades of cavalry, in all a force of more than ten thousand of all arms surrounding our two divisions of cavalry, numbering less than five thousand.

Kilpatrick, finding that he was completely surrounded, ordered his division and brigade commanders to cut their way out. His cavalry had been up to this time fighting almost entirely as infantry, but they soon were going to be given the privilege of drawing their sabers from their rusty scabbards for a cavalry charge, and the opportunity was hailed with delight. Saddle girths were tightened, revolvers examined, saber belts and spurs adjusted, and all equipments were made taut for the shock and melee of the charge. When all was in readiness and the order was given to mount, many a brave trooper sprang into his saddle for the last time and rode to his death in that wild charge, cheering his comrades on to the front as he fell.

Kilpatrick, a cavalry general, remembering the mistakes which had been made on a former expedition for the same purpose, instead of scattering his troops, massed them. The brigades of Minty and Long were formed on the right of the road, and one regiment of Minty's brigade formed in the road. The Third Division, under Colonel Murray, formed on the left of the road, all facing toward McDonough, while the artillery, ambulances filled with wounded, and ammunition wagons, were formed in the road with orders to follow up the charging columns as closely as possible. The troops were formed in columns of fours or platoons with the proper intervals, as it was thought best to strike the rebel line and pierce it in several places rather than charge in line, as it was a long distance to charge, and in some places the ground was cut up by ditches and washouts, with two or three fences between our forces and the rebel lines.

During the time the troops were forming the surgeons and ambulance corps were busy gathering up the wounded, and caring for them as best they could. The rebels had formed two or three lines with infantry behind barricades of fence rails and logs, as it seems they had anticipated a charge, and they were not disappointed in their expectations. When our troops were forming two batteries opened up on our lines from the front, and the infantry was closing up from our now rear from the railroad. When all was ready every eye was turned intently toward the line of barricades in front, from whence shells were now coming thick and fast, and through this line and over these barricades we must cut our way out, or surrender, and, perhaps, starve in Andersonville.

Draw saber! and forty-five hundred sabers ring out as they are drawn from their scabbards, the reins are tightened, the horses are excited, with nostrils extended as if they "sniffed the battle afar off."

It was a glorious sight, with horses stamping and champing the bits as if eager for the fray, standards and guidons flung to the breeze, with the dashing here and there of staff officers carrying orders, the serious face of the commander, the stern, quick commands of the officers as the squadrons are forming. Many of the boys who witnessed and participated in that charge, but whose hair is now silvered with gray, can feel the flush of youth again mount their cheeks, and the blood course more rapidly through their veins, as they go back in memory to the day they charged with Kilpatrick, August 20th, 1864.

The command "Forward!" is given, the bugles ring out "Trot! Gallop! Charge!" in quick succession, and the columns swept forward under the spur with a yell, scaling fences, jumping ditches, in that wild and reckless charge; the shells

2

from the batteries were sweeping the lines, while troopers and horses were falling on every side.

The First Brigade struck the rebel line at and just to the right of the road, and Long's brigade struck farther to the right, and Captain W. H. Scott, of the First Ohio, fell mortally wounded in front of one of the guns of a rebel battery. When our columns struck the barricades, the rebels retreated in great confusion, but a lieutenant, commanding a section of artillery, who gave his name as Young, was mortally wounded just in front of where Captain Scott fell, as he was attempting to fire one of his pieces after all of his men had deserted their posts. Both brigades urged their horses over the barricades, cutting right and left. Many of the prisoners had saber cuts on their hands, arms and heads, and it is estimated that from six to eight hundred prisoners were sabered. Infantry, cavalry, led horses and artillery were fleeing in confusion, and at one time we had at least one thousand prisoners, but they nearly all escaped in our rapid march that dark night following.

After this long charge over broken ground, ditches, fences, and woods, the regiments and brigades were considerably broken up, as many horses had been shot, troopers wounded or killed, and some horses falling in a ditch that we crossed were with great difficulty extricated, so that many of the men were dismounted.

Before Long's brigade could get into position, as Colonel Long had been ordered to cover the retreat, Minty's brigade and the Third Division having moved out on the McDonough road, Long's brigade was furiously attacked by Pat Clebourne's division of infantry, and a battery of artillery, and this fight lasted about an hour, with a part of the brigade dismounted. In this assault Colonel Long was severely wounded, but rode his horse to the rear, supported on either side by two mounted orderlies from his escort.

The First Ohio was forming on some high ground just as

Colonel Long rode to the rear, pale and bleeding. As he passed by the regiment he smiled and bowed, and was given a rousing cheer by the boys. The Third Ohio was still fighting, dismounted, and the brigade was falling back by alternate regiments, and just at this time the Chicago Board of Trade Battery came galloping back, dashed through a gate and into the dooryard of a plantation house on the opposite side of the road from where the First Ohio was forming. On the long porch in front of this house there were twelve or fifteen women and children wringing their hands, while some were crying, others were praying.

The battery opened up at once, and the rebel battery in our rear soon got range and sent the shells thick and fast, and at least one of them struck the roof of the house, thus adding to the terror of the women and children. While our battery was firing one of the guns burst, injuring two of the gunners. There was not a grim veteran of our command whose heart was so hardened by the every-day scenes of carnage that it did not go out in sympathy for those mothers with their children, and who would not have freely risked his own life to have saved them; but no aid could be rendered those helpless ones, as no soldier could be spared from his post of duty.

The enemy was crowding the rear guard, and making a desperate effort, by shot and shell, to create a panic and stampede in the brigade. Never were the words of General Sherman more truthfully demonstrated that "War is cruelty, and you can not refine it," than by this incident. Lieutenant Bennett, who commanded the section of the battery in this fight, informed the writer the next day that all of the women and children escaped injury, which he considered almost a miracle under the circumstances, as the shells tore up the ground on all sides of the house.

Soon after Colonel Long was wounded his brigade fell back in column through the lines of Minty's brigade immediately in the rear, and Minty's men covered the column during the afternoon and had some sharp skirmishes with Clebourne's division, following up with infantry and artillery.

The whole command moved rapidly toward McDonough. Both men and horses were tired out and exhausted, and after the excitement of two days and nights of almost continuous fighting, there was a complete collapse when the fighting ceased, and the men had lost so much sleep that they seemed perfectly indifferent to all surroundings. The command marched all night in a drenching rain, but it was utterly impossible to march in any kind of order or to keep out an advance guard, as men and officers would go to sleep. In some instances the horses would halt along the road in fence corners, and the riders would either unconsciously dismount, or fall asleep until dragged out by the rear guard and compelled to mount and move on with the column. Many of them lost their hats, and no doubt others were taken prisoners by the enemy, and the column moved on silently, horses exhausted, half of the men and officers asleep, and the night as dark as pitch. About 2 or 3 o'clock in the morning of the 21st the column halted.

We were ordered to unsaddle, as we had not unsaddled since leaving Sandtown on the evening of the 18th, and as soon as the saddles were removed the men tumbled down among the trees on the wet ground at their horses' heads, and were soon sound asleep. We halted there until 6 o'clock, about three hours, then saddled. Moving on about half a mile, we found ourselves on the bank of a stream called Cotton Indian Creek, at high flood, the banks full to overflowing, and no bridge. We had to swim our horses across this stream, and, as the banks were steep, there was a deep cut on either side of the stream, leading to the ford, and it was not possible to get up the bank only at one point, so that the process of crossing the stream was tedious. Picket ropes were stretched across the stream, and General Kilpatrick and his division and brigade commanders were on the bank superintending the crossing. Men, horses and mules were floundering around in the stream, and it was no doubt the first attempt of some of the horses to swim, and in some instances the men would get frightened, pull on the reins, and as a result many of the riders were unhorsed, and were saved only by the ropes. A number of soldiers were drowned. Forty or fifty horses and a number of mules were lost, and the dismounted gun, hauled in an ammunition wagon, was abandoned. But the ambulances, carrying nearly one hundred wounded, were all safely crossed. Having crossed this stream, we were not again troubled by the enemy; they did not follow us up, as they were in no better condition for fighting than our own forces. Guns and ammunition were soaked with water, as every man in the command was wet above the waist after fording the creek.

The command marched on all day, and about dark reached Lithonia, on the Augusta Railroad, and went into bivouac for the night, rejoicing to have the opportunity for a much-needed rest, as we had now been out three days and nights, had only unsaddled once, and had not more than two hours' sleep, excepting what we had snatched in the saddle. The next day the command marched through Lattimer and Decatur, and reached our old camp at Buck Head about sundown of the 22d, having marched completely around Hood's army in five days.

General Kilpatrick, in his report to General Sherman after the raid, stated that the defeat of the Confederates in the charge "was the most complete rout that the rebel cavalry had sustained during the war."

In summing up results he stated that "four miles of railroad track was completely destroyed, and ten miles badly damaged. Two locomotives with one train of cars were totally destroyed, and another train partially destroyed. A wagon train and many ambulances were captured, and a large amount of army supplies burned at Jonesborough. One four-gun battery, three battle flags, with a large number of horses and mules, were captured, and one hundred prisoners of the eight hundred to one thousand taken at Lovejoy were brought into our lines, the balance having escaped in the darkness during the rapid march in a pouring rain on the night of August 20th."

General Long, in a letter written to the writer a few years ago, stated that in the fight with Clebourne's infantry, after the charge, and when Long was severely wounded, that he "maneuvered his brigade by bugle commands or signals as he had never seen done before or since in a battle."

The losses in killed, wounded and missing in the two divisions was 326, of which 216 were in the brigades of Minty and Long, Second Division, and 110 of the Third Division. Among the officers killed were Captain W. H. Scott, of the First Ohio Cavalry, Inspector-General on the staff of Colonel Long; Captain James G. Taylor, Seventh Pennsylvania Cavalry; Lieutenant C. C. Hermans, Seventh Pennsylvania Cavalry. The Confederate losses were heavy, but could not be ascertained definitely, but they were, no doubt, as heavy as our own.

A dispatch sent from Atlanta to the *Memphis Appeal,* and published a few days after the fight, gives the Confederate side, and is herewith published:

"The newspapers have lately been full of accounts of how Martin's division of cavalry was run over by the Yankees at Lovejoy on the 20th ultimo. The writer was on the field on that occasion, and in justice to the much-abused cavalry states the facts in the matter.

"Martin's division, supporting the battery, was formed on the McDonough road. Ross' and Ferguson's commands on foot were in front and on each side of the battery, behind rail breastworks. A brigade of Clebourne's infantry was on the left of the road in three lines, the last one in a piece of woods. About one hundred yards in rear of the position of

228

the battery, on the right of the road (east side) the State troops were formed in line. When the Yankees charged they came in a solid column, ten or twelve lines deep, running their horses and yelling like devils. They didn't stop to fight or attempt to keep any kind of order or formation, but each fellow for himself rushed on, swinging his saber over his head.

"They rode over Ross' and Ferguson's men in the center, and over and through Clebourne's lines, one after another, on the left. Clebourne's first line, they say, tried to use their bayonets, but the Yankees cut them to pieces. After the Yankees had cut through all the other forces and captured the battery, Martin, seeing the field was lost, retreated in good order to the east and joined Clebourne's main body, and aided in the final defeat of the enemy on the McDonough road that evening, and pursued them to and through McDonough that night, recapturing nearly five hundred of our men, which they took in the charge. The effort to arouse the people against Martin and his brave division is more disgraceful and demoralizing than the Yankees' charge itself, and should be frowned upon by all who wish well to our cause."

The distance marched by Kilpatrick's command was about one hundred and twenty miles, and the route can be traced on the accompanying official map.

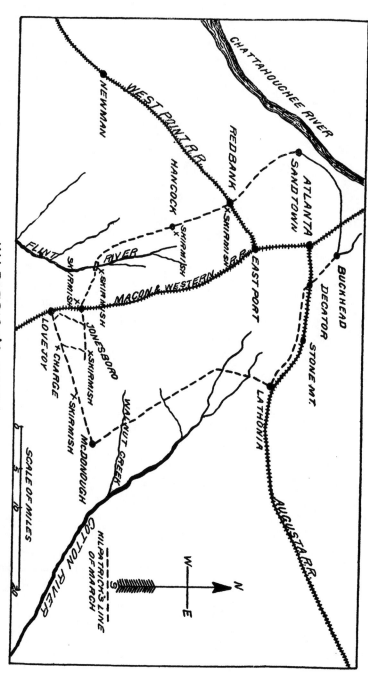

KILPATRICK'S RAID

CHATTAHOUCHEE RIVER

WEST POINT R.R.

NEWMAN

HANCOCK

REDBANK

×SKIRMISH

×SKIRMISH

ATLANTA
SANDTOWN

FLINT RIVER

MACON & WESTERN R.R.

EAST PORT

×SKIRMISH

×SKIRMISH

JONESBORO

×SKIRMISH

CHARGE

LOVEJOY

×SKIRMISH

×SKIRMISH

McDONOUGH

WALNUT CREEK

COTTON RIVER

BUCKHEAD

DECATOR

STONE M.T.

LATHONIA

AUGUSTA R.R.

SCALE OF MILES

0   5   10   20

N
W   E
S

KILPATRICK'S LINE
OF MARCH

INDEX